S0-ATY-534

"Yes Dear"

FREDDY & MARLENE,

Best Wishes to you
and your Family!

AUTOGRAPH 2-

In Memory of My Loving Wife
BRENDA SUE VOSS

"Yes Dear"

WRITTEN BY
HER HUSBAND:

MITCH V. FREIMARK

Inquires regarding book signings and speaking engagements, contact:
MVF Productions
Ph: 651-452-5380
Email: MVFProductions@aol.com

Copyright © 2002 Mitch V. Freimark

ISBN: 0-9718969-0-9

First Edition, May 2002

All rights reserved.

Printed in Canada by Friesens.

Prepared for Mitch V. Freimark by
North Star Press of St. Cloud, Inc.
P.O. Box 451, St. Cloud, Minnesota 56302

Published by
MVF Productions
867 Mendakota Court
Mendota Heights, Minnesota 55120

When someone has such a dramatic impact on your life that changes you forever, you're moved to tell the world how lucky you were to have known her. Brenda's life and the way she lived it inspired me to share her story. This is our love story. I hope she can help teach you the lessons of life she taught me.

Thank You!

First and foremost to my family: my mother, Barb, and her husband, Don Martin; my brother, Todd Freimark; my sister, Shelly, and her husband, Jamie Macdonald; my father, Del, and his wife, Ramona.

To Brenda's family: her mother, Donna Voss, her four sisters and five brothers, sister-in-laws, brother-in-laws, (especially my brother-in-law Wayne "Cowboy" Webster), and to all our nieces, nephews, and cousins.

And to all my friends, who are my extended family.

This book is dedicated to the memory of Brenda, but would not have been possible without the love, support, generosity, and kindness you have all shown me.

Contents

Preface

The idea to write this book came to me three weeks after my wife, Brenda's, death on Sunday, September 2nd, 2001. I was traveling to Watertown, South Dakota, to see my brother Todd Freimark on Friday September 21st, 2001. The four hours it took to get from Mendota Heights, Minnesota, to Todd's front door allowed me time to think about her and reflect on the eleven years we spent together. As I thought about it, I can only say that it was like yesterday when we first met. A blink of an eye, and eleven years flashed before me. I laughed out loud at all the funny things that happened to us, and I cried for over thirty minutes, missing her deeply, knowing she was never coming home.

I decided to write this book first for myself as a self-help book, but as I got deeper and deeper into each chapter, I realized the gifts Brenda shared with me and everyone she touched would also enrich others. This is a love story about how two people came together and became one. I laughed and I cried while writing this story, but, more important, I hope to pass on to you my understanding of the true meaning of life.

If you've never experienced the feelings of losing a loved one, a soul mate, a best friend . . . if you're wondering how anyone can possibly move forward after a tragic loss, then allow me to share some insight into my world during those first few days after Brenda's death.

I'd close my eyes and imagine the feeling of never being able to hold her hand or tell her how much I loved her. I knew I had to face the fact I would never again hear the daily routine of the garage door open and close as she drove her car in and shut off the engine, then hear the car door open and close as I anticipate the sounds of her footsteps on the hardwood floor as she arrived home from work, looking for me to give her a hug and ask her how her day had been.

As I glance outside into our beautiful backyard, I would imagine it being a sunny day in June and know I'll never again see her standing there, wearing her white tank top, cutoff blue jeans, her sunglasses, with her beautiful blonde hair pulled back in a pony tail and tucked under "my" baseball cap doing what she loved . . . gardening, planting flowers, or just enjoying the fruits of her labor.

I know I'll never hear her voice . . . never hear her tell me, "I love you," and never smell the back of her neck or be able to kiss her as I always did. I know the pain of her loss will always be deep inside my body because the loss will never go away. Thoughts of her image would stay in my mind twenty-four hours a day, seven days a week during the first month after her death. I cried so hard I couldn't see because my eyes were too puffy to allow me to put in my contacts. I'd try to sleep at night, but knowing she wouldn't be lying next to me only kept me awake. I'd call out to her, thinking she would respond, and I'd hear nothing.

I'd be surrounded by family and friends who I know love me, and still I felt entirely alone. That was the world I lived in during the first few days, weeks and months after Brenda's death. The only reason I was able to function during that time was because Brenda and I had such a solid relationship, and I have no regrets of my time spent with her, none.

The pain of losing Brenda, the love of my life, cuts so deep I often wonder, "Why her and not me?" How could someone as loving as my wife be taken from me at such a young age? That's when I hear her telling me, "Mitch, it's going to be okay." Then the tears stop, the questions stop, and my life goes on for another day. That's how I manage the pain: one day at a time.

Brenda and I had talked about this very thing, the "What if something happened to me. I want you to..." We didn't talk about it often, but we did tell each other that if anything did ever happen, the other one must go on. Live life to the fullest was our motto. Our plans were never to be without each other. I just never figured on it being Brenda to go first; I always told her it would be me. She would shrug off my comments as nothing, because she knew how hard it would be for her if I were gone.

I am a survivor, but in order to survive the loss of a loved one, you need to have a lot of friends, true friends. My advice is to make sure you take time out of your busy schedule and know who your true friends are. I suggest that those who have not experienced losing a spouse read this carefully. If you are ever in my position, you will thank God for the friends you can count on to be there for you because eventually the phone calls stop as people get back into their daily routines, while your life is still upside down. It's the silence which you are left to face alone, and the sound silence makes is as loud as if someone is beating a drum inside your head. And, just when you think you can't stand the pain, it will be your friends who remember to call; and if they don't, you need to pick up the phone and call them.

Brenda and I were so blessed; we have so many friends who love us and care about us. Friends can be lifelines to recovery. Without all our close friends, I know I wouldn't have made it. They cared for me in ways I couldn't have imagined.

God bless you, honey. I will always love you.

"Yes Dear"

Chapter 1

The "Fugitive"

Saturday September 1st, 2001, Brenda got up at 5:00 a.m. This was "normal" for her, if it can be called normal getting up at 5:00 a.m. and working until 9:00 p.m. "normal." As one of the top cosmetologists or hairdressers, as she referred to herself (I called her a "hair bender"), she needed to leave for Shear Madness by 6:30 a.m. to open the shop for her first customer, who would be arriving by 7:00 a.m. It takes about twenty minutes to get from our house to the salon. This was "normal" for her. Up at 5:00 a.m. everyday and off to work by 6:30 or 7:00 a.m. Tuesday through Thursday, she worked 7:00 a.m. to 9:00 p.m. Fridays had a shorter day, 7:00 a.m. to 7:00 p.m., and Saturdays she cut back, 7:00 a.m. to mid-afternoon, which meant she'd be home anywhere between 2:30 and 4:00 p.m. After twenty-six years in the business, the last ten in the Twin Cities, her customers had become an extension of our family; they depended on her to be there for them and the eleven years I knew her, she was always there for them even if she didn't feel well.

Saturday mornings I usually got up with her, and we'd have a cup of coffee and watch the early morning news. This particular morning I just lifted my head from my pillow and said, "See you later this afternoon."

"Don't forget we're meeting Mom, Kim, Lil, and Harry at Jensen's tonight for dinner," she reminded me as she kissed me on the cheek. Her perfume was still lingering in the bedroom when I got up around 7:00 a.m. to get ready for my 8:30 tee time with "the boys" at Mendakota. All I needed to do was walk across our backyard, across the parking lot and I was on the first tee box. It's a rough one when my wife is working and I'm playing golf, but somehow I managed to get used **to it**.

The round was typical for us, playing in a group of five meant there would be lots of laughs as we strolled around the course. The first hole is a short par five, measuring 510 yards. My drive was okay. In the left rough (imagine that). I was about to hit my second shot when I couldn't help but notice in my peripheral vision a Highway Patrol car pulling into the parking lot. I stopped concentrating on hitting my second shot and turned around to see were it was going. I usually don't pay attention to the traffic going in and out of the parking lot, but I'd never seen a Highway Patrol car at Mendakota before. I watched the patrol car head toward the clubhouse were I could see a Mendakota Police car was parked. It wasn't odd to see the Mendakota Police patrol the parking lot, but the Highway Patrol? I decided to watch to see if the red lights were going to come on, but nothing happened. I blew it off and hit my second shot. This time I hit a good one and only had fifty yards to the green. I made par on hole one and two.

Our third hole is a par four with out of bounds on the right, and trees on the left. Four of us hit it straight down the middle. Roddy hit his drive left into the trees and had himself in a little trouble. As the four of us headed to our tee shots, we could hear the sound of a helicopter getting closer and closer until it was hovering directly overhead. The word SHERIFF stood out on each side of the chopper as it made two turns, obviously observing us.

"Must be looking for you, Roddy," I yelled over to him as he was still searching for his ball. We all wondered what was going on, but no one really made a big deal of it. I was thinking, "Why would the Sheriff's helicopter be hovering so close over-head, especially at 8:30 in the morning?"

It took ten minutes for us to finish our third hole. By the time we reached the fourth tee box, Roddy and Aggie had started badgering each other as they always did when playing togeth-er. Mark, Mike, and I were laughing so hard at those two, we completely forgot about the helicopter.

Three hours had passed from the time we meet on the first tee to arriving at the fifteenth tee box. I was in a little bit of a hurry to tee off first. I needed to let a little anger out on the ball for not performing very well on fourteen. As I bent over to tee up my ball,

I noticed a guy standing in the pine trees staring at me. I didn't think anything of him standing there; I thought he was the owner of the house I could see behind the pines. As soon as our last player hit his tee shot, the guy walked out of the pines and headed up the fairway staying close to the right side tree line. I told the group my guess was he must be looking for his dog. There used to be a black lab that got loose and ran around on fifteen, so he must be the owner of the house next to fifteen, I told myself. I decided to keep pace with our new friend to see what he was up to. When he didn't stop and go back through the trees, back to his side, that's when my gut told me this might be the guy the authorities were looking for this morning. Why he decided to start walking along the outside edge of our fairway was beyond me, but if he was the "fugitive" as I could hear the group behind me saying, then I was going to keep pace with him and see where in the hell he was planning to go.

Hole fifteen has a severe dogleg right, and, as we both reached the corner, he kept walking next to the right side out-of-bounds markers, which is all woods and water. I sat my bag down next to my tee shot and watched him walk around behind the fifteenth green continuing past the sixteenth tee box and back toward the clubhouse. I saw my opportunity to cut him off before he got down sixteen's fairway, but I would need to move fast. I started walking straight for him. In seven years playing golf at Mendakota I had never seen anyone wearing work boots, blue jeans, t-shirt and a baseball cap following the outside edge of fairway fifteen and sixteen, heading directly toward the clubhouse. Since we don't allow blue jeans at Mendakota, I guess I had a pretty good idea he was the man the officers were searching for. The confrontation would be interesting since my gut told me he really was the "fugitive." My only fear was he might make it to my house. Why that thought ran through my mind, I'll never know. As I approached him, I figured the best thing to do was ask him a non-threatening question, but I needed him to know by my body language that I wasn't afraid of him. I walked straight at him, my rooster tail in the air, strutting confidently to show him I had no fear. He stopped, and I walked right up to him and asked, "Can we help you!"

He started shaking and told me he had a friend that lived "over there" pointing, in my mind, right at my house. "I was cutting across the golf course to save time," was his short story.

"Sorry, I said, you're on private property, and you need to go back the same way you came."

"But that's a long way to walk," he said.

"Too bad," I told him as I stood my ground and pointed in the direction he needed to go. The thought of him entering my home and harming my wife was the only thing pressing on my mind, even though she wasn't home. He looked at me and maybe knew he better not f--- with me. I meant business. He turned around and started retracing his footsteps. I walked back to my tee shot on fifteen and noticed everyone was standing on the green kind of dumfounded at what just took place. I hit my second shot onto the green and two-putted for par.

"What did you say to him?" they all wanted to know.

"I told him to leave the golf course."

That's when one of the guys in our group started acting all tough and said, "We should've tackled him and held him down until the police got here."

Roddy immediately shot back at him, "Sure, now you act tough once Mitch has confronted him."

I didn't listen to their jabbering and went off to sixteen and hit my drive and nonchalantly asked if anyone had a cell phone. Out of five guys one would think someone would have brought the technology along. As we watched him walk off the course into the trees where the fifteenth hole dogleg started, I saw three ladies coming up fifteen. I picked up my bag and walked down the middle of fifteen's fairway. When I reached the three of them, I asked Cheryle Kristal for her cell phone as I knew she always had hers along. I called the pro shop and talked to Dale Jones, our Golf Professional. I asked Dale if they were still looking for a guy wearing blue jeans, t-shirt, boots, and a baseball cap.

"Yes we are. Where did you see him?"

I quickly told Dale the story, that I had just spoke to the guy and told him to leave the golf course. After I hung up, I asked the ladies if they had seen this guy walk around the dogleg while they were teeing off. They said they hadn't, but I think

I must have scared them with the seriousness of my body language and voice. I told them what had happened, and one of them said, "Mitch, you're a hero!"

This was exactly what I didn't want to hear. "Ladies, it was no big deal." I was hoping to stop the potential "Did you hear what happened on fifteen today" story from spreading.

I headed back to my tee shot on sixteen, which managed to stay out of the water, and played my second shot to the green, thinking the incident was over. We putted out on sixteen and started walking to the seventeenth tee box. The cart path between sixteen and seventeen splits two lakes and it's about a 200-yard walk from sixteen's green to seventeen's tee box. The clubhouse sits on a hill above seventeen's tee box. In order to walk or drive a cart from the clubhouse to hole fifteen you needed to pass by us. We watched as the cavalry arrived—three golf carts moving as fast as they could, our head pro in one, followed by police officers in the other two. I had to chuckle to myself because it was one officer per cart—these were big guys, and I'm not so sure the cart would have made it if they both had jumped on one. They didn't stop to say anything to us, just gave the usual one-hand wave and continued on their mission.

We finished our round and headed for the clubhouse to get something to drink. As we walked into the lower level lobby, I had this weird feeling that word had already spread that I had confronted this guy, and people were going to blow it out of proportion. I went to the men's room to wash my hands and returned to the grill when people started asking me, "Mitch, did you see the guy?" "What did he look like?" "How old was he?" "What did you say to him?"

I didn't want to answer any of the questions, so I said he was a young guy, and I asked him to leave, that was it. I turned around and went home, not wanting to listen to the "What if he had a . . ." or "What if he would've . . ." stories.

Brenda normally worked from 7:00 a.m. to 3:00 p.m. on Saturdays. When she got home, it was around 4:30 p.m. We both sat around and did our normal chitchat about each other's day . . . except I couldn't tell her about my encounter . . . not yet anyway.

It was around 5:30 p.m. when we both started getting ready for dinner. Brenda was still upstairs "putting on her face," as she called it, when I took the opportunity to use the phone without her hearing me. I called the police department and introduced myself as the guy who talked to the "fugitive" that morning. I wanted to find out if they apprehended him or not. The dispatcher started laughing and said they still hadn't caught the guy.

"Is he dangerous?" I asked.

"No, not at all," was his reply. "He was pulled over early this morning for a felony he committed, and he fled his vehicle. I guess he didn't want to spend Labor Day weekend in jail."

"I didn't think he was dangerous," I said. "You wouldn't have allowed anyone to play golf if he was dangerous was what I had figured."

"You're right about that."

"So you never caught the guy?"

"No, he's still out there."

"We don't have to worry if we leave the house empty for a few hours do we?"

"No, don't worry about a thing."

Brenda came downstairs and asked who was on the phone.

"The police dispatcher," I said.

She gave me one of those "What are you talking about" expressions, and I knew I had to tell her what had happened earlier that morning.

Her first reaction was exactly what I thought she would say, "He could have pulled a gun on you or a knife!"

"Honey, I had already figured that the authorities would have cleared the golf course if he was dangerous. Besides, he was much more scared of me than I was of him."

I could tell Brenda just chalked it up to another one of my crazy antics. I explained what the dispatcher said and reassured her there wouldn't be any problems with leaving the house even though he was still at large. We got in my Yukon and took off to meet Brenda's mother Donna, our thirteen-year-old niece Kim, Brenda's Aunt Lil, and Uncle Harry for dinner at Jensen's

Supper Club in Eagan. Lil's brother John Voss, Sr., is Brenda's father. Lil is in her seventies, and her husband Harry, "old one-eye," as I call him because he can only see out of one eye, is in his eighties. As we approached the final stop light before turning left, I saw "old one-eye" coming the opposite direction.

"Hey, look Brenda. There's Lil and Harry in their new Caddy." My Yukon, which is a large SUV, is very hard to miss due to its size, but, of course, they didn't see us. I told Brenda, "We better follow 'em because you know they don't know where they're going."

Sure enough, they missed the right turn to Jensen's and drove north an extra block turning left into a strip mall. Both Brenda and I were laughing so hard at the fact that one day it would be us who would be old and lost. We decided to stop the Yukon and watch the humor unfold. They drove all the way to the end of the strip mall and turned around heading right at us.

Lil and Harry Weinandt.

I figured they couldn't miss a large, black SUV stopped in the middle of their path. So I made it even easier, I rolled my window down and started waving my left arm out the window, trying desperately to flag them down. Sure enough they drove right by . . . almost hitting us in the process.

"Honey, this is too funny. Do you think we should go after them?" I paused as I looked at Brenda, who couldn't answer me because she was laughing so hard.

By the time I had turned the Yukon around to chase them down, we could see the bright red brake lights come on, and we figured Kim or Donna must have said something to Harry. When we pulled up alongside their car, Brenda's mom, Donna, and Kim were laughing as hard as we were. I think Harry was a little embarrassed, but he couldn't stop laughing at himself. We told them to follow us to Jensen's, and we had a wonderful evening together.

Chapter 2

Sunday, September 2nd, 2001
The Day My Life Changed Forever

Sunday morning September 2nd, 2001, Brenda actually slept in until 6:30 a.m. I asked her if she wanted me to spend the day with her, her mother, Donna, and our niece Kim at the Mall of America or would it be "okay" if I went golfing with the boys.

"Go golfing," she said in an encouraging voice. "We're going to run around all day anyway. I'll see you this afternoon when we get back."

"I think I'm going to bake chocolate chip cookies this afternoon to take to DeLaney Lake on Monday," I told her. She looked at me and smiled, knowing I wouldn't get those cookies baked.

I was headed to the practice range to hit a few golf balls before we teed off, when Kenney Z. stopped me in the parking lot and stated, "I hear you're our hero."

I knew immediately he was referencing the "fugitive" episode from Saturday. "Kenney, that's exactly what I didn't want to hear. It was no big deal." I told him. I have a pretty good wit about me, so I decided to tell Kenney something to make him laugh and forget about the fugitive episode. Since Mendakota Country Club has a "no denim" policy, I just blurted out, "Kenney, I stopped the guy because he was wearing blue jeans and everyone knows blues jeans aren't allowed at Bushwood, sir," acting like it was a quote from Caddy Shack.

I teed off around 8:30 a.m. and was home by 12:45 p.m. I needed to start cleaning my Yukon and get her ready for our Monday departure for Canada. This was the "guys" annual fall fishing trip to Delaney Lake Lodge in Ontario. I was taking three buddies in my truck, and we would be meeting the rest of our group in Nester Falls, Ontario, Monday evening.

9

It's a tedious task cleaning a large SUV by hand, but I had invested a lot of money into extras like chrome wheels, meaty tires, fender to fender flares and running boards. Plus, I added dual pipes (chrome of course) to give that extra growl. By the time the "girls" got home from their day together at the Mall of America, all I had left to do was put on the liquid glass and rub it off. Of course I hadn't baked the chocolate chip cookies. Part of my plan was to plant the seed in her head earlier that morning. I knew once she found out I hadn't baked them, she would end up making her world famous cookies for me.

It was 4:30 p.m. Sunday afternoon September 2nd, 2001, when Brenda drove her black BMW into the driveway. Since I had my Yukon parked at an angle taking up the whole garage making it easier for me to clean her, it meant Brenda would need to park in front of the third stall. When she got out of her car and walked towards me, I immediately noticed how beautiful she looked, strikingly beautiful. It was almost as if I was seeing her for the first time and saying to myself, "Damn, that sure is one fine woman!"

She was wearing an orange tank top with light tan shorts and those sandals she favored with no backs. She still had her sunglasses on, and her gorgeous blonde hair blew in the wind as she walked toward me. Her luscious lips matched her shirt and she kept her fingernails perfectly painted. She looked stunning with her jewelry and that smile of hers. She was always smiling, especially when she saw me. I must have been staring at her in a daze because it took me a second to answer her when she asked me how it was going.

"She looks great doesn't she, but so do you, honey," was my comment to her.

"Wow, you're really doing a great job, honey," she said. Her next question was, "Did you get those chocolate chip cookies baked?"

I had to hesitate for the effect. "Aaaah, no I didn't," I said, saying it in just a way that told her I needed her help. She understood my madness. You don't spend eleven years living with someone and not know what they're up to when it comes to baking chocolate chip cookies. Mine would suck; hers were the best. She just smiled as I watched her walk into the house, her hips swinging back and forth as they always did when she was on a mission. God, how I loved watching her strut!

A few minutes later her mother, Donna, joined me in the garage and asked me what I using on the truck to make it shine. I told her it was Liquid Glass. She asked me if it would be okay if she helped me.

"Sure you can, Donna. I'll put it on and you can follow behind me wiping it off."

As we made our way around the passenger side to the back end and around towards the driver's side, we were discussing various subjects, none I can recall to this day except for the one question I asked her. "Donna, how did Carla's husband die?" I wanted to know the answer, but, to this very day, I don't know why I even asked the question. Carla is now married to Brenda's brother Jack.

"You know, Mitch," Donna said, "Carla's husband was a hay man, and one day he had a round bale on the loader, and it tipped backwards and rolled down onto him and crushed him." Donna's comment had barely enough time to sink in when the garage door that goes into our kitchen opened.

The time frame between Donna's answering my question and my hearing the garage door open was maybe *five seconds*. My niece Kim stood holding the garage door open and said to me in a very calm voice, "Mitch, you need to come inside. Something is wrong with Brenda."

I'll never forget those words as long as I live. I didn't run to the door. I just set the Liquid Glass down, put the rag beside the can and walked inside. My brain was telling me "No, you're not hearing this. There's nothing wrong with her."

Flashbacks started happening to me before I even made it to the kitchen. You see I had been having premonitions all year long that something was going to happen to her. I didn't know what it was, but for some reason these feelings had been with me for months. I never shared those thoughts with anyone because to me it was sick, demented. Why did I have these feelings that something was going to happen to her? Now the nightmares that haunted me were about to unfold right before my eyes.

11

It was so surreal to hear those words come out of Kim's mouth. "Mitch, you need to come inside. Something is wrong with Brenda."

Nothing was ever wrong with my wife. As I opened the garage door to the hallway that leads to the kitchen, I immediately saw her legs sticking straight out from behind our island bar. My peripheral vision also picked up the large bowl on the kitchen counter, and I knew she had been baking chocolate chip cookies for me to take on my fishing trip. When I got to her, I could see she had managed to position herself on two of our high back barstools, her butt on one chair and her shoulders on the other, laying face up with her arms at her sides, her hands clenched into fists. I touched her and could feel she was as stiff as a board, her head thrown back with her chin in the air, and she was gulping for oxygen. I placed both my hands on her face and slowly moved them behind her neck for support. I noticed right away that her eyes were rolled back in her head. She had lost all the color in her skin, and I knew she was in deep trouble.

"Brenda, can you hear me honey? Just relax and breathe," I told her, hoping she could hear me. "Just relax, baby. You're going to be okay."

My brain was going a million miles a second. I was very calm, which to this day still amazes me. I continued to speak to her, not knowing if she could comprehend anything I was saying. I looked at Donna, who had followed me into the house, searching for answers. "Donna, is she having a seizure?"

Although Brenda had never had a seizure, another of our nieces, Melissa Voss, Jack's daughter, had had seizures since she was six months old. At eighteen, Melissa was still struggling with them.

"It looks like she is, Mitch."

"What should I do?" I asked Donna as I tried to get my fingers into Brenda's mouth because she had her teeth clinched together.

"Don't put your fingers in her mouth!" Donna yelled at me.

I wasn't sure what I could do to help Brenda, so I continued talking to her, telling her to relax and breathe. The whole time I was keeping my eyes focused on her lips. I knew any sign of blue lips meant she was in deep trouble. Within seconds, she quit gulping for air, and her lips turned blue.

"Call 911, Donna!" I yelled. I turned to Brenda not knowing if she could comprehend anything that was going on and put my face next to hers and told her, "Honey, I'm going to give you mouth to mouth." I picked her up off the chairs, she was still stiff as a board head to toe and I laid her on the floor. My brain was racing so fast I couldn't believe the thoughts I was having as Donna tried to hand me the phone. I was thinking, *Why is Donna handing me the phone?* I said to myself, *I need to give Brenda mouth to mouth not be talking to a 911 operator.* There was no time to be angry or panic . . . all those thoughts ran through my head in a split second. I put the phone to my ear as I heard, "911," as the operator answered.

"I need an ambulance at 867 Mendakota Court immediately. My wife has collapsed."

When the 911 operator tried to ask me questions, all I could do was tell her, "Get them here NOW!" I hung up the phone and immediately began mouth to mouth.

The first puff of air I sent into her lungs caused her chest to heave, just like it was suppose to. The second puff did the same thing, and she immediately responded by breathing on her own. Her lips were no longer blue, her eyes rolled forward, and she looked straight at me. Her body was no longer stiff. I had her back, and everything was going to be okay. "Brenda baby, you're doing great. Keep breathing, honey. I want you to hold my hand and squeeze it."

She put her right hand in my left and squeezed with so much strength, strength I never knew she had. Her eyes were so full of life, I believed the scare she gave me was over. She was going to be "OKAY!" For a split second, I had convinced myself she was back to normal. I decided to ask her a few questions to find out how her brain was functioning. "Honey, do you know who I am?"

"You're, Miiittttccch," she said in a very slow and slurred voice.

All I could think was that she had had a stroke.

My mind flashed back to the conversations Brenda and I had had over the years about getting old and what would happen if one of us had a stroke or became bedridden. We both decided we wanted the other one to "pull the plug" vs. being incapacitated. But there's a huge difference between talking about what we thought we would or should do, especially when we were both healthy, verses being put into a situation when my spouse might die. The reality of hearing her voice and thinking she had had a stroke didn't bother me. My brain was off to the races again. I could only think of *her*. Of her not being able to walk, not able to go to work and "do hair" which she loved, and not able to hold my hand or feed herself. I could only think about her losing her will to live because she would no longer have the ability to garden or decorate our home, the two things she was so passionate about. But she was alive, and I thanked God she was alive. I'd take her anyway God would give her back to me.

My second question to her was, "Do you know who this is?" I was pointing at her mother.

"Mooommm," she said in that same slurred voice.

"Do you know where you are?"

"Home," and she said it perfectly. She loved her home because she made it the most peaceful, loving place on earth. She looked right into my eyes as she squeezed my hand again for what became the last time. I could hear her telling me how much she loved me even though she wasn't saying a thing. It was the look she gave me that meant so much . . . the most comforting look she had ever given me, telling me everything would be all right.

From the time I brought her back to life, asked her those three questions, and received "the look" she gave me, it had only been one and a half to two minutes. That was it, and I felt her leave me as her hand went limp. The love she showed me in her eyes was gone. The love of my life, my best friend, my wife, was dead. I was the only one who knew she was gone, and there was nothing more I could do for her. It was the most helpless feeling I have ever felt in my life.

The paramedics walked into the house only seconds after I felt her go. The reason they arrived so fast was that we lived less than a mile from the fire station. I sat there holding her hand and talking to her.

"Sir, we need you to get out of the way."

But I wasn't going to move that easily. This was *my* wife.

"Sir we need to remove her shirt." With scissors in hand the paramedic was about to cut my wife's shirt from her body.

"I'll take her shirt off her!" I told them. I knew Brenda wouldn't want her clothing cut. The second I got her shirt off they told me the bra had to be removed. I must have hesitated because they didn't ask twice, and they cut it off before I could say a thing. To watch a complete stranger cut her bra off and expose her was unbearable at first. I was thinking, *My wife is one of the classiest women I have ever met. How can they do this to her, expose her like that.* That's when I realized these people were professionals, and they were just doing their job. It's hard for me to explain why all these thoughts raced in and out of my head. I wanted to make them stop, but I wasn't in control; I wasn't able to shut them off. *Brenda, I know if you had a choice, you wouldn't have wanted the paramedics to do what they did, but I couldn't do anything about it, honey.*

There were so many people at the house, firemen, police, paramedics, and a neighbor I didn't know who helped with heart massage. They all did what they could for what seemed like an eternity. I didn't want to believe that she was dead because I could see on the heart monitor they had hooked up to her that she had a heart beat. I didn't realize that the blips I was seeing on the heart monitor were being artificially produced by the heart massage.

"Is she okay?" I must have asked this five times without a response from anyone.

"Is she breathing on her own?" I asked with still no response. "Someone please tell me what is going on!"

"We're breathing for her, sir," was the only response they would give me.

"Brenda, keep fighting!" I yelled at her. "You're strong, baby. You can make it!" But deep inside my heart I knew she was gone. It must be the bond two people have when they are so in love. They share each other's feelings. I also knew she didn't suffer. But why? Why did this happen to someone like her, and not me? Brenda was the healthiest person I knew. She just had her annual exam on July 16th, and the results proved she was in perfect health.

While the paramedics continued to work on her, I picked up the phone to call one of my best friends, Mike Chase. While I stood there staring at Brenda lying on the floor, my emotions started to well up inside me, and I felt as if I were starting to have a panic attack.

"Hello?" It was Jackie, Mike's wife, who answered.

"Jackie, I think Brenda just died. Can you please tell Mike I need him to get to the house right away."

"What do you mean died?" Jackie asked in a voice filled with total disbelief. It was only two weeks earlier that Brenda and I were at Mike and Jackie's for a barbeque along with the rest of the gang we hung out with.

"Brenda collapsed in the house. The paramedics are here and, Jackie, I know she's dead. Please tell Mike I need him."

"I'll get hold of him right away, Mitch!"

I hung up the phone with tears streaming down my face.

The paramedics continued to work on her for several more minutes before getting her ready to take to the hospital. During the whole ordeal, they had hit her three times with the paddles with no response, nothing. At one point in time, I'm not sure when, but one paramedic requested someone write down a specific time. I believe it was that moment it hit me, those feelings I had when her hand went limp in mine were being confirmed as true. She really was gone. I just started sobbing out of control as my mind flashed back and forth from the reality of Brenda being dead to "This must be a dream."

Chapter 3

The Hospital

It was such a helpless feeling as I watched the paramedics put her on the stretcher and take her out to the ambulance. I didn't go with her to the hospital. Brenda didn't want me to. She told me to stay behind and clean up the mess before I left the house. She didn't want anyone coming over to a messy house that evening. I know it sounds strange, but Brenda started talking to me the very moment they put her in the ambulance.

Brenda was taken to United Hospital, in St. Paul. As the ambulance pulled away, Mike came into the house, looking white as a ghost. Fortunately for me, Mike had just finished playing a round of golf and was in the grill when Jackie called the club to have him paged.

"Mitch, what happened?"

"Mike, I found her in the kitchen. She had managed to get herself on these two barstools . . ." I finished telling Mike the story, reliving the ordeal once again. "I can't believe this is happening, Mike. Brenda may be dead."

"Come on, let's go, Mitch," he said.

"Mike, before we leave, we need to clean up this mess. You know Brenda. She wouldn't want anyone to see the house looking like this."

Scattered about the floor and on the island were empty plastic containers that once held syringes and whatever else the paramedics had used to try to save her life. The hardwood floor where she had lain was sticky from the fluids that must have spilled. Mike and I cleaned up the mess and put the kitchen back in order. There was one item I just couldn't touch—the stainless steel mixing bowl next to the stove, the one filled with cookie dough and chocolate chips. I could see the labor of love she had put into getting those cookies ready. Now they just sat there, waiting for her to bake them.

Before we left for the hospital, I asked Kim if she would do me a favor and stay home with our dog Einstein. I wanted to protect her from the words we would eventually hear at the hospital.

Donna had gone ahead of us with a police officer. When we arrived at the hospital, admissions needed information that only I knew. In between giving the hospital admissions person the information about Brenda, I kept asking if I could see her. The lady behind the desk kept reassuring me I would be able to see her "But at the moment there are twenty people in the room working on her."

I didn't know what that meant, but it didn't do anything to calm me down. Jackie arrived moments later, and the four of us where told we could wait in a room around the corner.

"Mike, I know she's gone," was all I kept repeating.

"Mitch, you don't know that."

But I did know it and so did Donna.

In the waiting room, there was a couch and a couple of lounge chairs, a telephone and the obvious box of tissues. I sat on the couch, and Donna sat next to me on my right. Mike was on my left, sitting on one of the chair arms in order to stay close. Jackie sat next to Donna. We had just managed to get comfortable when a nurse came to the room to explain the situation. She hesitated to say anything for at least ten seconds, and then told us, "It's not looking good. We are doing everything we can. The doctor will be in to tell you more."

Before she could turn around to leave, I told her, "I know she's gone."

She didn't say a word as she kept walking towards the door; she just gave me a look that told me I was right.

"Mitch, don't give up hope. There's still a chance she'll be all right." Mike was trying his best to keep my spirits up but I knew, I just knew she was gone.

The doctor entered the room no more than five minutes after the nurse left to tell us the same story as the nurse had. "Folks, it doesn't look good. I'm waiting for the cardiologist to get here, and we'll be back as soon as we know more."

Ten minutes later, both the doctor and cardiologist came into the room to tell us, "I'm sorry, we did everything we could, but we never did get a pulse."

Just the words, "I'm sorry," was the reality no one wanted to hear. Donna yelled out something and started crying on my shoulder.

"I know," I said to both doctors, "I knew she was gone at the house." It was all I could say as the river of tears I cried for her continued to flow. As both doctors departed, we were joined by two women dressed as nurses, but I'm not sure whether or not they weren't staff members who are sent to help the families during a crisis.

"I want to be with her," I blurted out, looking right at the two of them.

"I'm sorry but you'll have to wait for the room to be cleared before you can see her," one of them quickly answered, making it appear she was in charge and the other one just an observer.

"How long will that be?" I wanted to know right away.

"It won't take long," she reassured us. We waited for ten minutes before they would allow us to go to her. Mike asked me if I wanted to go alone or if they should go with me.

"I want all of you to go with me," I requested, as I knew I needed their support.

When we entered the "area" (It wasn't even a room. Instead sheets were used as walls.), my eyes immediately focused on the "device" still strapped to her face. The paramedics had strapped this to her mouth before they put her in the ambulance. It looked like a mouth guard with straps. I believe the purpose was to support the tube they had inserted into her throat. I had overheard the paramedics at the house say, "We need to make sure her throat is clear before we take her to the hospital."

Since no one had taken the time to remove the apparatus, I felt as if Brenda had been violated in some way. It was very upsetting to me. I took it very personal seeing her lying there covered in a white sheet with this "thing" still strapped to her face.

19

"Please remove this immediately," I said to the three nurses who were standing outside our "walls of cloth" making idle chitchat.

"I'm sorry, but legally we can't remove it. Only the coroner can," was their quick response.

I decided it wasn't worth the argument and went to Brenda's side. I walked over to her and put my hands on her face and kissed her cheek. I started stroking her hair and telling her how much I loved her. "You're such a good person, baby, and I love you so much." It was so strange to touch her and not get a response. I kept thinking to myself as I held her, *This can't be happening; we are in the prime of our lives.* My brain was once again hitting me with all these thoughts that were driving me crazy. After spending no more than five minutes with her, I felt a sense of urgency to leave, and do so as quickly as I could. As I stood over her body crying, I could hear her telling me it was okay, that I wanted to go, that I should go home, to our home. But before I left, I noticed she was still wearing her jewelry. I removed her bracelets, earrings, and rings and asked one of the nurses where her clothes were.

"We had to cut them off, and we threw them away."

Her response to me was so cold, so callus, yet the words didn't seem to bother me, even though they were very harsh. I imagine people in medicine at some point in time become immune to all feelings and forget this is our first time experiencing a tragedy. How else could they function? Now, all I wanted to do was leave the hospital and go home.

As we were getting ready to leave the make-shift room she was in, I recognized the belt she had been wearing that day lying on a table next to her, it was one of my belts she had worn. As I picked up the belt and held it in my hands, I became very emotional. "Mike, I want to go home, now!" I demanded.

"If that's what you want, then let's go." One of the staff overheard our conversation and stopped us. She asked, "We would like you to try and answer some questions before you leave, if that's okay?"

"No!" I said. "I want to go home."

"Mitch, let's sit down with them and answer their questions," Mike said in a very calming voice.

That was all it took for me to settle down. It all seemed to be okay if it was okay with Mike. I can't recall what the first question they asked me was, but I do remember being asked, "Which funeral home would you like us to contact?" With everything happening so fast, all I could think was, *At age thirty-nine I'm not suppose to be doing this. I'm not supposed to be at this hospital. These things happen to other people not to us. Someone go get my wife and tell me everything is okay. And, exactly how am I suppose to know which funeral home I want her taken to?*

I turned to Mike and gave him that helpless look that I'm sure he was too familiar with by now. Unfortunately, Mike had experience dealing with the passing of a loved one. Mike's father had passed away several years earlier, and only recently I was at his mother's services. Mike was able to suggest a funeral home that would be close to our home.

As we were making our way out of the hospital, we were stopped by the two ladies with us earlier in the waiting room. They said they needed us to answer a few more questions before we left. The four of us followed them back to the waiting room, and they started pelting me with question after question.

I'm not sure how many questions they asked me because I don't recall all of them. There is one that sticks out in my mind. It was the easiest question for me to answer. "Where would you like Brenda to be buried?"

Without one second of hesitation, I looked right at Donna and said, "I would like Brenda buried next to her father, John Voss, Sr." Only someone who has experienced the loss of a child knew what that must have meant to Donna. As she wept, Donna asked me if I was sure I wanted her buried next to her father. Johnny, as we all called him, had died five years earlier from brain cancer.

"Donna, Brenda loved her father so much. I know she would want to be buried next to him." Johnny and Brenda loved to dance together. Johnny was a big man, six feet, four inches and strong as a bull, but always had a smile on his face. Brenda was five feet, ten inches, a beautiful stunning blonde, and a smile that came right from her father. I can still see them dancing together at the wedding dances we attended. I would watch her and Johnny dance together, and it looked like they were floating on air. "Donna, I know they are dancing in heaven right now, smiling their big beautiful smiles and laughing."

"Yes, they are. Thank you, Mitch."

It was time to leave the hospital, time to go home and start making phone calls. There would be so many calls to make. We walked out of the hospital, Donna with Jackie, me with Mike. I just wanted this horror film to stop, to rewind and give us a different ending. This wasn't supposed to happen to her, or to us. This happened to other people, people we didn't know. Not to us. I just couldn't shut my brain down. I remember turning to Mike right before we left the hospital and telling him, "Mike don't let me do anything rash."

I don't know why I said it or what I meant by it, but Mike reassured me he wouldn't let me to anything crazy.

"Mike, it's going to get really bad for me. I mean really bad. In two weeks when everyone is back into their old routines, I'll be all alone, and then it's going to get bad." I already had this empty

Mike and Jackie Chase.

feeling in the pit of my stomach, my heart was already broken, my head was spinning, yet I knew there would come a day when people would forget to ask, "How are you doing?" I couldn't figure out why all these thoughts kept bombarding me. I shouldn't be thinking about me. I should be thinking about Brenda. I kept asking myself, *Why is my brain doing this to me?* That's when Mike made a promise to me.

"Mitch, we won't let that happen to you."

Thank you Mike and Jackie for being there for Donna and helping me through the night of September 2nd, 2001. We will never forget what the two of you did for us.

Chapter 4

Hardest Thing
I've Ever Done

When I walked into our house, I felt like Brenda was with me the whole time. She was almost guiding my every move, every word. The only thing I can say is that it was so comforting to be back at "home." I completely forgot about our thirteen-year-old niece Kim and our dog, Einstein. When I saw Kim, I didn't have the heart to tell her that her Aunt Brenda had passed away. Kim really looked forward to her annual trip to the Twin Cities to stay with her Aunt Brenda and me. I couldn't find it in my heart to tell her, not yet anyway.

I still can't recall how long we were at the hospital nor what time it was when we got home. Time for me was standing still. I still can't recall how long we had been at the hospital nor what time it was when we got home. I do know this much: I felt like I was in my own dream, and Brenda would be walking through the front door telling me, "I'm home. Wake up, honey. I was just kidding about the dying thing." When my mind would clear from those thoughts I'd find myself looking for her, at times believing she really was coming home. Then I'd hear her talking to me, in an angel-like voice, so calm, and always smiling. "Mitch, you need to start calling our friends and family. I'll help you through this."

I turned to Mike and Jackie and told them, "I need to start making phone calls."

"Okay, whatever you want to do, we're here for you," and I needed them to lean on.

Brenda and I kept a black book with names, addresses, and phone numbers of our family and friends in the top drawer of our desk in the kitchen. The first person I called was my brother Todd. I didn't think about the emotional impact the news of Brenda dying would have on him. I was having enough trouble comprehending in my mind, she was never coming home.

Todd and Brenda had a very special bond. She was his only sister-in-law, and my emphasis is on the sister part. I believe for Todd, Brenda was like having the big sister he never had, someone he looked up to, respected and loved. She was always taking care of Todd when we were together. Especially when it came to helping him buy clothes for himself. Brenda loved to spend Todd's money, mainly because Todd can be an extremely frugal person when it came to spending his cash. I told Brenda, "I'll bet you Todd still has the first penny he was given as a child."

"Don't worry," she said. "I'll show Todd how to spend his money." Not only could she spend his money, Todd let her do it.

It must have been horrifying for Todd to receive my phone call telling him someone he loved, who was very special in all our lives, had died. Todd didn't know how she died, I didn't tell him any of the details. All I told him was, "I need you here with me as soon as possible." Our phone conversation didn't last very long. The shock of the news was enough to end the call.

"I'll be there as soon as I can." Todd told me. He left Watertown, South Dakota, immediately after our conversation. He didn't even take time to pack; he just drove. It's a four-hour drive from his driveway to mine; I estimated he would arrive around 1:30 a.m. I was informed by our mother that Todd had called her on his cell phone while traveling and needed to know how Brenda died. Mom said to me that Todd thought Brenda had been killed in a car accident. I can't imagine driving four hours thinking my sister-in-law was just killed in a car accident. It makes sense to me why Todd thought it must have been a car accident. I hadn't given him any details, and he knew Brenda hadn't been sick a day in her life. Mom also told me that Todd was crying so hard when she talked to him, she was worried he wouldn't make it to our house. I can't ever remember seeing Todd cry, but it didn't surprise me because Brenda meant so much to him.

I'm not sure what kept me going that night, but dialing number after number and telling the same story seemed to be therapeutic. Whoever answered the phone, I would first let them know who I was and then followed it with, "I need to tell you that Brenda died tonight."

The normal response from the people I spoke to was dead silence. I didn't know what else to say to them. I was doing what I felt I needed to be doing, letting people know what happened to this very special person in all our lives. After the initial shock wore off, the first question I was always asked was "What happened?"

I'd spend a few minutes explaining as much as I knew without going into to many details, but I passed on enough information to satisfy those who pushed for more answers. For those not home, I left a short message. After each call I'd hang up and glance back at Mike and Jackie who were "watching over me." It was so very comforting to have them with me.

One call in particular still stands out among all I made and received that night. It was to Carla and Dwight Kuyper. Dwight answered the phone, and I told him what happened to Brenda and asked him to tell Carla. "I don't have the heart to tell her myself Dwight. I need you to do it for me."

"I will, Mitch, I will." I could tell he was in shock from our conversation, but the terrible news he would have to relay to Carla would be better coming from him.

Brenda and Carla had known each other since 1978, and they were very close. Two weeks before Brenda died, on August 16th, 2001, Brenda had planned a special trip to Sioux Falls, South Dakota, just to see Carla. They hadn't seen each other since the day we were married on August 1st, 1998, when Carla sang at our wedding reception.

After I hung up with Dwight, I had made one or two more calls when the phone rang. It was Carla, and she was so angry with me.

"Mitch, what do you mean Brenda has died!" she demanded to know. Her voice was full of disbelief and anger. "No, no, this isn't true, Mitch!" she shouted at me.

"I'm so sorry, Carla, but it is." I didn't know what else to tell her.

"Oh, my God!" she yelled into the phone, and I could hear her start to cry. The anger left her voice and I could feel the compassion set in. Sobbing and trying to compose herself she told me, "Mitch, I'm so sorry!"

"I know you are," I said to her as I could no longer hold back my tears.

"Mitch, you know we love you!"

As we both hung up the phone, I knew how much pain she was in. I still hurt for Carla. I know how much Brenda meant to her.

Chapter 5

The Red Cross &
Social Security

American Red Cross

We'll be there.

here were only so many phone calls I could make before I needed to take a break and try to regroup my emotions for the next round of calls. What I found myself doing instead of relaxing was pacing back and forth from room to room. When I finally was able to sit down next to Mike, it only lasted for a minute or so when the phone rang, and I was up again. This time I was completely taken off guard by the voice on the other end of the line. It was the Red Cross.

The lady who was representing the Red Cross was extremely polite and very sensitive to the current situation. I could tell this was not the first time she had made a call like this. She was very professional in her explanation as to the purpose of her call, which was to ask for permission to obtain certain body parts from Brenda. She told me I had the right to say "no" to anything she asked for. She explained very delicately that under the current circumstances, Brenda had been gone too long for them to take any of her vital organs. What she asked for was her eyes, her legs below the knee, her upper arm bones and skin off her back. She started with the upper arm and asked if that would be okay. I told her no. My reasoning was simple, Brenda had the most beautiful arms in the world, and I wanted an open casket. The second request was for her eyes. Before she asked me for a yes or no answer, she

28

said she needed to explain that there would be a high probability Brenda would have severe puffiness around her eyes afterwards. After her explanation, I just couldn't allow them to take her eyes. I told her no. Then she asked me if they could take her legs below the knees. That was an easy one for me. "YES." Brenda would want someone to benefit from her legs. She had the greatest legs. In all the years I knew Brenda, she always wore her skirts above her knees, never afraid to show off those legs. And, of course, she loved to dance. I knew if Brenda could help someone else walk, run or become a dancer, she would be all for it. Next I was asked the question regarding the skin from her back. Again, this was easy for me because I was told it would be used to help children who were burn victims. Brenda loved children. For Brenda to be able to contribute to a suffering child's life was such an easy decision, it made me cry.

The toughest part about the Red Cross interview came next. She started asking me very personal questions about our sexual habits, if We had multiple partners during the past five years, if we engaged in drug use . . . and it only got worse. I thought these questions she was asking were crossing the line of decency, and it made me want to throw up, I was so disgusted. I wanted to yell at her on the phone and tell her, "My wife was a princess. We were faithful to each other for eleven years. She was the most beautiful person both inside and out. How dare you ask these types of questions!" But I kept my composure and answered each and every one of her questions; it seemed like fifty of them. We ended the interview with her thanking me for my patience and my time. She said she did need to inform me that, by law, Brenda's blood would be tested for AIDS before any donations could occur. I would only be informed of the results of the blood tests if they were found to be positive, which, of course, I knew wasn't an issue.

Two months after Brenda's death, on October 30th, 2001, I received a packet from the Red Cross. Inside was a booklet designed to help me understand the emotional roller coaster I'd been going through. It had information on support groups found locally in the Twin Cities. After reading and rereading the booklet they sent me, I felt really good about myself and the direction

I was going. I now had a deeper understanding that my decision to move forward and be happy was the right decision. My "choice" to be "okay," was, for me, one big step in the right direction toward getting on with my life. I've always believed that we individually have choices about how we live our lives. In my opinion, each person has the right to choose to be happy or to be sad. When it came to how I was going to deal with Brenda's death, I decided I was going to follow the path of happiness; it was how Brenda would want me to act.

I've found it very interesting how so many people have opinions when it comes to the grieving process. My take on grieving is: how we wish to grieve is personal and no one has the right to tell someone else how to grieve. Everyone grieves differently. There are no right or wrong ways to grieve, but there are healthy and unhealthy signs you need to be aware of. I have included a complete list of healthy and unhealthy emotions people will experience during their own personal grieving process. This isn't a rule book on grieving, but a guide the Red Cross has published. If there are any words of encouragement I can pass along to those who have lost a loved one, I would say first and foremost make sure you understand where you are in the grieving process.

I've included my own experiences, which I hope will give you a better understanding of what I've gone through.

Initially after a death of a loved one, a person will go through **numbness and shock** especially if your loved one died sudden and unexpected, which was my case with Brenda. I had so many conflicting emotions running through my head. As I now look back, it's hard to realize how I managed during those first few days.

Anger: It's possible to feel anger at the time or soon after a loved one's death. It's perfectly okay. I found myself extremely angry eight days after Brenda's death and needed to forewarn all those around me that my anger was not aimed directly at them. Everyone understood, but I know it wasn't a pretty sight. I can guarantee other people will expect a person to handle grief a "certain way," according to them. This may cause the grieving person to become angry with them or to distance themselves from those who believe they are trying to help. Expressing anger is one way of relieving the pent-up emotions that are kept deep inside. Of course, if the anger is allowed to turn inward, a person could become hateful toward themselves, and this is not healthy. Healthy anger is good; unhealthy anger can delay the journey through the grieving process. Seeking professional help if anger is getting out of hand and interfering with life is a good plan.

Grieving people may find themselves in a state of **denial or lack of closure,** especially if they were not present when their loved one died. People who do not get to see the deceased's body experience a strong case of denial. This situation often occurs during war, following a fire or accident (if the body is badly burned or not easily recognizable). Going through old pictures or preparing a special memorial may help get a handle on the loss.

Of all the emotions that surface after a loved one's death, feelings of **hopelessness** are probably the most strongly felt. And it's perfectly understandable. When I felt Brenda leave me, it was the most hopeless feeling I have ever felt in my life. I just lost a person very important to me, my "center," my "balance." Looking into the future and not being able to see her with me gave me a feeling that nothing I had thought was important mattered anymore.

Loneliness is another part of the emotional journey of grief. It's very hard to overcome. Loneliness may bring on emotions of blame and anger towards friends and family. The best advice I can give is to reach out to others, don't wait for the phone to ring, pick it up and make the call. Blaming or being angry with others for not calling, writing or stopping by are not healthy emotions to harbor.

Withdrawal or **emotionally distancing** oneself from others. People who are grieving may find themselves withdrawing from others because they feel more comfortable dealing with their grief in private. While this is understandable, it can also reinforce loneliness, the sense of helplessness, and feelings of anger. Extra effort should be spent reaching out to others and allowing them to help in the grief process.

With almost every death, there are feelings of **guilt**. Sometimes these feelings are very powerful and may make people feel that they've reached an emotional dead end. People may feel guilty that the loved one died instead of them or they may not have done enough for the deceased when they were alive. My feelings of guilt were, "Why her and not me?" I didn't feel it was fair to have Brenda taken when her life was hitting its peak. Talking about these feelings was my personal way to overcome the guilt I had inside. I realized early on after her death how important it was for me not to feel guilty but to be happy for having spent the time I had with her on this planet. That is how she would have wanted those who knew and loved her to act.

Regret is a very powerful part of the emotions we all feel after a death. I can honestly say the only regret I can think of is not marrying Brenda five years earlier. We were truly blessed in our relationship.

Fear often follows death, especially an unanticipated one. Fear of being alone, sleeping in an empty house or fear of death are common feelings. Talking about fears with friends is the best help a person can get. My biggest fear hit me at the hospital. I felt I was going to be abandoned one day by my friends. I confronted my fear by telling them how much I needed them in my life.

Hostility rears its ugly head in ways I will not understand. A person who is grieving may find themselves being mean and hostile to other loved ones. Hostility usually grows out of the unexpressed anger over the loss. If hostility causes family and friends to shy away, a person may need to discuss this with a counselor.

Panic, thoughts of self-destruction, or **wanting to run away** may occur. People may feel so overwhelmed by grief that they feel unable to cope any longer. Sometimes just taking a few days away alone in a place that holds great meaning may help relieve these emotions. Spending some quiet time alone or away from everyday life is not running away if used for renewal or to prepare to deal with the future.

Lack of motivation and an **inability to concentrate** are natural emotions that occur in the grief process. It's a paralyzing feeling that "Nothing matters anymore," or that "nothing is important." A person may not feel like getting up in the morning, getting dressed, going to work, or taking care of chores around the house or may have **excessive energy** accompanied by a need to "keep busy" so as not to have time to think about the situation. Sometimes both of these conflicting emotions surface—an inability to concentrate followed by a burst of excessive energy—all within the same day or same hour. I've had this happen to me all in the same day—the passing of time has helped alleviate these up-and-down emotions.

Uncontrollable crying occurs with some people. For me, I had a bout with this on Monday morning September 3rd, the day after Brenda died. I cried for over three hours. I can't explain why it happened. The uncontrolled part hasn't happened since. Crying is a great emotional release. I'm usually alone when I shed my tears.

Many people experience an **unhealthy attachment** to the deceased or their possessions. In some instances, a person may only remember the loved one's accomplishments or think of him or her as a saint or a superhuman who never made a mistake or said a cross word. To help put the unhealthy attachment into perspective, spend a moment or two thinking about one of the worst memories you may have about your loved one or re-live a very humorous or embarrassing moment. In my case, I thought about a trait of Brenda's I didn't appreciate—her stubbornness. She knew it, too. She also had a bad habit of putting too much value in keeping things in perfect order and not allowing herself to "just relax." Others may choose to leave a loved one's room or possessions in place for a long time, not allowing anyone to move them. This is exactly what I did with her clothing for the first six months.

A person may experience **changing feelings about spiritual beliefs**. Some may question God as to why this has happened; others may become fanatically religious, often to the exclusion of others. For me, I do believe in God but I do not ask the question, "Why?" I can say this: people who push religion on you, thinking it is the only way to help you grieve, are not looking out for your best interest. I do appreciate and respect others opinions, but I do not necessarily have to agree with them.

Many people who are grieving express excessive **curiosity regarding the details of a loved one's death**, especially if the death was due to an accident. Some people may feel a **compulsion to talk about the deceased** or walk around the house talking to him or her. Some may even "hear" a loved one talking to them. I had both experiences during the first week. I needed to talk about Brenda with my friends and family, and I could hear her talking to me, but it was usually in private. As time has passed, my emotional roller coaster has leveled out. I no longer hear her talking to me, and I believe it is because she knows I'm going to be okay. She told me over and over again during those first seven days, "Mitch, everything is going to be okay. You're going to be okay." Once again, she was right!

* * *

Mike and Jackie had been sitting on the couch in the hearth area listening to everything that was going on. I turned and looked at Mike and asked him to do me a favor.

I hate to talk about this next part, but it happened and I need to say it. My brain went into overtime, and I was completely out of control, not physically but mentally. First of all, I need to clarify a couple of things: One, a big thanks to my wife for always having our finances in order and, two, it's my fault for not paying attention to how she did it. It was the not knowing how she did it part that caused me to panic. For some dumb reason, and it hit me out of the blue, I needed to know whether or not I had to continue to pay rent for her station at ShearMadness. I also needed to know whether or not there would be any Social Security benefits. When I look back on this memory of how I acted, Mike and Jackie must have thought I had lost my mind. I started digging through the bottom drawer of the desk in the kitchen, the same desk I had been sitting at making all the calls, searching desperately for the ShearMadness contract she had signed. Once I found the contract, I read it over, and there wasn't a clause regarding death, which meant I would need to pay $9,600.00 in rent to fulfill the agreement. I asked Mike to look it over (Mike's an attorney), and he told me not to worry about these things right now. But it did worry me, and I made a note to myself on the inside cover of the folder the contract was in. My note read, "Negotiate the $9,600.00." But it never came to that. The owners of ShearMadness, Rose and Jodi, never said a word about the rental agreement Brenda had signed. They even gave me Brenda's security deposit back. Talk about business owners with class! *Thanks, you two, for being such wonderful people. I know why Brenda was so happy renting from you.*

"While Mike glanced over the ShearMadness agreement, I continued digging for the Social Security file Brenda kept on herself. "Here, Mike, here is her Social Security statement. What benefits are available?"

"Mitch, you need to stop worrying about all this."

"But I need to know," I said. "What about the Social Security benefits, Mike?"

In my mind, the Social Security issue wasn't about me, it was about Brenda. She had paid so much money into Social Security over the past twenty-six years, and I wanted them to pay her back. After all, it was her money! I wanted to know how much she would be getting, not that I needed or wanted the money. I don't. It was important for me to know her years of hard work meant something. I knew she would want it that way.

To appease my persistence, Mike looked over the statement. "Mitch, it looks like you're entitled to $255.00," Mike told me.

My brain started racing again. All I could think of was how hard Brenda had labored for twenty-six years in the hair industry. She was the best of the best. Top five percent in the world, I figured. Anyone who could earn six figures cutting, coloring, perming, listening, giving advice and whatever else she did for her clients must have been in the top five percent. All those hours she worked. Up at 5:00 a.m. every morning, to work by 7:00 a.m. to meet her first appointment. Not getting home until 9:30 at night, all because she loved her job and her clients. And now all her hard work was only worth $255.00. What an insult to my wife's career! I said it before; I didn't care about the money, but I felt it belonged to Brenda, and she was entitled to it.

In order to collect the $255.00, I had to call Social Security and set up a phone interview, which I scheduled for

Friday September 21st, 2001, at 9:00 a.m. (The number is: 1-800-772-1213. Also use this number to order "Your Social Security Statement," which is free.) I was given instructions on what I needed for the phone interview: They requested I have with me my bank statement or checkbook for the account I would like my payment(s) deposited, a copy of our marriage license (or a divorce decree, if that was appropriate) and proof of death (death certificate or statement of death from the funeral director). Friday morning, I called the offices right at 9:00 a.m. and told them I had all the documents they asked for. In my case, I was told the funeral home forwarded the statement of death to their offices. This meant I only needed to give them the bank statement. I can't reiterate enough that the sole reason I was going through with this was to find out if they owed Brenda anything at all, and, if they did, I was going to collect for her. Once all the standard questions were answered, they told me what benefits were owed. "You are entitled to a Social Security payment of $255.00 because of the death of Brenda S. Voss. Oh, by the way, Mr. Freimark (and I had to correct her, it's pronounced "Frymark"), you will be eligible for survivor benefits at age sixty, age fifty if you become disabled, but you must apply for the benefits. We won't remind you."

When I checked Brenda's statement, it showed I would be eligible for $1,499 per month at age sixty, but only if I remembered to contact them. A lot can change during the next twenty years. Thanks, Uncle Sam!

* * *

With the phone calls pretty much done, I sat down and tried to relax. It must have been 10:30 p.m. My brain continued to go into rewind . . . showing me the same movie over and over again. It started the same every time. I saw Brenda laying on the floor in our kitchen, breathing normally after I gave her mouth to mouth, holding my left hand in her right and squeezing with the strength of ten men, looking deep into my eyes until she could see my soul, and showing me so much love. Believing she would be all right, believing she was safe. I was overwhelmed by the feeling running through my body as she left me, not wanting to believe it was true, that she was gone, gone forever. I tried to focus on something else, anything else. Then the phone rang; it was my niece Carrie returning the urgent message I had left on her answering machine. She had just moved to California August first, and I knew this would be hard for her.

"Mitch, I can't believe it," she screamed in the phone. Carrie was sobbing so hard she could barely speak to me. I immediately knew one of the family members had already told her the news. "I'll be there as soon as possible," she said. "I'm so sorry I wasn't there with you. I can't get back until Tuesday morning, but I want to be with you now."

By now she was sobbing out of control. I tried to calm her down by telling her it was okay she wasn't here with me and I'd be looking forward to seeing her Tuesday morning.

Chapter 6

The Websters and Our Relationship with Carrie

A person never knows what impact or influence you will have on a child's life until the child becomes an adult. The greatest compliment in the world was paid to Brenda the day Carrie decided to become a cosmetologist. At first Carrie's news didn't sit well with Brenda . . . she was actually angry. Brenda's frustration came from what she thought was good advice she had given Carrie regarding how difficult the hair business could be, how hard it was on the body, standing ten to twelve hours a day. Behind the scenes, I was settling Brenda down, and after we had a few long conversations regarding keeping her opinions to herself and letting Carrie do what she

Left to Right: Justin, Matt, and Carrie

wanted to do, Brenda finally accepted the fact this was what Carrie wanted at this particular point in her life. I could always tell how proud she was Carrie had decided to follow in her footsteps, even if she never told anyone. Personally I'm not sure if Carrie would make a career out of cutting, bending, curling, coloring, etc., etc. . . . but I know in my heart Brenda will always be watching over her.

Brenda was raised on a farm in southern Minnesota. She was the fifth child of ten. There are five brothers and four sisters. We also have twenty-two nieces and nephews on Brenda's side of the family and one nephew on my side of the family, born October 14th, 2001. *So, Brenda, honey, you now have one more nephew, and his name is Cameron Macdonald.*

Brenda's younger sister Becky is married to one of my favorite people in the world, my brother-in-law Wayne Webster. The Websters only live forty-five minutes from our home. Our decision not to have children is one of the reasons why, over the past eleven years, we've become very close to their three kids. The oldest is Carrie, followed by Justin (JJ) and Matt.

I remember the first time I met the three kids. Carrie was thirteen, so cute, so bubbly and full of life. JJ was ten and extremely outgoing, always talking, even if nobody was listening to him. JJ and I have hunted and fished together over the years, and he has become one of my fishing buddies when Wayne can't get away. Matt was seven when I first met him; he was one of Brenda's favorites, mainly because he was so cute, according to her. At nineteen, Matt has become a handsome young man, but he was still cute according to his Aunt Brenda. Matt was always and still is Mr. Independent.

Brenda and I looked forward to spending Christmas Eve with the Websters. It had become a tradition we hadn't missed it for the past ten years. I knew that the first Christmas without Brenda would be difficult for all of us. Brenda loved to spoil those kids at Christmas. She always went overboard, but it was worth it. She loved them like her own. "Poor Matt," she would always say, "Everyone forgets its his birthday on December 25th." Not Brenda, she made sure we all made a big deal over his birthday. We weren't just celebrating Christmas according to her; we were celebrating Matt's birthday.

We are so blessed that she got to see each one of those kids graduate from high school. We couldn't believe it when we watched Matt graduate in June 2001. That's the funny part of growing older; time keeps moving, even when when we believe it's standing still.

After Carrie graduated from high school, she decided to attend the University of Minnesota. Since living on campus was not her idea of a good time, and though I don't know how she pulled it off, but she managed to secure an apartment off campus and needed to furnish it. It was perfect timing for Carrie. We had just moved into the home we had built and all our old furniture was stored in the basement. Brenda and I decided to give Carrie our old bedroom set along with an old TV and whatever else she needed to set up house. I put one condition on the gifts we gave her, "As long as you stay in school and graduate, you can keep everything."

I know it's difficult going to school and holding down a job, but Carrie, like Brenda, couldn't stand having any free time just to relax. I'm not sure where the extra time came from between going to class, studying, and her regular job, but I remember Brenda telling me, "Carrie now has another part-time job." She continues to remind me of Brenda's work ethic, never able to sit still, always having to find something to do.

I believe it was the end of Carrie's sophomore year that she decided to transfer to another college. I found out later from Brenda that Carrie called and was crying because she didn't want to disappoint me by leaving the University of Minnesota. I called and told her that I didn't care where she graduated, just as long as she graduated from a college. Carrie never did leave the University of Minnesota. Her junior year she was accepted into the Carlson Business School. We were so proud of her.

It was March of 1998 when Carrie moved in with us. I was never sure why she needed a place to stay, but I do remember Brenda hinting that Carrie was looking for a place. I told Brenda that she should stay with us. I do remember Brenda saying, "I didn't think you would want her staying here."

My response was, "Are you kidding me? Carrie is like our daughter." That was the only conversation we ever had about her moving in.

It was the end of March, only a month after Carrie had moved in. My best friend, Jimi, and I had taken advantage of the warm weather and played golf at one of the local municipals. After our round, we stopped by Al Baker's in Eagan and had a few cocktails. it was after our second Bloody Mary that I turned to Jimi and said, "Hey, Jimi, I just remembered that Carrie is working at Old Chicago tonight. Maybe we should stop by and say hi to her. What do ya think about that?"

"Sounds like a plan. Let's go!"

Still dressed in our golf attire, we headed to Old Chicago to surprise Carrie. She noticed us right away as we followed the hostess to a pool table. Even tough we weren't in Carrie's "section," she would still stop by and visit with us. After an hour or so of drinking and playing pool, we started thinking about finding our next watering hole. That's when we both came up with the same idea, "live music."

"Let me grab a city pages and see who's playing tonight," Jimi said as he headed to the front entrance to find a paper.

We were busy trying to decide on which band to see when Carrie stopped by. "What're you boys doin' besides drinkin'?" she said.

"We're trying to find a band to see tonight," I told her.

"That sounds like a great time."

"Do you want to go with us?" I asked her.

"I'd love to, but I don't get off work until 9:45." She sounded disappointed, as I'm sure she didn't expect us to stick around for another hour.

"We'll wait for you. Won't we Jimi?"

"Yes, we will," was his three-word answer.

"Sounds great, you guys."

She must have mentioned the idea of seeing live music to a few of her friends, because as soon as 9:45 rolled around, not only was Carrie ready to go, but so were two of her girlfriends. I drove, mainly because my Durango was big enough for five people. Our destination was Bogart's in Apple Valley.

Bogart's was packed, but we managed to get a really good table right behind the dance floor. After an hour or so of good music, laughs, and drinks, Carrie and I decided to dance. At the end of the song, the guitar player announced they would be having a "hot babe" contest. He was looking for four "babes" to come up on stage, and the audience would make the final decision as to who was his new "hot babe." I'm sure Carrie thought we were "just going back to our table" when I grabbed her and announced to the guitar player, "She just volunteered."

A little stunned by the announcement, yet bold enough to take the challenge, Carrie got up on stage and strutted her stuff. Of course, she won the "hot babe" contest.

Once "last call" was announced, Jimi and I were ready to leave. "Where's Carrie?" I asked Jimi.

"She's down by the stage talking to the guitar player."

I took off after her, determined to interrupt any ideas she had about getting to know this guy. You see, I understood these things, unfortunately too well. I played guitar in a band during my college years, and I knew she was messing with trouble. "Carrie, let's go!"

It was too late; I could see they were exchanging phone numbers. He took one look at me and knew I wasn't happy. He tried to smooth over the situation by telling me, "I make $70,000 dollars a year!"

Like that was supposed to impress me, dude. "I don't care how much you make. It's not enough," I said and immediately turned to Carrie and repeated myself: "Carrie, let's go!"

This time I grabbed her by the hand and pulled her out of the bar thinking that would be the end of it. Ya think? Wrong again!

I tried to convince her, on the way back to her car, which was still parked at Old Chicago, that she was making a big mistake. My only advice to her was, "Guitar players have their pick."

She didn't listen, and, of course, they started dating. Matt was his name. Since her younger brothers name is also Matt, I decided to differentiate between them by calling her brother, Matt and her new boyfriend MattMatt. "How's MattMatt doing Carrie?" I would tease. To my surprise, the relationship grew throughout the summer of 1998.

After graduating from the Carlson Business School at the University of Minnesota, Carrie decided to go back to school to pursue her new career and become a Cosmetologist. She enrolled at Aveda, one of the top schools in Minneapolis. When Brenda first heard the news, she was upset with Carrie's decision. Carrie had worked for Brenda as her receptionist when Brenda managed Regis in Burnsville, so the news that Carrie was "throwing away four years of college to go to beauty school and start over" was too much for Brenda to handle. "Doesn't she know how hard you have to work in this industry to make any money?" Brenda asked. "It must be Matt talking her into it."

All I could do was keep reminding her that Carrie was an adult and was going to make good and bad decisions throughout her life. "Brenda, just listen to me for one second." Once I finally had her attention, I said to her, "My advice to you is to stay out of it and support her decision."

To my amazement, Brenda didn't say a word. One of the few times I must have made sense to her.

I don't know a lot about Carrie and Matt's relationship other than we all thought they would get married. Matt had other plans, and one day Carrie came home to find that he had moved out. Matt left Carrie with all the bills and a broken heart.

After graduating from Aveda, Carrie worked in one of the Aveda salons in Minneapolis. During the summer of 2001, she decided she needed a change of scenery. Our guess was she needed to get away from the area, explore other parts of the world while she was still single and maybe get away from some of the bad memories. Her decision was to move to Hollywood, California, on August first, which was still a couple of months away. The news did not sit well with most of her family, but she did have two people supporting her decision and telling her to go; Brenda and I were all for it, and why not? "Why not go while you're young," we told her. "You have nothing keeping you here, no boyfriend telling you to stay, and the worst-case scenario: if you don't like it, you can move back." Those were our words of encouragement.

When it came time to make the trek to California, Carrie informed us that she wouldn't be moving any of the furniture we had given her. She asked if we wanted it back. Of course we didn't, but Brenda called and left a message for our niece Kelsey, who was getting married the second week in August, thinking she might be able to use the bedroom set, TV, table, and chairs.

Kelsey called back to tell us that she would accept the generous offer. She and her husband-to-be, Kent, would pick everything up the last week in July. When moving day finally arrived, Brenda made sure she was at Carrie's apartment to help in any way she could. When Brenda got home she told me how appreciative both Kelsey and Kent were. Kent told Brenda, "I can't believe you are giving all this to us. Nobody has ever done anything like this before." Of course, I wasn't surprised by Brenda's actions. To me that was who Brenda was, always giving so generously, almost to a fault. It's one of the traits we shared together, our ability to give.

* * *

The last time Carrie saw Brenda was at her cousin Kelsey's wedding.

On December 10, 2001, I received the following letter from Carrie:

December 10, 2001

Dear Mitch,
I have always said that Brenda was like "my mom away from mom." Don't get me wrong, I have the best mom in the world. I just got lucky. I had a spare.

• Second grade, the first time my finger tips touched my eye-balls, with Brenda's hard contact lenses following. Even though I was a little stinker, she took me to McDonald's for an Egg McMuffin anyway.
· Third grade, a picture to prove it, my first mullet hair cut.
· Fifth grade, a summer day, driving down Grandma's dusty gravel roads in a brand new Riviera, with a DIGITAL dashboard.
· Sixth grade, cruising around Mazeppa, Minnesota, in a brand new BMW, me in the driver's seat.
· Seventh grade, "You're reading *Cosmopolitan?*"
· Ninth grade, a basketball game. She sat in the front row with my mom. My little boyfriends thought she was beautiful.
· Grade twelve, my grandfather's funeral, a sleek, classic up-do, AND my senior prom, all in one day. She said, "Grandpa wouldn't want you to miss prom."
· Freshman year of college, "I wonder how long I really am going to have to store my car in Brenda's garage."
· Sophomore year of college, she took me to Target. We picked out rugs, plants, knickknacks, towels, everything you can imagine to decorate my first apartment. I thought, "How much money does she think I have?" I needed none.
· Senior year of college, I spent the summer at your house. My car broke down. I paid nothing. She paid for my repairs before I even had the chance to pick up my car.
· Beauty School—She wasn't sure that I made a good choice, after all of the years she had spent on her aching feet.

Mitch, I could go on and on about Brenda. But, I think that everyone can relate to just a few of the memories that I stated above. She was all of these things: fun, energetic, spontaneous, hip, smart, giving, vivacious, respectful, and spirited.

"Yes Dear"

When I came back out to California, the best way that I explained who Brenda was and how much she meant to me was like this . . .

Think of the person you admire the most. It might be your mother, sister, or friend. Think of the one person that, when you were a child, you always looked up to in awe. You wanted to be like her, funky shoes and belts and all. Think of a fish without a backbone, a garden without bright colors, a cookie without sugar. Then, think of a woman and add these things: a beautiful personality, long legs, perfect hair, so smart it is wicked, and last but not least, a never-ending smile.

Chapter 7

Weekend of
August 18th, 2001

renda couldn't wait for August 18th, 2001, to arrive. She had been helping her sister Bonnie Puck prepare for that day for the past eight months. It was our niece Kelsey Puck's wedding day. Brenda was in charge of the flower arrangements, which meant Birds of Paradise were sure to adorn each and every table at the reception.

Brenda was leaving for Sioux Falls, South Dakota, Thursday afternoon, August 16th, to meet Carla Kuyper on Thursday evening. I knew the two of them would have a lot of catching up to do since they hadn't seen each other in three years. Any changes in my plans would have to be communicated to her Thursday evening when she called me at home. Brenda expected me to meet her at her mom's farm in Lakefield, Minnesota, on Friday August 17th, which was sort of okay with me (She new I wanted to play golf in our club championship that Saturday morning). The original plan Brenda had laid out was for me to pick up our niece Carrie at the airport on Thursday evening and bring her to Lakefield Friday afternoon so the two of them could "do hair" Saturday morning.

Early Thursday evening, my sister-in-law Becky called and explained that Carrie was flying into the Rochester airport vs. Minneapolis. Therefore, "there's no need for you to pick her up or take her to Lakefield." I immediately saw an opportunity to play golf on Saturday morning in the club championship, but I'd need to get an approval from the boss before I made any final plans. When Brenda called Thursday night around 10:00 p.m., I first asked her, "How was your day with Carla?"

"We had a great time together. I really miss seeing her," Brenda said.

"What are you doing going to bed so early? I thought you and Carla would be out late."

"I'm tired, and both of us need to get up early tomorrow morning," she said.

"By the way, Becky called me today and said I don't need to pick up Carrie or bring her to Lakefield, so I was just thinking maybe it would be okay if I played golf on Saturday morning."

"I don't care if you play golf Saturday morning, just as long as you are here by 3:00 p.m., no later." She usually fudged by fifteen minutes, but this time, I knew she meant 3:00 p.m. "sharp."

"Don't worry, I'll be there on time. I love you. See you Saturday." I was so excited that I didn't have to take a vacation day from work and I could play golf.

My tee time Saturday morning was set for 7:30 a.m., and in my mind there was the possibility we could be done around 11:30 a.m. if everything went well, and we didn't run into any slow play. I knew I needed to be on the road no later than 12:00 to make it to the farmhouse, pick up Brenda by 3:00 p.m. and be to the church no later than 3:30. That was the original plan as long as Mr. Murphy didn't interfere.

When I got up Saturday morning, it was raining. I got dressed and walked over to the club to find out whether or not there would even be a tournament. I was informed at the Pro Shop that there would be a delayed start of thirty minutes. This wasn't any good, especially for a guy who promised his wife he wouldn't be late. I thought, *What the heck, maybe we'll get done early.*

Our group of three started on the backside, hole number ten for you non-golfers. And since we were the first group off the back, we were able to dictate our own pace of play . . . which was fast. When we finished our hole number nine and made the turn to the front side, now our back nine, our rapid pace of play came to a halt. Our next three holes took over an hour to play, making the idea of me finishing the round a little up in the air. "If this pace keeps up I'm not sure I'll be able to finish the round," I told the guys.

We continued to play the next three holes as slow as the last, and as we approached the tee box on hole number eight, our seventeenth hole, I looked at my buddy Joe's watch. It said 11:50 a.m., "What the heck, I'll tee off and see what happens," I said to Joe and John. Immediately after I said it, I knew I was pushing the envelope. We drove our carts down the fairway to our tee shots and sat there waiting for fifteen minutes as the group in front of us putted out. "Guys, I gotta go, there's no way I'm going to get divorced over a game of golf."

I packed up my rain gear, towels, umbrella, and removed the golf tees and ball markers from my front pockets and put everything into my golf bag. I moved John's bag to Joe's golf cart, said my thanks and goodbyes, and took off across the golf course, waving at the other players as they gave me the strangest looks. On my way by the clubhouse, I spoke to our head pro, Dale Jones, "Dale, DNF me. I ran out of time!" (Did Not Finish)

It was 12:30 p.m. when I left the house. Fastest shower I ever took. I now needed to make up some lost time or face a very disappointed spouse. The one thing I had going for me was that I knew Brenda wouldn't be angry if I was only a few minutes late. But I didn't want to have her mad at me because I knew how much Kelsey's wedding meant to her, so I was determined to make it on time. Heading down the highway, looking at my predicament in 20/20 hindsight, I was telling myself, *You dummy, you shouldn't have played. You should have slept in and taken your time or drove down on Friday night.* But it was too late and it made no sense to beat myself up about it.

Now I was forced to exceed the speed limit by fifteen to twenty miles an hour in order to make up for lost time. I know speeding isn't the smartest thing to do, but it did get me back on track. Feeling much better about my chances of at least showing up around three-ish, I called Brenda on my cell phone at 2:15 p.m. and told her I was an hour out. "No problem," she said. "Just make sure you get here safe and sound." The good news is I made it by 3:10 p.m.

Brenda greeted me at the front door of the farmhouse, the same farmhouse she grew up in. "Hi, Hon. Nice to see you," she said as she gave me a kiss and a quick hug.

She quickly pushed me away after the hug, so I knew something was bothering her so I asked her, "What's wrong?"

"I can't find my other diamond earring." I could hear it in her voice; she was about to panic. Holding one earring in her hand, she turned around and went upstairs to search for the missing one. These were her favorite "fake" diamond earrings. "Help me look for it and then we gotta get going."

We both searched and searched until the clock on the wall told us we had to leave for the church. "Those are my favorite earrings in the world, I only paid $25.00 for them when we were in Arizona last year," she kept telling me over and over again.

"Relax, we'll find the missing one later," I told her, trying to calm her down. "It's probably right in front of our noses. Eventually it will show up. I'll help you look tomorrow morning before we leave." Convinced I was right, she put on another pair of earrings and a different necklace, and we took off, once again speeding to make up for lost time.

When we arrived at the church, Carrie and Becky were waiting for us. The three of us sat together during the wedding ceremony and at the reception. The ceremony was beautiful and the reception included more food than we could eat. The flower arrangements looked exactly how Brenda described them to me earlier with Birds of Paradise as the center of attention.

During the ceremony, I leaned over to Brenda and whispered, "Where is Wayne, Justin, and Matt?"

The story Brenda whispered back was, "Wayne wanted to bring his boat along and do some fishing before the wedding. Becky got her panties all in a bunch and told him he might as well stay home if he thinks he's going to bring the damned boat along. So, he stayed home."

Brenda told me she was mad at Becky for not bringing Wayne along. *Wayne, why is it Brenda has always stuck up for you? You got your dumb ass in trouble just as much as I did over the years, and she never stuck up for me!*

After the ceremony, everyone was invited to the American Legion for the reception and dance. The dance started around 9:00 p.m., and Brenda, who loved to dance, was dancing the night away with her mom. It was great watching her have so much fun. She kept asking me to dance, so I told her the next slow one would be ours. It was the only song we danced together that evening, even though she wanted me to stay with her on the dance floor. I encouraged her to dance with her mother. I don't know why, but I don't regret making that decision.

Between dancing with her mom and sitting with her brother Bernie, his wife, Linda, and their daughter Jennifer, Brenda told me she was hoping to see one of her nephews, Travis Harmening. Travis is the son of Brett and Betty; Betty is

Brenda's youngest sister. Travis, a college freshman, had been recruited to play football at Northern State University in Aberdeen, South Dakota. Travis told his parents he didn't think he would be back for Kelsey's wedding since they had three workouts a day in August and it was a four to five hour drive to get home. "You never know about Travis. He may just show up," Brenda kept telling me.

Around 10:00 p.m., sure enough, Travis walked through the door and sat with Brenda and me. She was so excited to see him; I was, too, as Travis is a joy to be around. We sat and visited for forty-five minutes. I still remember Travis handing Brenda his football schedule and watching her expression as she announced, "We'll go to as many games as we can, Travis."

Travis, I guarantee she would have gone to all of them!

That evening was the last time Brenda's family and relatives, with the exception of her mother and our neice Kim Puck, saw her alive, and I mean *so* alive, *so* full of life. Dancing, smiling, enjoying the best conversation. It was exhausting watching her with so much energy, but she always had that extra spark, never wanting to slow down.

We stayed overnight at her mom's that evening. Brenda being five-foot-ten and I'm a shade under six three meant we needed a bed long enough for the two of us to stretch out. Since the bed we were going to sleep in is only a full, we needed to find a place for all those arms and legs. She always enjoyed it when I would "snuggle" as she put it, but I give off so much body heat, she normally can't stand me next to her for more than a few minutes, and then I get pushed aside. For some reason she slept on my shoulder the whole night, it was the greatest feeling in the world when I look back and think about it.

The next morning, we got up and got ready for our three-hour drive back to the "Cities" as the southern Minnesota people call the place we live. Brenda was still looking for the one fake diamond earring she had misplaced the day before. "They look so real I can't believe I lost one," she told me.

"Brenda, stop looking for a minute and listen to me. Forget about the earring. Let's go downstairs and get something to eat, visit with your mother, and we can look for it later. If we don't find it, I'll buy you a new pair." (If you look closely enough at the picture on the opposite page, you will see one of those "fake" diamond earrings she loved so much.)

Travis and Brenda after a high school playoff game in November 2000.

She agreed to take a break and get something to eat. We had a very nice breakfast with her mother and went back upstairs to finish packing. "Is that everything?" I asked her.

"Found it!" was her reply.

"I told you that damn earring would show up once we quit looking for it."

The relief on her face said it all. It was time for us to go home.

Chapter 8

How We Finally Met

Jn 1990, Brenda and I were both living in Sioux Falls, South Dakota. It was a mutual friend, Barb Westra, who kept encouraging each of us to meet the other. "Mitch, you need to meet my girlfriend Brenda. You two would be perfect for each other," Barb would tell me every time she saw me.

My response was always the same. "Barb, I'm not interested in dating right now." I found out from Brenda that Barb had been telling her about this friend Mitch and how he would be perfect for her. Brenda would tell Barb the exact story I was telling her, how she wasn't interested in dating. It's still funny, when I think about it, neither one of us were interested in meeting the other. What's even more amazing was how close we worked to each other. Located in the Empire Mall in Sioux Falls, Regis and Helzberg Diamonds were separated by four or five stores, which meant we must have passed each other a dozen times a day while I was working for Helzberg and she was working for Regis. Yet we never noticed each other.

Prior to meeting Brenda, I was involved in a three-and-half-year relationship with a woman I thought I was going to marry. It had been my decision to break off the engagement and part of my sabbatical was to take a year off from women. *Sorry, ladies, but you sometimes drive us men crazy.* I didn't quite make it to the twelve-month mark when I met Brenda. She made it easy to forget I had promised myself "no dating."

The day we met, I was sitting with a couple of buddies at Chi Chi's having a beer or two during happy hour. While we were talking I noticed this really good-looking blonde sitting with my friend Barb. Interrupting Tom in the middle of his conversation, I stated, "You guys! See the blonde sitting over there? I'm going over to introduce myself." I excused myself from the table and walked over to say hello to Barb and, of course, get the introduction to the blonde who was sitting with her.

"Mitch, how are you?" Barb said my name with enough emphasis to make her point to Brenda that I was the same Mitch she had told her about.

"I'm fine, Barb. Who's this you're sitting with?" I asked her grinning from ear to ear.

"Mitch, this is my girlfriend Brenda Voss. She's the one I've been telling you about." Barb turned her head toward Brenda and said, "Brenda, this is Mitch Freimark. He's the gentleman I've been telling you about." Without allowing Brenda or me to say a word, Barb quickly said, "Mitch, sit down and join us for a drink?"

"Thanks!" I said. And that was how we first met.

To me, what was even funnier about this story was that, during my sabbatical from women, I would go to a few of the local bars and "people watch." One of the "babes" I noticed, only a week before our actual meeting, turned out to be Brenda. The bar where I was sitting was horseshoe shaped. Brenda and her girlfriend were sitting across from me but facing the dance floor so they didn't see me. I was so impressed with this gal not because of her looks but how she handled the three or four guys who continued to hit on her. I could tell by her body language that she politely said no to every advance. It became obvious to me she was more interested in enjoying herself and the company of her girlfriend than all the men who were interested in her.

After Barb had made the introduction and asked me to sit with them, Brenda smiled and said, "Sit down and join us," reassuring me that I wasn't infringing on their "girl time." I'm not sure how long our initial chitchat lasted, but my memory of this next story is crystal clear.

After a couple more beers (a few more margaritas for the ladies), I gave Brenda a compliment on her looks. At first she thanked me for the compliment, but soon afterwards we were engrossed in this conversation about age, which prompted her to start bragging about how much older she was than I, a lot older according to her. I wasn't sure where she was going with this "I'm older than you are" stuff because I was twenty-eight and guessed she was probably the same. She continued to challenge me to guess the differences in our ages that made me want to know exactly how much older or younger she really was. I knew better than to even make an attempt at guessing for fear I might get into trouble . . . like guessing too high. Instead, I told her, "I just don't believe you're older than I am. You'll have to prove it."

Brenda sat back in her chair, took one drink of her margarita, started waving her finger at me and said, "Honey, I guarantee you this much. I'm a lot older than you think I am."

In order to discreetly find out everything about her, I said it again, "Okay, if you think you're so much older than I am, you need to prove it by showing me your driver's license."

She fell for my little devilish trick hook, line, and sinker. My objective wasn't to find out how old she was. I didn't care about her age. I wanted to know how tall she was and how much she weighed! Even if she lied about her weight on her driver's license, at least it'll be within ten pounds.

I was so impressed with her looks, personality, her smile, and her friendliness that her age didn't matter to me. She was seven years my senior, five-foot-ten, weighed 135 pounds—everything was perfect in my book. I know it wasn't love at first sight for either of us, but we had this connection going, and I knew I would see her again. I just didn't know when.

Mitch, Brenda, and our good friend Jason Cox on November 10th, 1990.

A few years later, Brenda told me she really didn't like me at first. I'm not sure why she didn't like me, and I never pushed her to find out. Over the last eleven years, she never explained why. When I would tell the story of how we first met to friends, she always added "I really didn't like him at first," and all along I thought I had made such a good first impression on her.

As our conversation continued, we exchanged information on where we worked. We were both amazed how two people who worked four or five stores apart had never met, let alone seen each other. I guarantee we not only noticed each other after our first introduction, but we became good friends.

As our friendship grew, I was becoming more and more attracted to her. Deep down I wanted to ask her out, but, for the first time in my life, I didn't know how. When I think about it now, I would say the main reason I never asked her out on an official date was that I didn't want to risk losing her friendship, especially if she wasn't interested in dating me. Since I've never been "just friends" with a woman without sex getting in the way,

Mitch blowing out the candles.

55

it was important for me to hold on to this relationship even if we were only friends.

Brenda was special, and I have to applaud her for the way she handled me. What was most difficult for me during our "friendship" had to do with the fact that I was falling for her, and I had no idea how she felt about me. The turning point came when I invited her to my twenty-ninth birthday party. I remember she agreed to be there, but I couldn't remember if she actually had made it until I found a picture of the two of us sitting on my couch next to each other in my "dumpy" little apartment. I was blowing out the candles on my birthday cake my sister Shelly brought, while Brenda sat there laughing. That birthday party was on November 10th, 1990.

When Brenda first met me at Chi Chi's, she didn't know I was as poor as a church mouse. I had made and spent a fortune during the previous eight years working in the life insurance business. I was working hard on financially getting my life back together when we first met. Making ends meet paycheck to paycheck working at Helzberg Diamonds in the Empire Mall in Sioux Falls, South Dakota. It was an okay job, but I wasn't managing the store. I was just a salesman, which, in my opinion, wasn't going to impress anyone, especially someone like Brenda. I guess she must have seen something inside me that intrigued her because two weeks after my birthday party, on Thanksgiving Day, in my dumpy little apartment, my mother, Barb, my brother Todd, and I were sitting at my new card table, my mother had just purchased for me, giving thanks to family and friends eating turkey, potatoes, and pumpkin bread when the phone rang. "It must be Shelly calling us to wish us a Happy Thanksgiving," I said. Shelly is my beautiful baby sister.

"Hi, Mitch. It's Brenda. Happy Thanksgiving!" she said.

"Happy Thanksgiving to you, and where are you tonight?" I wanted to know.

"I'm here in Sioux Falls. I was with my family earlier today and just got back in town. Mitch, I have a really big favor to ask you," she said.

"Sure, whatever you need," I was just flattered she called me.

"Can you help me out tonight?" she needed to know.

Without hesitating and not thinking about Mom and Todd, I told her, "Yes. What do you have in mind?"

"I need to go over to my old boyfriend's house and get my moving boxes out of his garage, but I'm going to need your help."

I could hear it in her voice that she actually needed me, and, for this lady, I'd do anything. "No problem. Give me directions to your place, and I'll be right over."

After jotting down the directions, I hung up the phone and immediately turned to Todd and Mom to explain a little bit about who my friend Brenda was and the favor she asked me to help her with. Then I made this statement to my brother: "Todd, you're going with me because I don't know how big this guy is," and of course we all started laughing.

Mom wasn't satisfied with the short story I gave her about who my friend Brenda was. She had fifty questions that needed answering. "Who is this gal, and how do you know her?" Etc., etc., etc.. After explaining that Brenda and I were "just friends," Mom gave us her blessing to take off and help Brenda out. Mom told us not to worry about her. She would be just fine. "I'll clean up. You two boys get going."

Todd and I left for Brenda's no more than ten minutes after she had called. When we arrived, she was waiting for us by her garage with her black BMW already running. "Follow me," she said.

Once we were on our way I turned to Todd and said, "I really like her, Todd. She's independent, great looking, and the added bonus is she drives a BMW!"

Being a man of few words when it came to the chicks, all Todd replied back to me was "No kidding!"

We followed her to her ex-boyfriend's house, which was only a mile or so away from her apartment. He had left his garage open and the lights on but never showed his face. She told us she hadn't dated him in over a year and wanted to sever the last tie she had to him which was the moving boxes he was storing for her. Todd and I loaded the boxes in both vehicles, and within minutes the three of us were on our way back to Brenda's apartment. We unloaded the moving boxes and stored them in the rafters above her garage. She invited us in for a beer, and we stayed and visited with her for an hour or so. Brenda's apartment was awesome. Everything was in its place, and it felt like home. Now I was more interested in her than I had ever been.

Since I hadn't had the guts to ask her out on a date, I think the moving box episode was her way of telling me she real-

Here's a picture of myself with my sister Shelly and my brother Todd on June 20th, 1991.

ly liked me. The problem was I still didn't get it because I kept asking myself why she picked Thanksgiving to call me to help her move boxes, when she could have picked them up anytime, any day of the week. It took a few days after that evening for it to sink in, and I decided she must like me more than being just another one of her friends. I always told Brenda, "Sometimes you have to hit me over the head with a ton of bricks before I get it." If she were here today she'd agree one-hundred percent.

The following week, after Thanksgiving, I called her and asked if I could cook her supper.

"Is this a date?" she bluntly wanted to know.

"Of course it is," I said, taking a small chance and hoping it was what she wanted to hear.

"Okay. What are you going to make me?"

And that was when our romance began.

I decided to make Marie Schwebach's famous roast beef, a recipe given to me by Marie's son Jeff Schwebach, one of my oldest and dearest friends. I'll never forget Brenda trying to take over my kitchen. "I think the roast beef is done," she kept telling me. "How long has it been in the oven?"

"Brenda, it's been in the oven for three hours. You're just going to have to accept that this is a four-hour roast."

"I don't think so. It looks and smells done to me."

"I know it looks and smells done, but it's the fourth hour that makes it mouth watering, fall apart using only a fork, perfect! So, please sit down, get out of my kitchen, relax, and I'll fix you another margarita."

Oh, did I mention I was trying to get her drunk from the moment she entered my apartment? Anyway, after two margaritas and still one hour to go before the roast was done, she made it clear to me that she couldn't wait any longer and needed to eat. "Mitch, I haven't had anything to eat all day, just these two margaritas."

"All right, but I can't promise you it will be very good," I told her.

I took one bite and knew right away that we needed to put it back in the oven for another hour. We both sat there, chewing, and chewing—to me it was like trying to eat rubber bands. Of course, she never complained about how tough the meat was. I couldn't stand it, and I never said a word. I figured it would be a good lesson learned if there was ever a next time. Brenda would learn and appreciate over the next eleven years that my (Marie's) roast beef took a full four hours! (For the mouth-watering Marie Schwebach roast beef recipe, visit www.yesdearbrenda.com.)

As our affection for one another grew over the next three months, we both knew the next step was coming. Were we in love with each other? I can remember us having long conversations about my need to move on in my career. Selling diamonds wasn't going to make me a millionaire by any means, and Brenda kept enforcing the fact that I have so much talent I could be doing anything I wanted. With her encouragement, I decided I needed to start talking to a few friends about any opportunities they could think of for me. One of my buddies, Rick Krause, who worked for Honeywell at the time, told me I should apply for a sales job Honeywell had available. Rick told me HW was always looking for talented salespeople. I had nothing to lose by applying for a job, and Rick was right, Honeywell did have openings in Sioux Falls, South Dakota, and in Des Moines, Iowa. The Sioux Falls position was what I really wanted, but it was the Des Moines position they offered me. With the opportunity to move to Des Moines, Iowa, and go to work for Honeywell, I knew I needed to have Brenda's full support. Since we had become really attached to each other, we both knew this could be a relationship breaker.

Brenda and I talked about my career opportunity and our future together; the whole time she was very supportive of whatever my decision would be. "It's only four hours away. We can see each other on weekends," she told me in a very reassuring voice.

I told her it meant everything to me to have her support, which made it very easy for me to make up my mind and take the job with Honeywell and move to Des Moines, Iowa. "I know it will only make our relationship stronger," I told her.

As we embraced, I noticed she became very quiet and was shaking in my arms. When I pulled away, I found out what was wrong. I could see tears running down her face. It was the first time I had ever seen her cry. She looked me straight in my eyes and, for the first time, said to me, "I love you."

Chapter 9

My Move to Des Moines,
Then "The Cities"

he decision to move to Des Moines, Iowa, wasn't an easy one for either of us, but once we had talked about all the obstacles we would face and how we would manage to overcome them, I made up my mind to accept the Honeywell job and make the move. Now I needed to find a place to live. Before I even started looking for an apartment, Brenda told me she had spoken to a girlfriend of hers, Louise, who lived in Des Moines. Louise wanted to know if I would be interested in renting a room from her. The rent would be $300 a month, and I could move in right away. I decided to leave it up to Brenda to decide what I should do. After all, I had no idea who this friend of hers was nor did I want to see any problems result from my staying with her.

"Louise told me she could use the extra money so I think you should go ahead and move in." Brenda made it sound like it would be a piece of cake.

Taking the advice from someone I trusted, I went ahead with what was sure to be a "piece of cake." What I didn't expect to find upon my arrival, was Louise's daughter, who was over twenty-one, also living in the house. With only one bathroom on the second floor to share between her daughter and myself, I could see the writing on the wall from day one. There was going to be trouble with a capital T. I didn't express my feelings to Brenda, not at first, as the possibility the situation I was now in might work for all of us. As the month came to an end, I can honestly say: you should never take the advice from somebody who says, "It'll be a piece of cake," because that month was a living hell for all of us. To this very day, I have no idea why they resented me living there when I was the invited "paying" guest. I can venture to make an educated guess that it was as uncomfortable for them as it was for me. The straw that broke the camel's back and made me pack my bags occurred when Brenda came to visit me at the end of that first month. I was so excited when Brenda told me she wanted to come down to Des Moines and spend the weekend. Her plans were to not only be with me but to spend some quality time with Louise. When she first arrived, I was so happy to see her, but, for some reason, only God knows, Louise didn't give Brenda a very warm welcome, and both Brenda and I sensed it right away. To try and make up for whatever was bothering Louise, Brenda decided to make all of us dinner. She just made herself at home in the kitchen and whipped up some barbeques. After dinner, I excused myself and went upstairs to use the bathroom. When I opened the door to go back downstairs and rejoin the "fun," there stood Brenda in tears. She explained to me how Louise was really angry with her and with me. She was mad at Brenda for taking over her kitchen without permission and then proceeded to say some really nasty things that Brenda didn't want to repeat.

"That's it, I'm out-a-here tomorrow!" I told her. It was the perfect excuse I as looking for to make my exit.

I didn't waste any time finding a new place to live. During that same weekend, before Brenda left town, I found an ad in the Des Moines paper for a room renting for $300.00 a month. Before Brenda left on Sunday to go back to Sioux Falls, I called the number listed in the paper and made an appointment for Monday around 5:30 p.m. "Let's hope this place works out," I said to her as she nodded in agreement. We were still at Louise's house, trapped in my small bedroom upstairs, neither one of us willing to make our presence known. "Call me when you get home tonight."

"I will," she said. "Please, Mitch, don't say anything to Louise. Just find a place and move out."

"I can't promise I'll keep my mouth shut. I'm so pissed off right now."

"I know you are, but do it for me."

I promised to behave after she asked me to do it for her, so I bit my tongue, for a few days at least.

Monday afternoon couldn't get here fast enough. When I finally got off work, I drove up to the house, which was more the size of a mansion. A very professional-looking man in his late fifties with white hair and a matching white beard trimmed short to his face, met me at the front door. He was dressed in casual business attire and was extremely polite—one of those first impressions that made me feel really good inside. He explained that he was the owner of the home and also lived on the premises with five other tenants. He showed me around the first floor of the house, which included the community kitchen, dinning room and a very large library with the only TV. The home was very old and smelled musty but not disgusting enough for me to end the tour early. The woodwork throughout the house was gorgeous but needed a good dusting. We went upstairs to the second floor so he could show me the room available for rent. I immediately noticed three other doors, two of them closed and one open. I peeked into the open one to find a very small bathroom with one sink, a toilet and a tub, no shower.

"Do you have a shower available?" I asked.

"Yes, it is located in the basement." He told me.

When he opened the door to the room he had for rent, I was amazed at how large it was; eighteen by eighteen feet with a walk-in closet. It only took me a matter of minutes to tell him I'd take it. I now had six other roommates sharing an eight-bedroom house.

I asked him if it would be all right if I moved in right away. He didn't see any problems with me moving in that night. All I needed to do was pay a month's rent in advance. No contract, just pay the rent on time.

I drove back to Louise's house and packed my belongings in fifteen minutes and left, not saying a word to either one of them.

It took Brenda several years to forgive Louise for what happened that weekend in 1991, but I'm glad she did. As we always said, "You can never have enough friends."

I quickly settled into my new pad, and it was extremely easy to get along with everyone living in the house. My normal routine after work was to either stop by a local tavern with my buddy Bill Venhaus or go directly back to the mansion. In the evenings, I'd relax by reading, taking a drive or going to the driving range to hit golf balls. When I'd return home, I'd head to the library to vegetate and watch TV. Around 9:30 p.m., like clockwork, the owner of the home would come down to the library and read his paper and start a conversation with me. After a few weeks of this same routine, I felt I had a new friend with whom I enjoyed talking. During one of our conversations, I asked him if it was okay if Brenda stayed with me when she came to visit. He not only said it was okay, he made sure she felt right at home when she arrived.

"He's such a nice guy, Brenda," I told her that evening after he said it was more than okay for her to stay.

By the end of those first two weeks, I now knew he was a psychologist who specialized in helping rape victims, and just by the way he expressed himself, I could tell he was very passionate about life and his work. I found out he had been married and had children. When he spoke about his work, he would tell me about some of the women he was treating and the horrible things that had happened to them. The rape victim stories were very sad, and emotionally were hard on him. I once told him, "Who would have thought there are so many rapes in Des Moines, Iowa." I think his communicating these stories to me was his way of finding a release from all the stress he must have been under, even though he never showed it. I was really proud to know someone who was helping others who were in pain. It was a nice feeling to know there are people out there who do care and can make a difference.

One evening while I was watching TV in the library (this time alone), one of my roommates who lived in the basement came upstairs and started the conversation off like this, "Mitch, isn't it weird that you and I are the only two guys living in this place who are *straight*!"

"What!" I shouted. "Are you kidding me?" I asked.

"No, man, it's true," he said, laughing. "Come on, Mitch. You had to know, didn't you?"

"No way. You're so full of shit," I shouted back.

"Okay, I'll name them for you. The chick living next to your room is a lesbian. The Russian living next to me is gay, which you had to know about him."

"Yes, I knew the Russian was gay. That was way too obvious. I mean, he kept wearing his ballerina outfit around the house. That was kind of weird. He never spoke a word of English, but he did give me some of the best chocolates I've ever had."

"Ya, that's because he liked you."

"Hey, f— you, buddy."

"Look, those two guys living on the third floor are together, the Englishman, Clive, living in the guest house out back is gay, and the owner is gay. Everyone living in this house is gay but us. It's the big Gay House, dude."

All this information coming from a guy who did nothing but workout, who was a muscle head, who's six-foot python was still lose somewhere in the house. And he didn't think he was weird.

He made such a big deal out of the situation and made me sound like I was a moron for not taking notice of how others were living their lives. I guess it proves if you don't have any prejudices against how people look or act, we can all get along. My feeling toward gays is and always has been neutral. The one thing that did bother me was his statement that the owner was gay. When I analyzed the situation, I could agree with his assessment of all the others in the house, but the owner never showed any feminine traits nor did he ever allow me to see him with another man. Unlike the incident I witnessed a few weeks later with "Clive," who lived in the guesthouse out back. I happened to look outside just in time to see Clive plant one on his boyfriend. It was a real shocker because the "boyfriend" was our maintenance guy or handyman, who was always hanging around the house with his nine-year-old son.

After the initial shock wore off, I decided to call Brenda and tell her the interesting news. "Hi, hon. Do I have a story to tell you? I was just informed that there are only two of us living in the house that are not gay!"

"Let me guess, you and the owner," she said.

"Nope, it's me and the muscle man who lives in the basement with his lost six-foot python."

By now she was laughing hysterically. "So what are you going to do?" she inquired.

"I'm going to watch my backside and never drop the soap!" I told her, joking of course. "I'm not going to do a thing. As long as no one bothers me, and they don't throw it in my face, I don't give a rat's ass what they do." At first I didn't see the humor like Brenda did, but after looking back on the memories, it is absolutely hilarious.

The adjustment Brenda and I made to not seeing each other every night was hard at first, but after a few weeks of my driving back to Sioux Falls on Friday nights and us "catching up" on our time away, we knew we could make this new arrangement work. Since Brenda was busy Tuesday through Saturday with clients, I figured she never had time to miss me (so I thought).

My new job required that I spend my first four months in Des Moines and then five weeks in Minneapolis training at the Honeywell headquarters. The only time I'd ever spent in Minneapolis was on business, and it was always in the wintertime. It was the first of May when Honeywell sent me to the Twin Cities. I had never spent any significant amount of time in Minnesota, especially during the "warm season." It was easy to fall in love with Minneapolis/St. Paul. The weather was beautiful, with blue skies, bright sunshine warming into the seventies by mid-afternoon. I was also very impressed with the way the people of Minnesota treated me. They truly lived up to the name "Minnesota Nice." And all those golf courses. I love to play golf, so the idea of having more than one choice of course to play after training class was very appealing.

After my five-week training was over, I returned to Des Moines, but I couldn't stop thinking about making the move to Minnesota. I called Brenda to tell her I might need a place to stay for the next thirty to sixty days while I searched for a new job in Minneapolis/St. Paul.

"What did you do?" She was afraid of what I was about to tell her.

"I quit my job today. I've decided to move to the Twin Cities." Brenda knew how much I hated living in Des Moines. It didn't really come as a surprise that I all of sudden decided to quit and make the move. What did surprise her was I did it without having a job waiting for me. The only question she ever asked me was, "Are you sure you want to move the Cities?"

"Absolutely!" I had made up my mind.

Brenda had also made a move in May, not a job change, but she had moved in with her girlfriend Wendy a few weeks before I announced I needed a place to stay. Wendy was kind enough to let me stay with them during my "time off" while I was job hunting. It only took thirty days, using a placement firm from Edina, Minnesota, and I was back in business. Brenda and I made a promise to each other the day I moved. "Mitch, you need to make sure you like living there. If after a year, you're still convinced it's the place you want to live, I'll move there with you."

That was our promise to each other. She would stay in Sioux Falls, and I would spend the next twelve months making sure I had found my home.

I moved to the Cities on August 1st, 1991. Needing a cheap place to live, I answered an ad in the paper saying "room for rent." I had been down that road before. This time my roommate was a little old lady who needed help with her monthly rent. She seemed innocent enough; I could take her if I had to, and I could tell she liked me right away, so I took the room. My rent was $80.00 per week, no lease; I could leave anytime I wanted.

Two weeks after settling into my new room, Brenda called to inform me that Regis had contacted her and asked her if she was interested in moving to Burnsville, Minnesota, a suburb of Minneapolis/St. Paul, to manage the Regis Salon in the Burnsville Mall. She wanted me to help her make up her mind. "What do you think I should tell them?"

I sensed a little anxiety in her voice, almost like she was being asked to do something she might not want to do. I knew she had quit managing the Spencer, Iowa, Regis for certain reasons I won't mention, and I didn't think she would ever be interested in managing again.

The first thing I did was to remind her of our promise to each other, about my making sure I loved the Cities as much as I told her I did. The second was to remind her about the managing issues. Neither one seemed to matter to her. She wanted help in making up her mind. "Brenda, I'm not going to tell you what to do. This has to be your decision. I don't want you moving here and then regretting it. I feel you should think about it for a couple of days, and then let me know what you decide you really want to do."

That seemed to settle her down, and she agreed to take a couple of days to make up her mind. The next night she called to inform me she had made her decision. "I told Regis I'd take the job. They want me to start in two weeks, right after Labor Day weekend."

"Wow, that was fast, what made you decide to do it?"

"I love you, and I want to be with you."

That was her answer. I was speechless. I couldn't say anything except to tell her how much I loved her.

Throw out the idea of a twelve-month separation. We needed to find a place to live and find it quickly. I thought it would be easy for us to find a place to live within a two-week time frame, especially when I considered there were so many "nice" apartments and town homes available . . . until I found out my idea of a nice place and her idea of a nice place were miles apart. Fortunately for me, Brenda was able to take things into her own hands and find a town house she was comfortable with. One that fit our budget and would have enough room for all her furniture and her clothes. You see most of my stuff had been sold, without my knowledge, at the garage sale she and Wendy had earlier in the summer. This was just the beginning of my "training" as she put it. I needed to learn the difference between good taste and my taste, which at the time indicated that I didn't have a clue. She also got rid of most of my clothes, and replaced them with items that had this guy on a pony playing polo. It took me at least five years to understand why we would spend so much money on my clothing. Eleven years later I still have most of those polo shirts she bought me. They still look as new as the day she brought them home.

Now that we were officially living together, I wondered if our relationship would change. And it did. Our adjustment to living in the Cities was the easy part; we both loved living here. The real adjustment for us was living together.

I always knew she was a neat freak, but I didn't realize how crazy we made each other, I mean how crazy I made her with the things I'd do or, should I say, didn't do.

Here are a few examples of my bad habits:

The bed not being made if I got up last; the dishes not being washed or put into the dishwasher; leaving my clothes lay on the closet floor; hanging my shirts back on the hanger after only wearing them once; not going to the grocery store when I knew we needed groceries; not even attempting to do the laundry; laying around watching TV when the house needed to be cleaned; not learning how to iron; not cleaning my side of the bathroom after shaving; not remembering to leave the toilet seat down! That seemed to be the worst offense. There's nothing worse than a significant other going to the bathroom and "falling" into the toilet. Wow, did Brenda let out a scream.

Yes, I was a typical guy who didn't know shit about living with a classy lady like Brenda. But I was lucky; she was too stubborn to get rid of me. Unfortunately for her, I was a very slow learner. I mean very slow. My stupid stubborn brain didn't get it, didn't understand what she was trying to teach me, not for several more years at least. I look back now and can't believe she was that patient with me. That's why I loved her so much; she believed in me. She always, always, believed in me.

Chapter 10

Lessons Learned

It hurts when I think of how hard Brenda worked to ensure that we had all the good things life has to offer, and just when she had everything the way she wanted it, she was gone.

Getting up every morning at 5:00 a.m. to be at work by 7:00 a.m. and not get home until 9:30 p.m. She was working this hard because she loved *me*, she loved *me*! Wow, I still can't believe Brenda picked me to spend the rest of her life with.

The good news is, I did finally wake up and realize, "I'm the luckiest man alive!" That was in early 1995. The transformation from the person I had been to the person I am today took her almost five years. I don't know many people who would have had the patience to wait that long for their boyfriend or girlfriend to shape up. I was fortunate. I had Brenda as part of my life, and she was too stubborn to give up on me. She saw the potential inside my soul to be her perfect mate, and she wasn't going to throw all those years away no matter how difficult I made it for her. *Thank you for believing in me, honey.*

She taught me to be considerate of other people's feelings. I needed to be more patient (which I'm still working on); learn to compromise, which is when I learned the value of "Yes Dear." I learned to listen to her and really care about what was on her mind, to be *nice* to her twenty-four hours a day seven days a week, not just when I wanted something. I learned to show her how much I loved her by doing the little things like making the bed without her reminding me, doing the laundry without her asking me if I had done it, cleaning the house without her wondering why I haven't helped, mowing the yard without a subtle hint that "the yard is looking shaggy," putting my dirty dishes into the dishwasher without her doing it for me. I grew accustomed to making sure the house was clean and picked up before she got home from work—that was huge in her book. I got a lot of brownie points for keeping the house clean. When I learned how important it was to her to see me doing my chores without being reminded or told to do them; our relationship blossomed beyond my wildest dreams. In my heart I knew it was no longer about my way vs. her way, it was about *us*!

In February 1993, we decided we needed to get out of our town house and build or buy our "dream home." I didn't have a clue what that meant, "dream home," but Brenda had it all figured out. She would spend every Sunday and Monday scouring the area, looking at every house on the Parade of Homes. In the Minneapolis/St.Paul area each spring and fall, builders showcase their model homes. Brenda couldn't wait until the spring of 1993 for the Parade of Homes to start. When she found a house that was close to what she wanted, she would come home, get me, and off we would go so she could show me what she loved about the house. She never liked one-hundred percent of every home, but she would write down the "must have in our house" ideas from each one. When she got home, she transformed her notes into a drawing, and before long I could see her idea of what our house was going to look like.

There was one problem she had, and it didn't have anything to do with her ideas of what our home should look like. I loved her ideas. The problem was with me. I kept fighting this idea of hers that we needed to build or buy such an expensive home. "Why can't we buy one of these houses that's already built for a lot less?" I almost had her convinced that we should buy an existing home in Eagan, Minnesota, when she finally had had enough and told me, "Forget it! If you're not willing to work at this than neither am I."

I felt like I had crushed her dreams. It took me a few days to realize how "right" she really was. I apologized, and I told her she was right, and I was wrong. It was hard for me to do, but, after I said it, I felt better, and she felt better. It was so strange for us to fight, we rarely did, but when we did, I now know I was 99.99 percent to blame, although I didn't know it from 1991 to 1995.

Our search for a lot to build our dream home began, this time, as a team. In the spring of 1993, we found a lot in a secluded valley in Eagan. The lot and cost to build the home was included as one price in the bid. Convinced we had a great deal, we paid the builder one thousand dollars as a down payment.

The lot we chose looked to be very private. There was a pond directly in front of where the house would sit, mature trees surrounding the acreage and bluffs bordering the south side of our future home. The bluffs made us feel we had our own built-in privacy fence, but it was five stories high. One big concern we had was the potential for homes to be developed on the bluffs. This would completely take all our privacy away. The builder reassured us the bluffs wouldn't be developed as he and his father owned all the property. Three weeks later, after a little investigation by Brenda, she found out he had lied to us. We were heartbroken but decided the best thing to do was ask for our thousand dollars back and start over.

Disappointed, but not disheartened, we were more determined than ever to find a place we could call home. Brenda asked me if I was interested in looking at lots on a golf course in Lakefield, Minnesota. A client of hers had made the suggestion.

"What a great idea, do you know how much the lots are selling for?" I inquired.

"They're selling in a range between sixty-five and seventy thousand dollars," she replied without blinking and eye.

"What! Are you kidding me? I could buy a whole house in Mobridge, South Dakota, for that kind of money." Why I compared my hometown to the Cities, I haven't a clue.

"Mitch, this is the Cities, and property values are different here." She remained as calm as could be, which at the time drove me insane.

"I just can't imagine paying seventy thousand dollars for a lot," I told her. For two weeks I tried to convince her that we could find a lot in the twenty-thousand-dollar range. I have no idea where twenty-thousand dollars came from. I do know this: my stubbornness was driving her crazy. Like I said, she had a lot of work to do before she had me whipped into shape.

"Not around here we won't," she kept telling me. "You need to realize that, if we want a nice lot, we need to be prepared to spend around fifty thousand dollars."

Brenda knew seventy thousand dollars was out of our price range, but starting on the higher end was her way of proving her point. She knew it would only be a matter of time before I'd realize how "right you always are, dear."

Brenda kept pursing the dream of building our home on a golf course. It was late June 1993, and it must have been a

Sunday or Monday when she came home and asked me if I wanted to look at a lot she found in Mendota Heights next to the Mendakota Country Club. She told me how impressed she was with the lot, and, if I liked it, maybe "this would be the one."

"Honey, there aren't any lots on the golf course at Mendakota." I had played there the year before, and I knew there were only a few homes adjacent to the clubhouse.

"I know the lots aren't on the golf course, but wait until you see the location. Then decide for yourself, Mitch. All I'm asking is for you to keep an open mind." She must have had her intuition turned on full force because during our drive to Mendota Heights she was smiling the whole way.

As we wove our way around Mendakota Drive to Mendakota Court, the excitement was growing in both of us. "I completely forgot about Mendakota Country Club," I told her.

"So did I until I was driving by on 35E and remembered the house we had looked at earlier this spring before the golf course was open." Brenda had remembered this place because we had looked at the second house on the right upon entering Mendakota Court. I remember thinking that the guy wanted two hundred seventy thousand dollars, and there was no way that fit into our budget. I guess we both had written off MCC because we assumed we couldn't afford it.

As we made our way past the first few houses I wasn't sure which side of the road she was most interested in, but my gut told me this was going to be it. When she said, "Stop right here and tell me what you think about this one," she was pointing to the lot on the right side. There were six houses on the right side as we drove into Mendakota Court, then two empty lots side by side. Those two empty lots were the only lots available for sale with property adjacent to Mendakota Country Club. I didn't say anything for a couple of minutes. I got out of the car and walked around trying to picture our house and us living here. It felt right; it really felt right.

"I love it," I said. "We need to find out how much they want for it," which was my only concern.

Brenda was so excited about the fact I immediately agreed with her without first arguing about some minor issue. Another lesson she taught me; don't always disagree just for the sake of disagreeing, even if I was right and she was wrong. I found it was easier to agree with her and talk about all the positive things first, then ease into any points I'd have. It's funny how her listening mechanism would shut down when I spoke in negative terms and how attentive she was when I first spoke in positive terms. I really was starting to "get it" and that was causing me to rethink this attitude I had of "always being right." I was starting to change the way I dealt with her and how I dealt with others; but I still needed a lot more work.

Back in 1993, neither one of us owned a cell phone. Instead, we had to write the number listed on the real estate sign and drive home to make the inquiry regarding the lot price. When we got back to our town house, Brenda made the call. Her conversation was brief, and I could tell by her expression I was in for more good news. "The price they are asking for the lot is forty-five thousand dollars," she informed me with a huge smile on her face. "What do you think?" she asked me and without waiting for my reply said, "I think we should buy it!"

I'd realized there was no way we were going to find a lot for twenty thousand dollars, let alone an incredible piece of property on a golf course for under sixty-five thousand. But there it was; it was perfect, exactly what we were looking for and priced right in line with our budget.

I don't believe what I did next . . . I told Brenda, "We should offer them forty thousand and see what happens."

"Are you crazy!" she said in that tone of voice only used when I needed to explain myself. "What if someone else comes along and offers them forty-five? Then what are we going to do?" "Mitch, we've already lost one lot, and I don't want to lose this one."

I explained that I understood the risks, but I had a good feeling our offer would be accepted. "Brenda, you know when it comes to negotiations I'm one of the best (in my mind anyway). Besides, the worst-case scenario is they say no to the forty thousand and we pay them forty-five."

"I don't totally disagree with you," she said carefully, "but I don't want to risk losing this lot either."

On July 7th, 1993, we signed the Contract for Deed for Lot 7, Block 1, Mendakota Estates in Dakota County, Minnesota. The selling price was $40,000! The terms were our terms. We agreed to give them $5,000 down and $1,000 a month until paid. Our intentions were to start building sometime in late 1994 or early 1995. The time frame would allow us to pay down the Contract for Deed and save some money for everything new we needed to buy. Well at least our intentions were good. It was pure economics that forced us to move our home building project up twelve months. It only made sense that we take advantage of the low interest rates being offered and move quickly to secure a builder.

During the remainder of July and the month of August 1993, Brenda stayed busy on Sundays and Mondays going to open houses. Her goal was to find that one home that already had the floor plan she was looking for. In late August, on a Sunday afternoon, she came to the town house and announced that she found exactly what we were looking for. "I want to show you this house," she said. "It's got everything we want for our floor plan. The only problem is it's a half-million-dollar home."

"We can't afford a house like that, Brenda."

"I know, but come with me and take a look at it anyway."

She was right, the floor plan was awesome. Now we, or should I say, *she* needed to figure out how to incorporate a five-hundred-thousand-dollar floor plan into a two-hundred-fifty-thousand-dollar house.

Once we were home, Brenda went to work with her colored pens and paper. In three hours, she had managed to draw the front and back of our new home. She sketched the kitchen, hearth, laundry room, great room, music room, and dining room. For the upstairs she detailed the guest rooms, main bath, our master bedroom, master bath with a Jacuzzi tub, his and her vanities, shower, and a huge walk-in closet. It was exactly what she wanted, nothing spared.

As mortgage interest rates continued downward during the fall of 1993, we talked about the possibility of starting to build in the spring of 1994. Brenda told me that if we were going to make this happen, we needed to "get going" on finding a builder, and it had to be someone we felt comfortable with and could trust.

"I don't know any builders, Brenda. Maybe you should ask some of your clients to help us out."

With her diverse client base, it didn't take her long before she had a referral to someone she felt would fit the bill.

Prior to us visiting with any builders, Brenda called her oldest brother, Bernie Voss, who is a builder in northern Iowa.

She asked Bernie to help us with the dos and don'ts of building a home.

Bernie gave us a lot of really good advice, "Make sure you pay attention to all the little details, all the way down to the color of the outlets and face plates." Bernie also suggested we hire an architect to draw our plans. The advantage, he told us, would be getting bids based on exactly what we wanted and not what the builder thought we wanted. What most people don't realize is that, without blue prints, a builder can't give you an exact price. You can get an *approximation* without prints, but not an exact price.

Brenda's Aunt Lil, who came to see her every week to have her hair done, referred us to someone she knew who would draw our plans for $600.00. We were so fortunate that Lil knew this woman and knew she did excellent work.

Brenda spent a lot of time making sure all the details in every room were considered. She worked very close with our "draftsman" to make sure the prints would match the drawings she had sketched at home. It wasn't easy downsizing a half-million-dollar home, but, within three weeks, the prints were completed, and we could actually see the details of what our dream home looked like. Now we were totally prepared to find a builder.

Brenda's clients were always a great resource when it came to helping us. If we needed something, anything, someone knew someone or had the information for us. Finding a builder wasn't any different. Brenda's clients gave us names of some really good builders. One in particular stood out among all the rest.

"Do you remember meeting a guy named Rich Schaefer?" Brenda asked me.

"No, I don't. When did we meet him?" I said.

"About a year ago we were in Rosemount checking out model homes. He was the guy with the really deep, raspy voice who said he was going out on his own, and, if we were interested, to keep his name and give him a call."

"How did you remember him?" I wanted to know.

"Actually, I didn't. One of my clients knows his wife and said we should call him, that he used to work for so and so and that's when I remembered we met him and thought he was such a nice guy," she told me.

We put Rich on our call list of possible builders. We had three names that looked promising, all referrals. Rich would be the last one we contacted.

One of Brenda's clients was a real estate agent, and she was pushing hard for us to use her builder who was also a woman. I'm only pointing out the fact that she is a woman because it has significance to the story. Brenda took the initiative to have the first meeting with her client and the builder and kept me out of the loop as she wanted to test the waters before bringing in the "big gun." When she came home from her meeting, she told me how comfortable she felt with this woman and had given her a set of prints and was looking forward to getting back togethcr to see her bid. During that same week in September 1993, Brenda and I met with Rich and his partner, Keith. We also gave them a set of prints and told them to call us when they had their numbers ready, as we were getting two other bids. During our meeting with Rich and Keith, we found out that they would be working side by side with many of the subcontractors. In other words, they would be doing some of the hammering. The idea of having our builder do more than just hire the subcontractors, which is typical, really impressed me. It meant they would have an active role in the finished product.

We never did get a third bid, we felt between these two builders, one was going to build our home.

The following week, we met with Brenda's client, who was the real estate agent and the builder she had referred. One of the first things the builder told us was that our prints were wrong, and we would have to have them revised in order for her to give us a bid. The cost for the revision would be $1,000.

"I don't understand what you mean," I told her.

"Well, you see, you're trying to fit a half-million-dollar home into a quarter-million-dollar house, and it's just not possible," she said in a very condescending voice.

"Oh really, and what makes you believe we won't be able to build this house for $250,000?" I wanted to know.

She took out her red pen and started showing us. Marking up the copy of the print Brenda her given her the week before and making us feel like we had no idea what we were doing.

"How much do you estimate this house will cost us for you to build?" I wanted to know.

"My estimated guess would be around $300,000," she said. "I have a contract for you to sign, and we can get going on the revision of the prints."

I got very quiet and started thinking, *There was no way I'll do business with someone as arrogant as she is. What a bitch!* I didn't care if it cost Brenda a client. This was bullshit.

About the time I was going to tell the woman where she can stick her three hundred thousand dollars, Brenda chimed in, "I think we need to go home and think about it."

"Great idea. Let's go!" I said.

When we got outside, I turned to Brenda, and we both said the same thing, "We won't be using her for anything."

"By the way, I'm really proud of the way you handled yourself," she said.

"You know . . . I am too." I got in the car thinking, *I'm making progress.*

Brenda's real estate client, embarrassed by the total lack of professionalism displayed by her friend, called the next day to apologize for her actions and attitude and said, "I wouldn't blame you if you decide to look elsewhere.". By then, we already had a meeting set with Rich and Keith for the next evening at Rich's house. I couldn't wait to get together with them because they told us they were "hungry for business," which was exactly what I wanted to hear before we negotiated the price.

We arrived at Rich's house around 6:50 p.m., and, before we went inside, I turned to Brenda and made her promise me one thing. "Brenda, you need to promise me that you won't say one word during the negotiations."

"What negotiations are you talking about?" she asked me.

"What's going to happen is this: There will be some small talk, you and I will be offered something to drink, and eventually Rich and Keith will sit us down to go over the details of the bid. They won't show us their price until the very end of their presentation, so feel free to ask them any questions you want, especially for any clarifications on what you don't understand. I'll do the same. Once we're comfortable that they didn't miss anything, that's when I'm going to start the negotiations, and that's when *you must promise me* that you won't say a word, no matter how difficult the urge is for you to speak. You can't say anything, Brenda, not a word, you have to do it . . . *promise.* I need to hear you say it."

"I promise. I promise."

"You promise what?"

"I promise I won't say a word when the negotiations start."

I had only one more bit of information to tell you as we walked up the driveway to the front door. "Remember, Brenda, during negotiations, the first one to speak loses!"

Rich met us at the front door and was his normal talkative self. Keith was always smiling but was much more reserved. They were both very pleasant to be around, which gave us a good feeling inside. Unlike our previous experiences with builders, these two were genuine, down-to-earth people.

"Either of you want coffee?" Rich asked.

"Sure," Brenda told him.

"Just a glass of water for me, Rich," I said.

After a quick tour of Rich's home, we all sat down at the dining room table. Brenda was at the head of the table, and I was at her right. Rich sat on her left with Keith next to him. They were sitting directly across from me, exactly how I wanted it.

"Ok, you guys, we're very excited to go over our bid with you," Rich said.

For the next thirty minutes, Rich and Keith went over the details of how they arrived at their bid. No issues with our prints other than a few questions that Brenda was able to answer. With that part out of the way, Rich put a copy of the bid in front of us. $199,000 was the bottom line. I looked at Brenda and my eyes and facial expression reminded her that she needed to sit back and remember her promise, the negotiations were about to begin.

I sat there quietly paging through their bid, basically wasting time, waiting for Rich or Keith to say something, when Rich piped in, "What do you guys think?"

I kept my eyes focused on the paper. "Well, it's a lot more than we anticipated," I said. I looked at Brenda, and I knew she was ready to explode. This was the lowest price we had seen, and I was trying to work the deal lower. I knew it was killing her, but she managed to keep her promise. "Look, guys, we're working with two other builders, and one of them we want nothing to do with, that means it's you and one other guy," I told them. "We really like you guys, but the other bid is lower than yours," I added.

The sole purpose for saying that was to get their reaction. There wasn't another bid. These guys were it, and we didn't have time to find another builder. Brenda was doing her best to stay composed, and if Rich or Keith would have said, "I'm sorry this is our final offer," I know Brenda would have jumped out of her chair and signed the contract.

Instead, the buzz of excitement that was lingering around the room, the sound of our voices echoing off the walls, became silent. The four of us sat there looking at one another, and no one said a word. A few minutes passed without anyone saying a word . . . just dead silence. Those few minutes must have seemed like hours to the three of them, while I was completely content waiting it out.

"Where do we need to be to get the job?" Rich asked. The silence was finally broken as Rich asked the one question we needed to hear.

I looked at Brenda and could see that she was breathing again. Relief flooded her face.

"You're $10,000 too high," I said.

"Okay. Let me get this straight. If we can come down by $10,000, are you willing to sign a contract with us tonight?" Rich asked.

I didn't even get a chance to respond before Brenda said, "*Yes!*"

Rich and Keith excused themselves from the dining room and went into the kitchen to have some privacy. As soon as they were out of ear shot, Brenda turned to me and told me, "I don't care if they agree to come down on the price or not, I want them to build our house!"

"Relax, honey, they'll do the right thing," I said as the sweat poured down my armpits.

It didn't take Rich and Keith long to make their decision. They sat back down, looked at us and said, "Congratulations we're going to build your home for you!"

We signed the contract that evening, and the four of us celebrated by drinking a bottle of champagne Rich and Keith had on ice. We had our builders, and they were about to build their first custom home.

* * *

On the drive back to our town house, I told Brenda how lucky I was that she didn't allow me to convince her to settle for one of the models we looked at, especially the house in Eagan, the one I had pushed so hard for us to buy. She smiled and reminded me, "You just need to learn to listen to me. I sometimes know what I'm talking about." And she was right; she did know what she was talking about. I needed to learn to listen to her. That lesson was so important. I realized how right she always was. Her attitude was never, "I'm right and you're wrong." (Unlike mine.) It was far from that. She was just flat out right about so many things, and I needed to learn to listen and admit that her ideas and opinions count as much as mine.

Chapter 11

We Built Our Dream Home on a Budget, but the Stories That Followed!

J t was mid-November 1993 when Whitney Homes, the name of Rich and Keith's company, broke ground and began digging our basement. At the time, I was working for NewMech Companies, one of the largest Mechanical Contractors in Minnesota. The advantage of working for NewMech, especially during our building process, was that I had access to so many people who had a wealth of knowledge when it came to building a house. The advice was endless. One piece of advice came from Troy Pearson. He convinced me that I should make sure to stop by every day to oversee the work being done. I would be my own general contractor, making sure the subs were doing what we wanted. Troy's advice paid off several times during the next four months. *Thanks, buddy.*

The basement had been dug and it was two days before Thanksgiving, when my phone rang at the office. It was Rich, and he was panicking. "Mitch, the cement crew was due out here today, and they just called me to cancel!"

"They said their primary builder called and needs them as soon as possible. Since Keith and I are just getting started, they had no choice. Mitch, I don't know what to do."

"Rich, calm down and let me make a few phone calls and see what I can do. I'll get back to you as soon as I know something," I told him.

The first call I made was to Brenda to pass along the bad news.

"How did you handle yourself on the phone when Rich told you the news?" was her first question.

"What do you mean?" I asked.

"Well, did you get mad or did you remain calm?"

I had to think about why she was asking me this for a split second to understand what she was driving at. "You know, I was extremely calm and collected, I handled it just like you would, hon."

She told me she was proud of the way I handled the situation. If it were a year earlier, I probably would have had a fit and said some things to Rich I would have to apologize for later. Not this time, I was learning the lessons Brenda had been teaching me. Her easy-going personality was transferring to me, all the good stuff anyway.

"I'm thinking we should call David and see if he can help us out of this jam." I said. David Voss is Brenda's first cousin. He owns and operates a contracting business, Dave Voss Construction and specializes in cement work.

"Great idea. I'm sure he'll help us if he has time. Call me and let me know what David says. I got to get back to my client. Talk to you later."

I was fortunate to reach David on the phone later that morning and told him about our predicament. David, who is one of the nicest guys in the world, told me he would take care of it the *next day!* I gave him the phone numbers I had for Rich and Keith, and David said he'd call them right away. I called Brenda back to let her know how lucky we were that David was willing to help us out.

"According to Rich, if we don't get the basement poured tomorrow we'd be in big trouble trying to make the deadlines," I said. "I can't believe our luck, hon." I hung up the phone knowing we were in good hands. My next call was to Rich to let him know everything would be okay and to expect a call from David Voss.

"How the hell did you pull that off in one hour?" he asked me.

"Rich, my wife has connections in this town," I said, laughing the whole time.

"I guess she does. Who's going to do the work?" He wanted to know. I explained who David was and gave Rich his number to make sure those two made contact.

Within half an hour, my phone rang again. It was Rich. "Mitch, David said he would be coming over late tonight to survey the lot and get ready for the morning. Wow, is he a nice guy, Mitch."

David Voss had his crew on the job site within two days of my phone call.

"I know. We're very fortunate David was willing to do this for us."

With the basement walls and floor finished, it wouldn't take long for the shell to go up. By mid December the house was framed, and the inside work began. Our dream home was becoming a reality.

One of the reasons why our building process went so smoothly was Brenda's ability to communicate with Rich and Keith. After each conversation, she would write what was discussed in her notebook, detailing the date, subject, dollars, colors—all important information. Brenda was a stickler for details, and the smallest details were as important to her as the biggest ones. She was smart enough to know that one day her notes would save us from any disputes that may arise. Her notes were organized room by room, in her red Mead eighty-sheet, college-ruled, nine and one-half by six inch, one-subject notebook. Each section was tagged with brightly colored tabs she had made, sticking out the front, labeled by room or by location.

The little red notebook did come to our rescue during our closing the last week of February 1994. Keith and Rich told us

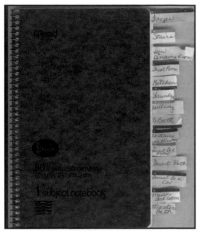

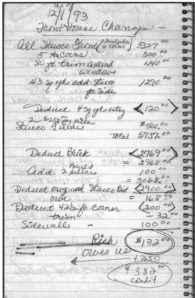

Brenda's Little Red Book.

Below are a couple of examples of her entries.

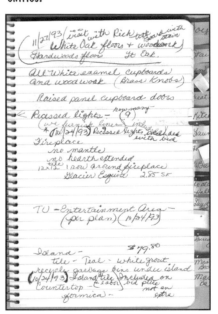

we owed them an additional $450.00 for the nine recessed lights in our kitchen. Brenda calmly turned to them and said, "I know you told me you included those in your bid. Let me get my notes and show you."

On the right page of the samples above is the notation about the nine recessed lights, dated October 23, 1993. They both sat quiet for a few moments, then Keith leaned forward, and said, "I do remember us talking about those lights, I'm sure she's right."

Above: Front of house. Below: Back of house.

Above: backyard left-side plantings. Below:backyard right-side plantings.

Backyard with ponds and walkway to club.

"I could have told you guys she's rarely wrong," I was just reinforcing what I already knew.

We moved into our home on March 1st, 1994. We had done it; we had built our dream home.

I learned a lot of lessons from our building experience. To this very day I still can't believe how talented Brenda was as an interior decorator and as a landscaper. The photos of our home and landscaping attest to how talented she was. She designed most everything except for the front of the house and the back-yard, which we designed together.

Over the next seven years, we continued to add and update both the inside of our home and our landscaping. Brenda's hobby was our home and gardening. She loved to decorate and always had an idea to enhance and keep our home looking updated. Because she had a perfect eye for color schemes (her taste was impeccable), she wouldn't settle for a piece of art or furniture with the slightest mismatch of color tones. What made her so unique was her ability to see the piece she wanted. If it was perfect for the house but had maybe the wrong colors, she'd buy it anyway and refurbish it to match our decor. Over the years, Brenda taught herself how to refinish any item she purchased to fit into her grand scheme of things.

The Furniture Is Gone!

October 1996 I walked into the house to discover all of our furniture in the Great Room was gone! I mean all of it. I walked around the house and took a mental inventory of everything that meant anything to me . . . all my CDs, stereo equipment, TVs, VCRs—all the stuff that really mattered—it was all still in its place. I thought we had been robbed, but what idiot burglar would only steal our furniture? Brenda came home an hour or so later and started laughing when she saw the expression on my face. "Where's all our furniture?" I demanded to know.

"I sold it," she said matter-of-factly.

"What do you mean, you sold it?" I asked, and she knew I was upset by the look I gave her.

"I sold it all for $500.00—the chase, the couch, the coffee table, and the painting on the wall. I'm buying all new furniture."

"When did you decide to do this?" I wanted to know.

"You obviously weren't listening. I told you I was going to buy new furniture."

"I know what you told me. I just didn't expect it was going to happen this month."

Brenda spent the rest of October and half of November looking for furniture in the Twin Cities with absolutely no luck. It was on our trip to Arizona over Thanksgiving to see my mother, Barb, and her husband, Don, that Brenda found exactly what she was looking for. "I've ordered everything I want, and it will arrive in three months," she said.

"Three months! Are you kidding?"

"No, I'm not. The furniture has to be made and shipped from the East Coast," she explained.

I didn't take the news very well at all. I wasn't too excited about watching TV sitting on the floor in a big empty room or having to watch her twenty-year-old nineteen-inch TV located in the kitchen. By the time the three months had passed and our

October 1996, our old furniture (above). The new furniture (below) finally came.

new furniture hadn't arrived, I asked Brenda to check on her order as I was sick of looking at an empty room. When she called the salesman in Arizona, he told her a couple pieces where on back order, and it would be another month to month and a half at least before it would all ship.

"I can't believe this!" I told her.

"Just be patient. It will be worth the wait," she said, trying to reassure me.

The month and a half extra wait turned into three more months. It wasn't until May 1997 that we finally had delivery of our "new" furniture for the great room.

Texturing the Walls

Brenda decided in 1997 that the walls of our home needed to be updated to something besides the color white, and I couldn't have agreed more. Since we both loved the way the builders in southern Arizona textured the walls, we thought we would hire a contractor to texture or "mud" our walls. It was February/March 1997 when we went to the Minnesota Home and Garden show, located in the Convention Center in Minneapolis. We found several contractors during our tour of the show. They all seemed willing to send us a price to do the work. But after receiving their bids in the mail and by phone, we decided their prices were extremely high in our opinion.

After thinking it over and not willing to give up, Brenda called her brother Bernie and asked him for advice on how to tackle this project on our own.

"I'd buy the pre-mixed mud at the lumberyard," was the advice he gave her.

She turned and said to me, "Let's try and do this ourselves. Bernie said we can handle it. We can start in the back hallway leading to the garage, and if we make any mistakes, it won't be so noticeable. Get your coat on and let's go to Menards."

The project took us four weekends to finish. I would trowel the mud onto the wall, and Brenda would add the texturing. The only tricky part of the whole job was when we needed to start the foyer, which is eighteen feet high. I rented inside scaffolding for our final weekend of this drawn-out project. Since I had to return the scaffolding by 8:00 a.m. Monday morning, it meant we needed to mud, texture, and paint the foyer by the end of Sunday night. The scaffolding came in two sections, each was six feet high, giving me a twelve-foot platform to stand on. Brenda, who I found out was afraid of heights, wouldn't climb up to the top to help me, so I was on my own having to add mud to the walls and do all the texturing. I asked to her to make herself useful by holding onto the bottom section so it would stop shaking when I would reach to the top of the wall just below the ceiling. She gave it her best effort but didn't have the strength to keep it steady, and she kept telling me she was terrified I was going to fall. "Please be careful, Mitch," she insisted.

Just to keep her on her toes, every once in a while I'd give the scaffolding a good shake by shifting my weight quickly back and forth, then act like I was about to lose my balance and yell "Hold her steady, honey!"

"I'm trying to, but I'm not strong enough," she'd yell back. "You're starting to scare me. I don't want you to fall."

So I'd give it another really good shake.

It didn't take long before she figured out what I was doing.

"Hey, where are you going?" I asked as she was walking away shaking her head and letting out a huge sigh. "I need you to hold her steady."

"Forget it. You'll be just fine."

I thought it was funny, but she obviously didn't see the humor.

When we finally completed our joint project, it looked like we had hired it done. We were both so pleased we had done it together.

The before shot of the hearth on page 92 shows our old wicker, old window treatments, no stone on the fireplace, a plant hanging above Brenda's twenty-year-old TV and the plain white walls.

The after shot of the hearth on page 92 shows the new wicker furniture, new window treatments, and stone work on the fireplace, beautiful glass cabinet above the new TV and textured walls.

Above: Before shot of the hearth. Below: After shot of the hearth.

Above: Before shot of Great Room. Below: After shot of Great Room.

The Rock Gardens

The front yard was Brenda's next victim for a facelift in 1999. She was determined to add on to our two existing (small) rock gardens and take half of my yard to do it! I'm the one who loves to take care of the grass, so the yard belonged to me, so to speak. I couldn't believe she was serious about doing this project. "Are you really going to do this?" I said to her. "There won't be any grass left in our front yard by the time you get done with your makeover."

I loved the look of all the green grass, and I was determined to change her mind. I tried to hold strong to my argument but I knew it was useless, especially when she told me. "You don't get it, Mitch. My plan will look awesome. I want you to take a few photos of the front yard for me, and I'll draw the size of the rock gardens so you can see what I'm talking about." It was always easy for her to visualize the project completed but I needed proof.

Of course I agreed to take the digital pictures and print them out for her so she could help me to visualize her great idea. What I didn't expect to see was Brenda in the front yard using a garden hose and a can of spray paint outlining the extensions to the existing rock gardens.

Rock garden drawings.

"So you really want to go through with this?" I asked.

"No, I *am* going through with this. You'll love it. Trust me."

"Okay, I trust you know what you're doing, but good luck just the same."

The next step was to remove the grass so I rented a machine from A to Z Rental to make the job go a lot quicker. Once we had the grass removed, the next step was to go to Hedberg Aggregate and bring home a few pieces of rock so Brenda could see if the physical size was the look she wanted. We used four-inch to nine-inch rock with the larger pieces as the border. "This is exactly as I envisioned it would look," she said.

We called and placed an order for nine ton of four to nine-inch rock to be delivered to our driveway. It was Sunday, the day of rest that Brenda picked to finish the project. I ended up moving each piece of rock one at a time into a wheelbarrow and then removed them one at a time—nine tons worth! Brenda helped as much as she could but the rock was too heavy for her so she would mainly point and tell me which pieces went where. It was better that she let me do all the heavy work, as I didn't want her taking a chance on crushing her fingers or her toes. Once the project was completed, our neighbor from across the street, stopped over and told us how awesome the rock gardens looked, "It looks like something you see in Arizona," he told us. Exactly what Brenda wanted to hear!

My job was always the grunt, the guy she told to move the heavy stuff, to do the digging. I never have cared much about

Front of house with finished rock gardens in place.

gardening, not like she did. I just loved watching her hard work blossom during the summer months.

The Wicker Furniture

It was August 2000, and we both agreed we needed a new couch and chair in our hearth area. Brenda had found the "look" she wanted and didn't hesitate ordering the wicker couch and chair from the furniture store just down the road from our house. She also special ordered the fabric to match the fabric on the window treatments. Of course it would take two months before we'd see any sign of the furniture. When the furniture store called and said the two pieces were in, I told Brenda I'd take care of it on Saturday morning. This particular Saturday she'd be home by 3:00 p.m. I decided to move our old wicker to the basement around around 11:00 a.m., then drive to the furniture store to make the final payment and arrange for delivery. By noon, I had the new pieces in the house and arranged exactly as I thought they should be. I plopped my butt down on the "new" couch, picked up the remote and turned on The Golf Channel. It was time for a quick nap before Brenda got home.

I didn't notice that these two wicker pieces didn't match the rest of the color scheme, or at least I felt they "looked good enough for me." It was a little after 3:00 p.m. when Brenda arrived home from work. The first thing she saw was the new wicker couch and the chair and immediately told me "They're the wrong color! But they have the right look."

"What do you mean they're the wrong color?" I knew what the next step would be if I didn't try and convince her to leave them alone; I'd be spending the rest of my Saturday afternoon laboring away changing the color.

"All we need to do is stain the wicker to match the hardwood floor." She said so nonchalantly. She also made it clear to me this project would be happening this afternoon, which was exactly what I feared.

So I said to her, "You go right ahead and knock yourself out; I don't see any reason why we should go to all the work of changing the color when they look fine to me!" What did I know about color schemes? What I did know was her idea sounded like a lot of work.

Brenda spent the next two hours running back and forth to Home Depot buying colored stain until she figured out which colors could be mixed together to match our "white oak" hard-wood floor (white oak doesn't have the pink color like red oak). She volunteered me to help her for the next five hours to transform the wicker couch and chair into the exact color she wanted. When it was all said and done, I stood back and announced to her, "Wow, you were right. They do look one hundred percent better."

"You see, Mitch, you need to learn that I know what I'm talking about!"

"Yes Dear, you do know what you're doing. I'm sorry I doubted you. Now leave me alone I have a severe migraine from the smell of the stain." With that said, I went to bed at 11:45 p.m. while Brenda cleaned up the mess we had made. She couldn't stand to see the house in a mess, not for one second. It was the one thing she always demanded of me: "Mitch, please keep the house picked up. You never know when someone might stop by."

Wicker Furniture on her new rug.

The Stone Floor

One of the ideas we had been kicking around for at least five years was to upgrade the tile in the foyer, master bath, shower, and tub to natural stone and replace the eight-inch tile in the main bath and shower with new twelve-inch tile. The idea became a mission for us in March of 2001 when, after searching for two months, we finally found the natural stone that matched the color schemes in our home. Brenda didn't expect we would start the project until the fall. So it was a shock to her when I went ahead and hired Lex, who owns Island Tile, to start the project as soon as possible. Brenda didn't fight the idea, but she thought we were rushing to get it done. My intuition was to go ahead and get it done before fall so we could enjoy ourselves during the winter months. Coordinating a project this big meant we needed to break it up into two phases. This was Brenda's idea, as she did not want have both the lower level and upper level of our home torn up at the same time. The first phase would include the foyer/dining area and the main bath, to start on May 7th and be completed by May 11th. The second phase would include the master bath, tub, and shower to start August 6th and be completed by August 17th.

The first week of May, I was scheduled to be in Switzerland for a management meeting, not the best timing in the world, but I assured Brenda everything would be fine. On Tuesday evening May 8th, 2001, I called her from Switzerland to see how the installation was going. "They finished the layout of the stone, and it's a good thing they didn't install it because I don't like the color of the pieces they are using!" she said and I could tell she was very upset.

"But you know each piece of stone takes on its own identity." I said to her.

"I know, but they could have spent some time picking pieces that matched. The foyer and dining area is the centerpiece of the house. It's the first thing you see when you walk in, and I want it to look perfect. I decided to go through all the stone in the garage and pick out the pieces I want in the foyer, and I arranged them so the colors would at least match or make more sense than the way they had them laid out." (These were eighteen-by-eighteen-inch pieces of limestone and extremely heavy. The foyer and dining area combined are 300 square feet.)

"You go, girl," was all could I tell her. When I called her the next evening to discuss the progress the guys had made she had calmed down and was very excited with the way the project was moving along. By the end of the week the foyer/dining area had been completed exactly how she had asked them to install it.

Foyer and dining room before shot.

Phase two began the first week of August, but we still needed the sealer applied to the foyer/dining area and that was when we found out Lex had not included sealing the floors in his bid, "I usually leave it up to the homeowner," he told us.

The idea of spending $15,000 on upgrading the tile to natural stone and not having the sealer included didn't sit well with either one of us. Instead of arguing, we asked Lex for a dollar amount to finish the job. Lex gave us a figure of $195.00, and we told him to go ahead. On August 9th, I came home to find a note that read, "Mitch, we put down the sealer, if you see any excess on the stone please wipe it off." I didn't see any excess so I didn't think there was anything I needed to do.

The next morning Brenda and I both got up at the same time anxious to see how the sealer had dried. We were both horrified when we looked at the floor and some spots looked wet, some looked dry and some looked like there was a shadow cast across the floor. It wasn't a shadow as we finally figured it out, it was the hone marks from when the stone was cut. "This looks terrible!" I told her. Later that morning I called Lex, and he said he might need to add one or two more coats to even it out. After the third coat was applied, and we could still see the hone marks we decided to contact the sealer company. I explained that the sealer Lex used looked fine when applied but once it dried it showed all the hone marks. "You may need to use a different sealer," they told us.

Sure, after spending $50.00 a quart and three quarts later, then they tell us.

The added kicker was when I was told, "You'll also need to remove the sealer that has been applied with phosphoric acid before you try applying a different brand."

"Great, now I need to buy phosphoric acid, how much is this project going to cost anyway?"

"Do you have rubber gloves and a scrubbing pad?" he asked me.

"No, I don't, so I guess I'll need to buy those too."

Back home with my new orange rubber gloves, scrubbing pad, bucket of water and phosphoric acid, I began the three-hour process on my hands and knees scrubbing 300 square feet of limestone one at a time. Once I was finished with the phosphoric acid part, I needed to use clean water and wipe the floor down three more times. "Well at least I have it looking the same as it did before Lex applied the sealer," I told Brenda.

Before I ran out to Home Depot and bought sealer off the shelf, I said I better call the people we bought the stone from and explain what had happened in case they had any ideas. They suggested we bring in a piece of our stone and test it with one of their products. I put a few pieces in the Yukon and I was once again going to the tile store. The lady that had originally sold us the stone explained that their product is a solvent-based stone enhancer, and they have never had any problems using it. She applied the enhancer on the stone I brought with me, and, of course, it looked great wet, but it would need time to dry. "It looks awesome. Why don't I go ahead and buy the enhancer so

I don't have to make a trip back," I said to her and paid another $50.00. This time we were on our own, just as Lex had originally planned, but $400.00 poorer for our effort. I went ahead and applied our new stone enhancer just as the woman had at the store. I didn't think a little extra left on the stone would hurt anything, I figured it would dry by morning. We went to bed, crossed our fingers, and prayed it would work. The next morning when we looked at the floor, it had a wet look to it. When I touched the floor to test it out, the stone enhancer was still tacky. It hadn't dried. "Maybe it needs more time," I said to Brenda, trying to convince myself that was the answer to the problem. We waited all day long, and it never dried, but remained sticky to the touch, and we could see our dog, Einstein's, paw prints all over the floor. Back to the drawing board, back to removing the sealer for a second time.

"I think the sealer I just bought is the right stuff. I'm going to try using it again, but this time I'm going to wipe off all the excess," I told her.

"You go right ahead, and if it looks the same when you're finished, you're going to take it up again," she said as she went upstairs to get ready for work.

After three more hours of scrubbing and cleaning, I was ready to apply the sealer, but this time I wouldn't apply so much, and I would wipe it down immediately and follow the directions to the "T." The next morning when I came downstairs, I was hoping things had changed, but it was the same damned results we had from the first sealer; we could see the hone marks in the stone. I didn't even say anything to her. I just put on my rubber gloves, got out the phosphoric acid and spent three hours cleaning for the third time! You'd think I'd have learned my lesson.

"Okay, I'm going to Home Depot and see what I can find," Brenda told me. She returned with a quart of stone sealer that cost her $8.00. "Let's test this and see what happens," she said.

To our amazement, the sample dried to the touch and looked fabulous.

"Let's give it a try on a small area and leave it overnight." I suggested. The next morning we both got up excited to see how the "cheapo" sealer had dried. "Take a look, hon. It appears we have a winner!" I said to her. We had achieved the look we wanted, and the hone marks were gone. We both declared Brenda's Home Depot idea of buying a cheap $8.00 bottle of sealer the big

Dining area is finished, the hutch is in place. Notice the statue of Aphrodite.

winner. I finished applying the sealer to the rest of the stone on Sunday August 19th, 2001.

New Roof in 2001

In between phase one and phase two, we scheduled the installation of our new roof. We decided that black shingles were more fitting than the drab gray-green shingles in the pictures. The old shingle tear-off and new install went very smooth, a first for us, and we were extremely pleased with the results.

The Hutch

During the summer of 2001, we had been expecting the delivery of a hutch for the dining area that Brenda had ordered eleven months earlier. I didn't stutter and it's not a misprint, you read it correctly, eleven months earlier! This story is as wacky as they come, I wouldn't believe it myself if it hadn't actually have happened to us.

Brenda had been saving her money to purchase this particular hutch because it matched our dining room table and server and was the piece our dining area was missing. The original retail price for the hutch was $10,000, so Brenda had been saving her tip money for over three years. She made the decision to purchase the hutch when she found out through a client of hers, who worked for Dayton's, that it would be going on sale, and she could save an additional twenty-five percent off the retail price. That was in October 2000.

Expecting the hutch to be delivered before Christmas 2000, we were both surprised when we called Dayton's to find out they had to re-order another hutch due to damage that occurred while shipping the first one. "When do you expect the next one to arrive?" Brenda inquired.

"End of January is our best estimate," was the reply.

By the end of January and now into the first week of February we couldn't believe we still hadn't heard anything regarding the delivery date. "Give them a call and find out what's going on, hon," I said to her.

Brenda took a few days to finally make the call, and once again she was disappointed to find out they had to send the second one back for the same reason, "It was damaged during shipping, but we expect the next hutch to arrive by the end of April."

"I don't know, Brenda. Maybe you should cancel this order and buy it from a different store."

"I'd love to but the piece is being discontinued, and I'm already saving twenty-five percent, so let's be patient and see what happens." She was determined to see this through to the very end with Dayton's.

"If you don't mind, I'd like to speak to someone at Dayton's and find out why they can't deliver a piece of furniture without busting it up every time they try and ship it." I was hoping she would let me get involved, as if my two cents worth would actually speed up the process.

"I don't care if you call them, but don't you dare piss them off."

She knows me too well, I thought. "Don't worry. I'll handle them professionally." *With boxing gloves* is what I was thinking. I made the call and amazingly my request to speak to the manager was granted. After telling Rich, the manager (his name really was Rich), our story of how the original delivery was a

Christmas gift, and, of course, they ruined our holiday (just a little white lie to soften him up), and "You're on your third attempt to deliver a hutch that I'm not so sure will ever arrive. Plus, the communication by your people has been horrible from the very beginning. What are you willing to do to ease our pain?" I asked him and sat silently waiting for an answer.

He first gave me the normal routine stuff, I understand, we're sorry, we should have done this and done that . . .

I stopped him. "You're not listening. I'll spell it out for you. What are you going to do monetarily for the aggravation you have put us through?" I could keep this up all day.

"Can I think about it and get back to you?" he said to me, which was a smart move on his part, I thought.

"Sure, but you better call me back!" I said it smiling. When he finally did return my call, he said he was willing to give us an additional ten percent off, which was fine with me and made Brenda feel better since she was the one paying for the hutch.

Eight weeks later and not a word from Dayton's about the latest delivery schedule. I decided to call and speak to Rich, the manager, to request the latest update. "It looks like they are scheduled to have it here next week. I'll call you once we have it inspected," he said sounding quite confident.

"Don't forget to call us, Rich. I'm not happy with the effort put forth in the communication department, if you know what I mean?"

"I apologize," he said. "I'll make sure and call you as soon as I know something."

"Thank you. Brenda and I appreciate what you're doing."

The following week I did receive a call from Rich while I was home in between appointments, but not with the news I wanted to hear. "Mitch, I have bad news. I was informed by the warehouse people that the hutch was damaged in shipping and will be returned. I'm not sure what to tell you at this point in time, maybe you want to cancel the order, and we'll return the money Brenda has paid us to date."

I decided to keep calm and try and talk this thing out. "That is a possibility, but I believe the manufacture can find a way to get this hutch to us without damaging it in transit. I have a suggestion, why don't you call the manufacture and talk to them about the shipping issues and see if they can pack it differently or ship it differently or maybe Dayton's should drive a truck to North Carolina and pick it up. Rich, at this point in time we are *not* happy with Dayton's. We've been customers for over ten years and have spent thousands of dollars with Dayton's and with Target. As a matter of fact, I challenge you to look back in your records to verify what I'm telling you is true! I also want you to think about how you would feel if this was happening to you and your wife and how patient you would be. I think we've been extremely patient with Dayton's and now you owe us Rich."

"Maybe you should consider canceling the order," Rich said.

"At this point in time we're not interested in canceling. We can't believe you won't get it right one of these times," I said to him.

"Here's our proposal, Rich. We are willing to offer you $4,000 for the hutch, and we'll forget all about the 'pain' you've put us through," I had no idea whether or not he would even try and reduce the price but it was worth a shot.

"Mitch, I won't promise you anything today, but I'll see what I can do." It was a week later when Rich called back. "Well, I did check to see how long you have been a customer and how much you have spent with us, and you were right. You are a valued customer of Dayton's, and we want to do everything possible to make this situation work. I spoke with upper management, and we all agreed we do need to do something for you. The best we can do on the price is $5,000. I know it's not what you wanted to hear, but it's the best we can do." He didn't say a word after that.

"Rich, I think we can live with your offer of $5,000. Now you need to get the hutch to us in one piece."

I was extremely pleased with the way the negotiations had gone. Brenda was ecstatic, as I had just saved her another $1,750. The next phone call we received from Dayton's (now Marshall Fields) was good news bad news—the good news was that the hutch was in; the bad news was the glass was broken, but it was being replaced locally, and they could delivery the hutch to us on August 9th, 2001.

Brenda only had a few weeks to enjoy her lovely hutch, her treasure, as she put it. All of her best crystal that she had collected from all over the world is displayed in "The Hutch."

* * *

The now infamous "Hutch."

It was March 1st, 1994, when we moved into our home, and here it was August 15th, 2001, with only one project left on Brenda's list, but it was a big one—she wanted to add on to our kitchen area. This was a subject we had debated for two years. I didn't want to lose part of our deck, which would happen during the expansion, nor did I really believe we needed to add on. Brenda was persistent with her idea of needing a "gourmet kitchen." She never gave up trying to convince me, which was part of her personality when she knew she was right. This two-year debate had turned into an agreement, on my part, of course. The real clincher occurred the week before she died. We were invited to Mike and Jackie's house along with several of our friends. Brenda was so impressed with the overall design and decorating of their home, that she couldn't stop telling me to "look around, and you can see why I want to add on to the kitchen."

"Yes Dear," I finally said to her. I told her to go ahead and start making plans for 2002.

"I already have. You just didn't know it." She said with a big smile on her face.

Now that she's gone, I'm not sure when I'll go ahead with her big dream of adding a gourmet kitchen. The biggest problem I face with adding on, is she had the design in her head. I'm not convinced there is anyone out there who would design it like she would have.

The year 2001 was a big year for renovation and change to our home. Brenda loved her home, and I'm thankful she was alive those last two weeks and two days to enjoy the complete five-year makeover.

Chapter 12

When I Finally Proposed, I Thought She Was Going to Kill Me

The holidays were a very special time for both of us. Brenda would spend three days after Thanksgiving transforming our home into a Christmas wonderland, both inside and out. She paid so much attention to the little details, making sure every room spoke volumes about the time of year. In 1994, our first Christmas in our new home, she was given one of the Heritage Village Collection pieces, which is a hand-painted porcelain building complete with plug-in for illumination at night. Each piece carries a Christmas theme and every year she would purchase a new one. It was Ming, who worked for Brenda at Regis before he followed her to Shear Madness in 2000, who got her started on the collection. We have a total of fourteen pieces that remind me of a little village in Switzerland when they are all set up and plugged in.

I've always enjoyed giving gifts, especially during Christmas Time. Brenda loved to try and guess what was in each package. Just like a little kid, she couldn't

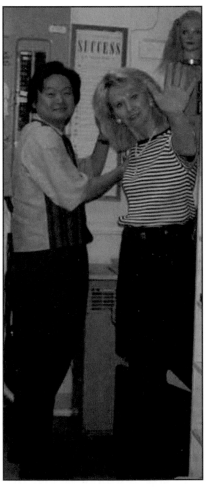

Ming Chu and Brenda.

wait for Christmas Eve or Christmas Day to open presents. I had rules for "The Guessing Game." They were very simple: The game couldn't start until the week of Christmas. I would give her three guesses per present, and if she didn't guess correctly, she had to wait until December 25th to open them. The problem was, she always guessed correctly. 1990, 1991, 1992, 1993, and 1994. I couldn't fool her. She usually had it right by the second guess, but only once in a while did she ever need the third one. I'll never know how she did it. When Christmas 1995 rolled around, I decided I'd had enough. This time I would make sure she wouldn't be able to guess what gift I bought for her. My strategy was to find something so unique and out of the ordinary that she wouldn't have a chance to get it right. The one place to find such a gift, in my mind, was the famous Mall of America. I fought my way through the maze of 125,000 people, who obviously were not aware of how important finding this special gift was to me. I didn't have a clue what I was going to buy for her, but I'd know it when I saw it.

On my third trip around the Mall, and feeling as if I wasn't going to find her anything, I decided to stop and look around at the Museum Shop to see if anything struck my fancy. I wandered over to an area that was made up largely of Greek Mythology figures. In first, second, and third grade, while living in Redfield, South Dakota, part of my grade-school curriculum was to learn about Greek Mythology. Don't ask me why they taught us Greek Mythology at such a young age because I had no idea when I would ever apply this knowledge. Until I saw the statue standing in the corner and I remembered who she was. Her Greek name is Aphrodite, and she is also known by her Roman name, Venus, "Goddess of Love." She is also known as the "Modest and Lovely Goddess." These descriptions touched me deep inside as I thought about my love for Brenda. Inside my head I kept saying to myself, *This is the perfect gift for Brenda, and the added bonus is, if I buy her, Brenda will never be able to guess I bought her a statue!*.

The replica stood a little over three feet, and, as I walked around the Museum Store, I constantly found myself looking back over my shoulder at her and thinking, *She's expensive, but she's worth it, and it's worth spending the money to keep Brenda from guessing what the gift is.* I started to envision her standing in our foyer greeting visitors, telling them to "please enter and enjoy your stay." Aphrodite was also known as the Lady of Kypros. Her gentle domain was intended to be "the sweetness of love." How could I not purchase her? She represented everything I felt about Brenda.

When the salesclerk brought her up front crated in a box that was five feet long and three feet high, I just knew, after the past five years of Brenda's guessing her Christmas gifts, I was finally going to see her wait until Christmas day to find out what was inside this large box. This would bring out the insanity, and I was going to enjoy every minute of it.

The salesclerk already had the box on a dolly and said he would help me load her into my Blazer. When I got her home, I decided I was going to have a little fun this year and yank Brenda's chain a little. I wrapped the box in two separate types of wrapping paper and wrote in large bold black ink, "Merry Christmas, Brenda. You're Not Going To Guess What's Inside This Year! Love Santa Claus."

I was getting cockier by the minute. I just had to rub her nose in it this year, so I picked up the phone and called her at work. It was around 8:00 p.m. and I knew she had about an hour to go before coming home, just enough time to drive her crazy. "Hi, hon. Guess what I did tonight?"

"Mitch, I'm really busy. What did you do?"

"I bought you your Christmas present, and you're never going to guess what it is!"

Her client was going to have to wait because I just hit her hot button. "You did! What did you buy me?" She was smiling ear to ear, I could tell by her voice.

"I'm not telling you, and remember you only have three guesses. See you when you get home."

"So you're not going to tell me?" She knew she had to get back to her client, and I knew the next ninety minutes would drive her nuts. We said a quick goodbye and hung up.

Around 9:30 p.m. I heard the garage door open, and Einstein did his usual barking routine until she opened the door. Then he couldn't wait for her to hold him. I walked over to her and gave her a kiss and asked her how her day was.

"Fine, now where is the present you bought me!"

"Well, hello to you to, dear." I said as I acted like there wasn't any present.

"You know this drives me crazy, so where is it and what did you buy me?"

"Come on, follow me. It's in the music room, and I'm not telling you what I bought you." The music room was so dubbed because I play guitar, and Brenda played piano. I had my guitars in the music room, but we hadn't purchased the baby grand. That came a few years later.

As soon as Brenda saw the three-by-five-foot box and read out loud, "Merry Christmas, Brenda. You're Not Going to Guess What's Inside This Year! Love Santa Claus," she immediately used one of her three guesses, "It's a piano bench! Where's the piano?" she screamed.

I started laughing. I didn't even think about the fact the box resembled a piano bench. "Excellent guess dear, but not even close."

So she tried to shake it, of course nothing moved inside. "It's my engagement ring!" She said using her second guess. Since 1992 she wanted a large 2K-diamond marquee for Christmas.

"Not this year, honey." I said, hoping she would drop the engagement idea.

"Mitch, are we ever going to get married?"

"Yes, of course we are," I said, trying to settle her down. "You need to focus on your third guess." I changed the subject for a little while at least. She pondered her next guess for about fifteen seconds then looked at me and said, "It's a piece of *art*." I couldn't believe what I just heard; she had done it to me again.

"You need to be a little more specific, dear." I was only being fair to her as she was in the right category.

"It's a statue."

"I can't believe you. Go ahead and open it. Six years in a row, you've done this to me." I was so disappointed, and she was elated.

She opened the box and lifted Aphrodite out and looked at her and told me how beautiful she was. "She's the goddess of love," I told her. "Her Greek name is Aphrodite, and her Roman name is Venus. She reminds me of you, honey."

"She's beautiful," Brenda said as she gave me a big hug and kiss. At least she forgot about the ring issue for another year.

Aphrodite still stands in the foyer, greeting visitors as they enter the house the "modest and lovely Goddess" Brenda built with so much love.

Christmas 1996 was the year I finally got her, and I got her good! The difference between 1996 and all the Christmases we spent together before 1996 was her attitude about getting married. This time she wanted that ring or else, I'm not sure what the or else entailed. I knew she loved me too much to ever leave me, so I knew that wasn't it, but I didn't want to push the idea of seeing how upset I could actually make her. I made up my mind that this year I would get her the diamond she deserved, but she would have to pay the ultimate price. The price she'd have to pay, in order for me to take away her "guessin powers" was to make her think we were never going to get married. Once she thought that, then I would pop the question.

I waited for her to bring up the subject of marriage, which she did every year about two weeks before Christmas. All year long, she never spoke about us getting married. She always waited until December, and then she'd badger me until I couldn't stand it any longer. My normal response each year was to tell her I didn't have enough money to buy the ring she deserved. By the end of 1996 I did have the money, and she knew it, but this time I was ready for her. Right on time, two weeks before Christmas on a Sunday afternoon she asked me, "Are you ever going to buy me a diamond so we can at least be engaged?"

Wow, it was amazing. Every year like clockwork, she'd hit me with that question. My response was so cruel, but I needed to do it in order for my plan to work. "Brenda, you know I think diamonds are a total waste of money. Besides why do we need to get married?"

Oh, my God. I thought she was going to kill me right then and there. The look she gave me was unbelievable.

"Fine," she said and went upstairs.

She didn't talk to me for three days. Not that I didn't blame her. But I needed to remain calm like nothing had happened even though her world had come crashing down. The end of the third day, she finally spoke to me. "Here's what I want for Christmas. I want the Big Green Machine," she said in a pissed-off voice.

"What the hell is a Big Green Machine?" I asked.

"It's a carpet cleaner," she replied.

I was having a difficult time comprehending what she just said to me. She had gone from wanting a diamond ring to a carpet cleaner. My brain kept telling my face not to show any signs of how funny this whole charade was. I knew I could play along because, according to my plan, she had swallowed the bait, *hook, line, and sinker!* I was doing everything in my power not to start laughing, but I couldn't help myself and just let it out. "Okay, where do we get this Big Green Machine?" I asked her almost peeing my pants I was laughing so hard.

"It's not funny," she told me. But it really was. "They have them at Montgomery Wards," she said.

"Well, let's go," I didn't want to waste any time if she knew what she wanted. So we drove to Roseville, Minnesota, to buy the Big Green Machine at Montgomery Wards. Believe me, there wasn't a lot of conversation during the twenty-minute ride it took to get there. We parked the Blazer, and, as we approached the store, she told me, "This won't take long. And you're paying for it," she made sure I was clear on that point.

"Not a problem," I told her, biting my tongue so I wouldn't start laughing again.

A salesman in a cheap brown suit approached us and asked if he could help us.

"Yes, you can, sir. I would like to see the Big Green Machine," I declared so everyone within the department could hear me and, at the same time, embarrass Brenda.

"Right this way," he said as he turned and walked away from us, assuming we would be right behind him, which of course we were.

The Big Green Machine was located in the vacuum cleaner section and, fortunately, I could get her again because we actually needed a new vacuum. He pointed to the Big Green Machine, not saying a word, as if pointing was all it would take to make the sale . . . *Oh, no, not so fast*, I thought. Brenda was thinking, *This isn't going to take very long* . . . but she was in for a surprise. I made him go through his whole sales pitch without letting Brenda say a word.

Before he could finish, I chimed in. "I'll take it," I said with a grin on my face. "And while we're here I would like to purchase a vacuum cleaner."

Brenda looked at me like I had lost my mind.

"And I would like to purchase this hand-held Dirt Devil as well." I walked over to Brenda and put my arm around her shoulder and stated, "Anything for you, honey."

If looks could kill, I was definitely a dead man. But how could my master plan work if I didn't put a dig in here and there?

We left Montgomery Wards with our new Big Green Machine for deep cleaning the carpets, our new Hoover Vacuum Cleaner, and my new Dirt Devil. When we got home, I had to try out both the Hoover and the Dirt Devil. The Big Green Machine would have to wait for the weekend. I kept trying to smooth the situation over since we did have another seven days to go before Christmas Eve, and I didn't want her so miserable she'd go into shock when I finally proposed.

Living with Brenda that week was a real treat. On day two, she finally broke down and told me she couldn't believe I actually bought her three vacuum cleaners for Christmas! "I can't believe you really think that's what I wanted for Christmas," she said.

Because I was being totally insensitive to the engagement situation, and I am a man, I decided to continue to play the jerk. "Honey, you told me you wanted the Big Green Machine for Christmas. I'm not a mind reader! Every year you give me a list of three to five presents to buy for you, and this year you said you wanted the BGM!" I was explaining this to her as if I really didn't know any better.

"You know I want a diamond. I want us to at least be engaged, and eventually I want to marry you," she said. For me those words were hard to take because I loved her so much. I never wanted to see her unhappy, but I was really making her unhappy by not agreeing to the diamond ring and marriage. What I had to say next to keep the surprise in place didn't do much to calm her down. "Look, I'll think about the diamond for next year. I just don't want to spend five-thousand dollars on a diamond; I just don't think they're worth it." This was probably not my best choice of words.

"So, what you're saying is I'm not worth it, is that it?" She shot right back at me.

"No, No, No, that's not what I'm saying, I'm saying we have allowed the jewelry industry to put such a high value on diamonds, and we're sucked into believing a piece of coal is worth paying thousands of dollars for." That statement didn't do me any good either.

"All I'm going to tell you is this: it's going to cost you a lot more than five-thousand dollars, mister, and you better start saving your money because the two carat marquee you're going to buy me will cost you $15,000 at least, and you better remember I'm worth every damn penny!" By the tone of her voice and the manner in which she walked away from me, I knew she meant it.

So, my plan worked, there was no way she would be expecting a diamond for Christmas. The next day was December twenty-third, and I needed to find the perfect marquee. Plan or not, I hadn't even looked for her diamond yet. I like to Christmas shop with a little pressure and no time left on the clock. Know anyone who fits that profile?

It was 7:00 p.m. on December twenty-third when I drove to the Mall of America; Brenda wasn't going to be home until 9:00 or 9:30 p.m. so I knew I had enough time. I figured if any place would have a large selection of loose stones it would be at the Mall of America. I wandered around between diamond shops for at least forty-five minutes not able to locate a single store that sold loose diamonds. I checked the information center and found I had missed one store on the north side. I didn't have a plan B to fall back on this year, so I crossed my fingers as I walked in. As luck would have it, not only did they have loose stones for sale, but they had a huge selection. Because I had worked for Helzberg Diamonds when I first met Brenda, I knew enough about diamonds to throw the lingo around and sound like I knew what I was talking about, especially when it came to the negotiating part. Buying her diamond from a retail store though, would mean the negotiations might take awhile. It was 8:15 p.m., and I wanted to be home by 9:15 to get ready for the ultimate proposal.

The store was packed with guys like me looking for that last minute gift. I was dressed in blue jeans a sweater and the black leather coat Brenda had bought me in 1992. I wasn't exactly dressed for success, so I was being ignored by the salespeople. I finally managed to get the attention of a very nice, attractive young saleswoman, and we started chatting about loose stones and marquees in particular. "I'm looking for a quality stone, something in the two carat range." I figured that would get her attention. Well it did get her attention but the problem was she didn't have any two-carat marquee diamonds with the quality I wanted.

"Let me show you one of the most beautiful marquee stones we have in the store, but it's only 1.51 carats," she said as she pulled the stone out of the case to show me.

It didn't take me long to realize how beautiful the stone was, and even though it wasn't two carats it had Brenda's name written all over it. "Okay, tell me what you're willing to do on the price," I stated. We went back and forth for ten minutes, until I made her my final offer.

"If my manager approves this are you willing to purchase the diamond tonight?" she asked.

"If you get his approval, it's a done deal." Ten minutes later, with the diamond in my hand, I was going home to prepare for my proposal to Brenda.

This diamond didn't come in a traditional box, oh, no. This box was three inches by five inches with a black crushed velvet exterior. When I opened the box, the diamond sat in the middle and on top was a large picture and full description of the stone staring right up at me. I also requested and was given a smaller more traditional box to take home. I was finally done with my Christmas shopping, birthday shopping, and any other holiday that would require a gift. *Spending that kind of dough*, I thought, *I was good for the next five years at least.* There was one thing I did know for sure, this would be a night we would always remember.

Once I got home, I needed to hurry to put my plan into action. It was 8:45 p.m., and Brenda would be getting home around 9:30 or 9:45 p.m. at the latest. The first thing I did was to take the diamond out of the three-by-five-inch box and put it into the smaller box I had requested. I found a gift bag from Garven, Inc., and filled it with the gift certificates I was given at the jewelry store. I found a large box and put the empty three-by-five-inch box inside and wrapped it. The diamond I purchased was preset in a thin gold band. I wanted Brenda to design her own ring so having this stone preset in the cheap band was perfect. I put the diamond ring in the small box, but I did not wrap it. I was ready for her to come home, but I needed to do one more thing. I needed to call Brenda while she was still at work to mentally prepare her for the evening.

"Hello, this is Brenda," she said after I was on hold for thirty seconds.

"Hi, hon. I just wanted to call you and let you know I just got home with your Christmas present!" I said it in one of those lovey, dovey, voices that would peak her curiosity.

"I thought you already bought me my Christmas present," she said, meaning the Big Green Machine.

"Just hurry home. You're going to love what I got you." I knew that would do it. She loved getting presents, and I knew the whole vacuum cleaner episode was now behind us.

Einstein heard the garage door open, and he started barking. Right on time I thought, it was 9:45 p.m., and I knew she would be dog tired. The whole month of December she worked from 7:00 a.m. to 9:30 p.m., and, after three weeks of those hours, she'd drive home change clothes and go straight to bed. Tonight would be different.

"Hi, hon. How was your day?" I said as I gave her the usual kiss and hug. She was actually receptive to me. I knew the phone call did it.

"So, what did you buy me?" She asked.

"How was your day, hon?" I repeated.

"Busy as usual. Now tell me what you bought me."

"I'm not telling, but why don't you go upstairs, change clothes, get into something comfortable and come on back down, and you can open it." No guessing game this year.

"I'll be right back," she said.

I knew it would take her at least fifteen minutes to wind down, change clothes, take off her makeup, wash her face, blow her nose, and use the bathroom before she would be back down. I knew her routine, and she never changed it.

Fifteen minutes later she was standing in our kitchen wearing her white sweats, white socks, blonde hair pulled back in a ponytail and looking like she could fall asleep where she stood. I had put the two gift bags on the island and decided to start with the empty box first. "Go ahead and open this one first," I told her.

She dug into the bottom of the bag until she felt the three-by-five-inch box and lifted it out. She held in front of herself as her hands began to shake. I'm sure in her mind all her dreams had just come true. She became so excited, she forgot how tired she was.

"Go ahead and open it," I said to her.

She lifted the lid of the box, and I could swear she was about to start crying when she saw the box was empty. "What's this? The box is empty!" she said in a shocked voice.

"I know it's empty, but take a look at the picture of the diamond on the inside lid and read the description." I stood next to her with my arm around her, letting a few seconds tick by as the stunned and bewildered look on her face made this all worth it. She wasn't able to say anything, so I broke the silence. requested. "I thought this year I would give you a picture of the diamond I'm going to buy you next year." That was my setup line. "Tell me. Do you like it?"

Still in shock from expecting to see a diamond ring, she really didn't know what to say. "I guess so," was about all she could manage to say. "What's in the other gift bag?" she wanted to know.

"Those are a bunch of gift certificates they gave me at the jewelry store. We can use them when we purchase your ring." I knew she was too confused to figure out I would have had to purchase something in order to receive gift certificates, even though she later explained she thought something wasn't quite right. I now had her exactly where I wanted her. The six years of her guessing what Christmas gifts I'd bought for her were over. I'd finally gotten her! She was standing in front of me, still in shock, when I opened the draw on the island and lifted the small box out and walked over to her. She didn't even notice what I was doing. She was just standing by the island not knowing what to do. I knelt down on one knee in front of her, took her right hand in my left as I brought the small box out from behind my back. I opened the lid of the box and turned it towards her as she started to tremble and cry, I asked her "Brenda, will you marry me?"

"Oh, my God, Mitch!" she shouted. She pulled me to her and hugged me for what seemed like forever. I had to ask her twice for an answer because she couldn't stop crying.

"Yes, Yes, of course, I'll marry you. I love you so much!" she told me as we embraced and kissed. "I have to call Bonnie and Becky." Bonnie and Becky were two of her closest sisters.

"Brenda, I think you need to call your mother first," was my advice to her.

"You're right. I need to call mom first." Repeating what I said because she was so excited. If I would have asked her to walk on water that night, she not only would have said yes, she probably would've been able to do it. That night was one the most memorable evenings we ever had together. I'll never forget how happy she was to finally get her diamond ring and be engaged.

December 24th, 1996, the day after I asked her to marry me, we were on our way to her sister Becky's in Zumbrota, Minnesota. Brenda couldn't wait to show everyone her new ring.

"When are you two gonna get married, or are we gonna have to wait another six years for that, too?" Our brother-in-law Wayne wanted to know.

Brenda smiled because we had talked about waiting at least a year. "We're thinking about mid to late July 1998," she announced.

I never knew how much I should spend on her diamond. Her idea was craziness in my mind. It was the advice from one of my co-workers two weeks earlier that helped me decide how much to spend. Scott Boehm and I had given a seminar to a group of engineers at the University of Nebraska. At lunch, Scott asked me if Brenda and I were ever going to get married. Typical question since everyone thought I was crazy not to have married this woman by now. "Mitch, take your bonus check and blow the whole thing on a ring for her. You'll be good for the next twenty years buddy."

"Good advice when you're spending my money, Scott."

"Believe me and just do it." Scott never mentioned another word about it, but I couldn't get it out of my head. He was right. Brenda told me I didn't have to buy her another birthday or Christmas present, but I think it was all the excitement talking. I had to remind her each year on February 5th, her birthday, and on Christmas that she was wearing her present. It did work for the past five years in a row. I'm not so sure how many more years I would have gotten away with not buying her a gift, she loved getting presents.

Chapter 13

Holidays

always knew Brenda was an excellent cook, baker, artist—you name it, she could make it. What surprised me the most about her was during the holidays, when she managed to work all day and still find time to bake all those goodies and do her crafts. Her main color theme was gold and silver but she always added the brilliant reds, whites, greens, and blues together so there was no doubt you knew it was Christmas. We always hung the Christmas wreath above the fireplace in the

Santa golf wreath.

hearth. This wasn't any ordinary wreath; it was one she created. Brenda didn't play golf but she loved to make things with a golf theme. Our Christmas wreath was thirty-two inches in diameter with multicolored golf tees, white golf balls, red and green ornamental balls, miniature presents, all hot glued to stay in place. Sitting on the bottom of the wreath was a two-foot Santa Claus wearing a golf hat, knickers, and a multi-colored golf shirt with a big smile. Brenda bought a little kid's golf set and hot glued the putter across the center of the wreath, which really added to the theme. When people saw the wreath, especially those who played golf, they wanted to know, "Where did you guys buy that?" I always got a good laugh out of that question because when I tell them Brenda made it, the next question they always asked was, "When did she have time to make it?"

The first Christmas in our new home was in 1994. I, especially, loved the tradition of buying a real Christmas tree and had done so each of the previous four years, so 1994 wasn't any different. Brenda had been trying to convince me for the past few Christmases that we needed to forget about the real tree and buy an artificial. I agreed with her analysis that the problem with a real Christmas tree was taking it down and getting it out of the house without making a huge mess. It was always easy bringing the tree inside the house when the branches were still folded together. The dilemma we had was figuring out how to successfully remove a Christmas tree without the inside of the house looking like a pine needle tornado had hit us. Don't get me wrong; I'm not trying to push artificial trees because, like I said, I always loved having a real tree, especially during those first few weeks when the aroma of pine filled the house. The "straw that broke the proverbial camel's back" occurred late one evening in 1994. The vacuum cleaner had obviously missed a few of the razor-sharp pine needles, as they were left buried in the carpeting, waiting for their shoeless victim. I was doing my normal late-night check, making sure all the doors were locked, wandering around the house half asleep, when I felt a sting in my foot, and the pain shooting up my leg was unbearable. My first instinct was to fall to the ground and reach for my foot, while simultaneously letting out screams that

I didn't know existed from deep down in my lungs. Talk about a wake up call! 1994 would be the last year a real tree adorned our home, even though my childhood memories were still fighting the idea of having a real tree the following year.

It was the first week of January 1995; we had just finished cleaning up the mess after tugging and pulling our Christmas tree out the front door. The pain in my foot inflicted from our tree had long been forgotten when Brenda asked me how I felt about an artificial tree for our next Christmas. I told her the problem with artificial trees was that they looked artificial. She quickly reminded me of the foot incident and the mess we were cleaning up and all the other reasons we should get an artificial tree. "It will be so much easier to take down, especially taking off the lights." She was right of course.

For me, pain is a hard feeling to remember, but when I thought about that needle stuck in my foot, I had to agree with her that the "artificial tree" was the way to go as long as she found one that looked real. Deep down I didn't think she could pull it off. It only took one week for her to find what she was looking for, "There's an after-Christmas sale going on," she announced, and the next thing I knew she had me standing with her in a large room filled with artificial trees. We must have looked for an hour before deciding to purchase a seven-and-a-half-foot Macon King Pine Tree. To me it looked artificial, but Brenda said she could see the most beautiful tree I would ever lay my eyes on.

A few days after Thanksgiving, in 1995, it was time to put our tree together. Brenda had been buying lights, ribbon, ornaments, and twigs, all to make this tree special. It was my job to read the directions, or "destructions" as Jimi says, so it was a good thing the assembly book came with pictures. I did exactly what the directions said, starting with the base and center poles. Before we added the branches, Brenda had a great idea on how to illuminate the tree. She had me wrap the center pole with over 500 small lights. The purpose was to illuminate the tree from the inside to take away the look of it being artificial. Her plan was awesome, and it worked. Once we had all the branches put in place, we then added another 1,000 lights on the outside. My job now complete, Brenda would spend the next hour and a half adding all the beautiful four-inch-wide ribbon, ornaments, and twigs. When we turned off all the lights in the house and turned on the Christmas lights, it was incredible how real our tree looked. When guests would first see the tree, they would ask us where we found such a "perfect" tree.

I've never missed having a real Christmas tree after that year. I can still see her standing on the step stool leaning forward adding all those decorations to that tree, watching her and wondering how one person could be so talented.

Part of our holiday tradition was to spend every Christmas Eve with the Websters—Wayne, Becky, Carrie, Justin, and Matt—at their home in Zumbrota, Minnesota. From 1991 to 2000, ten years in a row, we traveled the forty-five minutes from our home to theirs. We loved being with them, drinking wine, eating Becky's cooking (which is fabulous) and spoiling the kids with gifts.

I'm not sure about the year, but Brenda and I once played a really good practical joke on Matt. I'm guessing it was his fourteenth birthday. Matt's birthday is December 25th. He was notorious for telling his mother, Becky, exactly what he wanted for his Christmas/Birthday present. Matt didn't think small; he wanted the expensive stuff. This particular Christmas, he wanted a snowboard, not a used one, a new one, and it had to be a certain brand name, the most expensive one of course, around $600.00. When Brenda and I found out from Becky how much trouble she had trying to find "that damn snowboard" and "it cost me $600.00 bucks." I told Brenda, "I can make Matt a snowboard out of plywood. Hell, I won't even charge Becky more than five or six bucks tops.

"Do it, Mitch. That would be so funny. I'll call Becky and tell her you're going to make Matt a snowboard and to make sure Matt doesn't find the other one before we get there."

I spent the next hour cutting the shape of a snowboard out of three-quarter-inch plywood. I painted it red, white and blue. I stood on it barefoot and used a pencil to trace my feet. Next I outlined my footprints with black paint to make them look like Fred Flintstone feet. I added two leather straps; I figured Matt would need bindings, right? Brenda and I carefully wrapped the "biggest practical joke" and we were off to see the family.

Brenda told Becky to make sure Matt was pre-occupied when we arrived so I could hide the gift in the master bedroom. It was traditional for Becky to bring the big presents from the master suite, so we might as well keep with tradition, for Matt's sake anyway. The family went about the normal Christmas Eve celebration, acting as if nothing different was about to unfold. The routine for those over twenty-one was to have wine or beer, pop or water for the young 'uns, and we all nibbled on the goodies Becky and Brenda had made. We then ate a fabulous dinner, drank more wine and beer, all before gathering in the living room around the biggest damn Christmas tree Becky could fit into the house, it was "Chevy Chase like," as seen in the movie *Christmas Vacation*. Becky was in charge of handing out the presents, one at a time, and we'd wait for that person to open their gift and show everyone what they got and announce who it was from.

I'd never seen Matt so nervous; every time his name was called, he became more and more excited first he got the snowboarder's hat, then the snowboarder's pants, goggles, socks, and boots. This kid was going to look good, even if his snowboard didn't. Because it's traditional that we take our time when opening gifts, it had taken us a little over an hour to open all the presents that were under the tree. Matt knew Becky had bought him a snowboard, but he didn't know what it looked like, nor did he know what we were going to do to him. And, of course, I couldn't stand the idea of sitting still and not setting up my joke properly. I needed to start agitating Matt, get under his skin a little. "Matt, man you're making a haul on this snowboarding stuff. Where's your board at? I'd like to see it."

Matt had the biggest smile on his face as he announced as loud as he could, "I'm getting the snowboard for my Christmas/Birthday present. Mom, why don't you go to your bedroom and bring it out here."

Matt was so confidant Becky had bought him a snowboard that we had to try and shake him up a little. So I kept up the questioning. "Matt, are you sure you're getting a snowboard? I heard those things are really expensive, and it looks like you've gotten so much already."

"Oh, don't worry. I know she bought it for me." His confidence filled the room. "Mom, just go and get it," he said to her as he pointed in the direction of the master bedroom.

Now it was Becky's turn to take it up a notch, "Matt, what makes you so positive I bought you a snowboard? You might need to get a job to buy something like that for yourself. They're just too expensive."

We had him. We could see the doubt on his face as to whether or not the snowboard was going to make an appearance. Wayne was sitting next to the fireplace and had to turn his head so Matt wouldn't see him bustin' up. JJ and Carrie were both calm and collected, but I could tell they were laughing hard on the inside. Brenda played along as if nothing was going on. She put the icing on the cake when she said to him, "Matt, I don't know if your mom could afford to buy you a snowboard."

Matt actually looked disappointed. The doubts we had placed in his head were starting to show on his facial expressions.

Without Matt noticing, I got up as if I were going to use the bathroom. I went into the bedroom and retrieved the "practical joke." As I walked down the hall, I announced to Matt, "Is this what you're waiting for, Matt?"

When he saw what I was carrying, he went wild. To a normal person, even wrapped, the gag gift didn't look like a snowboard. But to Matt, his brain in overdrive, he was blinded with excitement. We had him tricked into believing it was a snowboard. I'm sure due to the weight of the plywood, he couldn't tell it was a gag gift. Everyone bit their tongues because no one wanted to start laughing. The spectacle was about to begin. Matt ripped all the paper off so fast he didn't even have time to analyze what it was before him. But man, the expression on his face when he turned to us and stated, "What is this?!"

I jumped right in with, "It's a snowboard, Matt. Your mom said she couldn't afford the one you wanted, so I told her I would make you one. Don't you like it? Look Matt, I even rounded the edges for better control." I got up and stood on the board and acted like I was a snowboarder.

He looked at me like I was insane, like I was some nut case who just landed on this planet. But I wouldn't crack, no way. Everyone in the room was busting a gut in laughter the whole time my conversation with Matt was going on. I still wouldn't crack. But as soon as I did, Matt knew he had been taken for the biggest ride of his life. It was one of the funniest things I have ever witnessed in my life. Becky brought his snowboard out from the bedroom, and all Matt could say was, "I knew you bought it for me."

Chapter 14

Einstein

J grew up in Mobridge, South Dakota, a small town located on the Missouri River in north central South Dakota. When I was five, I got my first dog. He was a French poodle, and we called him Peppie. When I was fourteen, I'd saved one hundred dollars and bought my second dog, a Doberman pincher I named Duke. My third dog was a German Short Hair. and my fourth dog was another Doberman. At eighteen I left for college and my dog days were over, for a while at least. The idea of having a dog around the house was in my blood. I loved big dogs, but owning anything other than a house dog was out of the question as I never had enough room needed when owning a large dog. Brenda knew how much I loved dogs, and I knew how much she was against having one. Since we were both in agreement that neither one of us wanted to have children, the idea of us owning a house dog seemed like a logical next step in our relationship, according to my way of thinking that is.

Brenda grew up on a farm in southern Minnesota and was used to having dogs and cats running around the farmstead. But to Brenda, the idea of us owning a dog never crossed her mind. I had asked her several times since moving to Minnesota if we could get a dog, and she always answered, "Dogs belong outside. We don't have room for a dog, and I don't want a dog in my house." This was her stance on the subject and that was it, period, end of story.

In this chapter are several short stories, starting with how Einstein became part of our family to how he tried to commit suicide. Enjoy.

After two years of me asking and her rejecting the idea of us owning a canine, I had given up on ever owning another dog. I don't know what changed her mind or if she ever did change her mind, but one evening after she got home from work (we were still living in our town house in Eagan at the time), Brenda told me this great story about a little old man who walked in the Burnsville Mall for exercise. Every morning he stopped by the Regis salon to visit with "the girls."

"Mitch you wouldn't believe it. Today he had a knapsack around his neck and inside was the cutest little dog I have ever seen. I asked him what breed the dog was, and he told me it was a Shih Tzu. I just loved that little dog. Now I could handle a dog like that."

I'm not kidding; she actually said, "I could handle a dog like that." Wow! That was music to my ears! That was all it took for the wheels in my head to start spinning. It was late January 1992, and Brenda's birthday was on February 5th. What a great birthday present this would be. I'd buy her a Shih Tzu puppy for her birthday! I'd get my dog, and she'd get a birthday present. We'd both be happy. *The way I used to deduce a situation wasn't very fair to my partner.*

I only thought about the idea for a few days and finally decided to do it. I purchased the Minneapolis paper, found the section, "For Sale, Dogs by Breed," looked up Shih Tzu and found several ads selling the puppies between one hundred fifty and two hundred dollars each. I made a phone call to the ad with the one-hundred-fifty-dollar pups. The woman I spoke to said they had five pups left, two males and three females. She said they were located about an hour's drive north of Minneapolis. I asked for directions and told her we would be up in the afternoon.

The day of the week I chose to pull this caper was Monday, a day Brenda had off. I asked her if she would want to tag along with me because I had found her birthday present and was going to go pick it up. Enough said; she was in the car and waiting for me after I said the words, "birthday present." Anyway, with her birthday a week away and an hour to the kennel, she immediately started bombarding me with questions.

"My birthday is a week away, and you've always waited until the last second to buy me anything. What did you do?" It was that guessing gene she had kicking in again.

I decided the best thing to do was to tell her what I was up to, but not until we were at least forty-five minutes into the trip. I'd make her guess what her present was until she was exhausted.

Oh, how I loved to keep her in suspense. It was all part of being a romantic. I also knew how much it meant to Brenda that I had taken the time to put her first, to make it all about her. She loved me more for those little things I did than any present I could have bought her. I firmly believe it is the little things we do for others that really count!

Tired of guessing and starting to lose her patience, it would be safe for me to discuss where we were going and what I had planned. I knew buying a pet for someone isn't cool if they're dead set against owning one. Which she was, except she did say, "I can handle a dog like that," and I hadn't forgotten what she said.

When I told her that her birthday present was a Shih Tzu puppy, I didn't give her a chance to say anything, I quickly followed up with, "You told me you could handle a dog like that." I was amazed at how she took the news. She was actually okay with the idea, which surprised me, to say the least.

I finally found the kennel but we were hoping we had the wrong address. Pulling into the farmyard was like pulling into a garbage dump. I was reminded of a documentary I saw on "puppy mills." The kennels were full of dog shit, and the dogs looked more like mutts than purebreds. The place was big enough to allow us to drive around looking at all the kennels, and we started thinking we made a serious mistake. I couldn't leave the place without at least meeting the low-lifes who were advertising themselves as professional dog breeders.

"Mitch, this place is disgusting! I don't want to be here."

I couldn't blame her. "I don't disagree with you, but my curiosity is killing me. I want to see what or who is behind this operation. Besides, we've come all this way. Let's at least see what the pups look like." Brenda agreed to go inside with me, but she looked like she was ready to gag, and we hadn't even gotten out of the car to get a good whiff of that "kennel air."

We walked up to the front door of what was supposed to be a house. It looked more like an old, weather-worn deserted shack I used to see on the prairies of South Dakota. The door opened, and the smell, or should I say stench, from cat piss filled our noses. The stench was so strong, we both almost gagged. Forget about the dog shit smell outside; this was a whole new experience! The woman who greeted us at the door was extremely overweight, and it was obvious she didn't know how to bathe herself. From the front entrance we could see her husband sitting in the kitchen trying to pull himself up off the chair with his crutches. We could see dirty dishes in the sink and on the kitchen table. To top it off the culprits of the cat piss were everywhere, and I'm allergic to *cats!*

Trying to breathe through our mouths only, I told her, "We're the ones who called about the Shih Tzu pups."

"Come on in," said the woman. "They're right here," as she pointed to a small wire kennel sitting on top of their washing machine located around the corner from the front entrance. I looked at Brenda, and we both were thinking the same thing, "Watch your step."

Inside the kennel were the cutest puppies I ever saw, and, amazingly, they were clean. I mean spotless. My knee-jerk reaction was to ask her, "Where did these puppies come from?" My question was more of a slam, the unspoken words I was thinking, *because they sure as hell couldn't have come from this kennel!* I could see Brenda felt a little embarrassed, so I quickly followed with, "The reason I'm asking is I didn't see any Shih Tzus in your kennels."

"Oh no, we don't have any Shih Tzus here. A friend of ours called us last week and asked us to sell them for her. She dropped them off earlier today." Brenda and I were so relieved to know the puppies came from anywhere but this place. We looked at each other as if it was now okay to go ahead and buy one.

"Brenda, go ahead and pick the one you want," I said to her in a tone meaning hurry up.

It only took about five minutes of handling each pup, and Brenda had made her choice. It was based on the coloring of the dog. She liked the pup with pure white hair, tan ears, and two tan markings on his body. He was so small she could hold him in the palm of her hand. "I want this one," she said, smiling as she held our new baby.

I paid the woman the one hundred fifty dollars and asked her for the papers, as these dogs were advertised as AKC registered. "I'll mail the information to you if that's all right," she said. Of course it was okay with us. We weren't going to stand around and argue. The stench was killing us.

Once in the car and on our way home Brenda turned to me and said exactly what I was thinking, "That was the most disgusting place I've ever seen or been in my life. How do people live like that?"

"Honey, you just experienced what the dog breeding industry calls a "puppy mill," a place were the dogs are never cared for properly and the people who run the joint are just like these two, they're *pigs!*" Our poor little puppy was sitting on

Brenda's lap not knowing what had just happened. "Hey little guy, we just saved you from the puppy mill," I told him.

Since I'd had experience raising dogs, I knew we needed to purchase a kennel, a clock that made a "ticking" sound so the pup could sleep at night, puppy food, and a combination bowl for food and water. Anything else he needed we could wing. During the trip home, we discussed naming our new puppy, but nothing we came up with seemed to fit. While we were at the pet store, we purchased a book about the Shih Tzu breed, and Brenda was reading it to me as we made our way from the pet store to our town house. One of bits of information she read to me about the breed, described them as "highly intelligent." That description inspired me to think about people I know who were intelligent, but we couldn't call our dog "Mike" or "Mark." "Doc" would work, but didn't fit his look; I'm saving "Doc" for when I own a lab. So I thought about intelligent people I'd heard of, and that's when the name "Einstein" popped into my head.

"What do you think about the name Einstein?" I asked her.

"Einstein, Einstein," she repeated. Then she looked at him and said, "Einstein!" and he turned and looked at her. That did it. He had a name.

The next day was Tuesday, and Brenda had worked all day. When she got home that evening, she did her usual change routine and came downstairs and sat next to me on the couch. I was watching the ten o'clock news, and she was reading her mail and not paying any attention to the TV, when the headline for the top story was read: "Puppy Mill" busted in Minnesota. She looked up and turned toward me with her eyes wide open. "Did I hear what I thought I heard?" she asked me.

"You heard it right," I said to her. "Wouldn't that be incredible if they busted the place we bought Einstein from?"

After the three-minute commercial break, the lead story started by showing pictures of the exact place we had been the day before!

"I don't believe it. We *did* save Einstein from the puppy mill," Brenda said as she held and petted him.

Those first few weeks were quite an adjustment for all three of us, but somehow we managed to get along just fine.

Brenda's motherly instinct had taken over, and she was a changed woman from the day we brought Einstein home, and, yes, she spoiled him rotten. Einstein had become her little baby, and the bond couldn't be broken.

"Mommy's Home!"

The move into our new home on March 1, 1994, meant a new environment for Einstein. Brenda and I would have to be

Einstein a few weeks after we brought him home to our town house in Eagan, Minnesota.

very careful with how much free time we gave him to roam around the house by himself. It didn't take him long to figure out his new kingdom, and, with only a few accidents here and there, he was fine. But in 1996, we still don't know why, Einstein started to pee on the carpet in the Great Room. He continued to soak the same area right in the middle of the room. The more we tried to clean it up the more he "let her go." After a week of his accidents, we took him to the veterinarian, who diagnosed him with a urinary infection. The cause was our own fault; we weren't paying enough attention to him and not letting him outside to go on a regular basis.

It really upset Brenda that "my dog" was peeing on "her" carpet. (Of course, he was now my problem.) I had now cleaned the carpet three times and, to both Brenda and me, the smell was gone, but Einstein, who has such a keen sense of smell, could still smell his scent in the plywood below the carpet and pad and continued to use the same area even though his urinary infection was gone. I had no choice but to replace the carpeting and pad. I also had to take a mandatory precaution and paint the plywood floor with KILZ in order to prevent any detection of urine by Einstein. Brenda was so furious with Einstein she actually wanted to give him away; or so she made me think she did. I decided to call her bluff, at least I was ninety-five percent sure she was bluffing.

"How can you think about giving your own child away?" I asked her.

"He's a dog, Mitch, and peeing on the carpet is the exact reason why I didn't want a dog in the house!" She said it like she meant it.

"Okay, honey, either we replace the carpet and pad or we get rid of Einstein. You tell me right now what you want to do!"

She knew I was dead serious. After a few moments of silence she said, "I guess we better go to Dayton's and look for new carpeting. Twelve-hundred dollars later, I installed the new pad and carpeting. Einstein has never had another accident, and Brenda loved him up even more during the next five years.

Brenda's habit of getting up at 5:00 a.m. every morning put Einstein into the same routine, up at 5:00 a.m. "every morning." Once she let him outside and fed him, she would lie on the couch in the hearth and watch the early morning news on TV with Einstein lying on her stomach, paws straight up in the air while she gave him a tummy scratch. On the mornings I'd get up with her, I always made it clear how much better Einstein has it than I did. "Hey, I don't even get a tummy scratch!"

"Oh, you poor boy," she always said. On the mornings I didn't get up with her, Einstein would get his usual morning scratch and then race upstairs to jump in bed with me. I didn't mind as long as he didn't move and just went to sleep. But at 7:00 a.m., right after Brenda would leave for work; I'd feel his wet nose nudging my back telling me it was time for me to get up. Einstein became my alarm clock!

With a name like Einstein, he better be smarter than the average dog next door. In order to prove how smart he was, I taught him how to count. It was a really easy trick to teach him, but when he performed for our friends, they would swear he knew how to count. The night I showed Brenda how smart Einstein was by having him count, she about lost it laughing. She was so amazed at this trick, she started showing him off every time we had company, especially for the kids. Here's how it works: First I taught him to speak, which took awhile for him to understand, but once he knew what the word "speak" meant, the rest was easy.

"Einstein, speak," and he would bark once. The trick was to cut him off after that first bark by telling him, "good boy," then I'd reward him by petting him on the head. Before he was ready to perform for Brenda, I had to interchange the word "speak" with the words "Can you count?" Once he learned I wanted him to bark after asking, "Can you count?" he was ready to make his debut.

"Einstein, can you count to one?" I let him bark once, and then cut him off with the "Good boy." "Can you count to two?" He barked immediately then sat there waiting for me to praise him. When I didn't do anything, he barked again, and then I immediately praised him. I continued doing the same thing until he could count to five. And this was the first time I showed the trick to Brenda. When we had company, Brenda couldn't wait to show everyone Einstein's counting ability. She always pushed him to make it to eight and he never failed her.

On August 14th, 2000, Einstein was scheduled for surgery to remove a tumor on the left side of his body. We had discovered a small lump on him about eight months earlier and immediately took him to the veterinarian, who said it was a small "fatty tumor." We were instructed to keep an eye on the size and if we noticed any change, it would have to be removed. By the first of August, the tumor had grown large enough that we decided it needed to be removed.

On the day Einstein was to have surgery I was originally scheduled to be out of town, but my plans had changed, so I was able to go with Brenda to pick him up. When we arrived at the vet's office they brought him to us, and the first thing we noticed was the bleeding from the incision. Even though the vet told us it was normal to see a little blood, one look at Brenda, and I thought she was going to faint.

"Mitch, I can't handle looking at him. There's no way I could have done this by myself."

"Don't worry, he's okay, all you need to do is hold him in your lap on the way home. Everything will be all right."

We had brought a towel and blanket along for the ride home just in case. Brenda put the blanket on her lap, and I laid Einstein on her and covered him with the towel so she wouldn't have see the blood. He was in so much pain, he whined every time he moved or we moved him.

Once home, we had the following letter from the vet on how to care for him during the next two weeks:

Einstein's larger mass was definitely invading the muscular body wall on his side. I removed all of it, as far as I could tell, and we should have a histopathology report on it in approximately two weeks. Meanwhile, since the muscle we had to cut is in a place where a lot of motion can seriously slow healing, keep Einstein as QUIET as possible: no running or jumping for the next two weeks until suture removal. If Einstein has a kennel or crate, that would be the best place for him when no one can watch him. Take him out on a hand-held leash to do his business. When you are home to watch Einstein, I strongly recommend hooking his leash to your belt so you are sure he won't go running off if the doorbell rings, or he hears a strange noise. We don't want him breaking any of the sutures I placed in the muscle and under the skin!

Don't hesitate to call with any questions or concerns, but he did great today, and I don't anticipate any problems. Be sure to follow the post anesthetic instructions we also are sending home with Einstein.

Doc T.
(JoAnn W. Taurog, DVM)

Here are the instructions we were to follow:
• Keep incision clean and dry.

- Observe incision for signs of irritation. Return pet if signs show up.
- The sutures are not dissolvable. Please return your pet in [fourteen] days, when the incision appears healed. Do not remove sutures at home.
- Call if your pet becomes ill.
- Strictly confine your pet in the house. Do not allow your pet to go up or down stairs without assistance, or to jump on or off furniture. Avoid letting the animal chase around in the house or run to the door.
- Do not allow your pet to lick, chew, or scratch the incision or sutures.

After the vet read us the instructions, I asked her, "Do I need to schedule a time to bring him back to remove the sutures?"

"No, just bring him in after two weeks, and we'll removed the sutures while you're here. It's not necessary to schedule an appointment."

"Great, see you in two weeks, and thanks for everything you did."

When we arrived home, Einstein was in so much pain, he could only lay wherever we put him. In order for him to "do his business," I had to carry him outside and gently set him down so he could go. That evening we brought him upstairs and kept him on the floor next to our bed. He slept in the same position all night, and the next morning he was still in pain whenever he tried to move. Brenda had to leave for work at 6:30 a.m., so I was on my own to play nursemaid. As much as he wanted to get up and walk around, it just wasn't possible without hearing him whimper. It was amazing to watch him during the day because as each hour passed by, I didn't know if he was going to make it or not.

Then around 4:00 p.m., only twenty-four hours after surgery, Einstein got up and started wagging his tail and moving around like nothing had happened. "Hey, big boy, what the heck do you think your doing?" I asked him. "You're not supposed to be moving around like that."

He walked over to the back door and wanted to go outside, so I let him out to see what he'd do. I couldn't believe my eyes as I watched him walk down the steps, appearing not to be in any pain.

He did his business and came back up the steps, which is a lot harder to do than going down, wagging his tail and wanting something to eat! "What the hell happened to you old boy?" It was like the drugs had worn off and he was ready to party. I had rehearsal with my band at 5:00 p.m., and the guys would be showing up between 4:45 and 5:15. I always left the garage door open on rehearsal nights, so I wasn't worried about the doorbell ringing and Einstein running to see who was there. Actually I wasn't worried about him at all. I decided to let him do whatever he felt like doing as I had completely forgot about the strict instructions the vet gave me. After I fed him, he came out from the laundry room and jumped up on the couch in the hearth area and lay there for a few minutes. I heard a thud, as he jumped down from the couch and turned to go upstairs. "Where are you going now?" I asked him. He just wagged his tail as he climbed the fifteen steps it takes to go to the second story of the house. When the guys all showed up for rehearsal, Einstein ran down those same fifteen steps and greeted each one of them. No one could tell only an hour earlier he couldn't even move without being in severe pain.

The garage door started to open at 9:00 p.m., and Einstein ran to the door and started barking. It was Brenda coming home from work. When she opened the door to the kitchen, Einstein greeted her just like he had for the past eight years. She couldn't believe her eyes. "How long has he been acting like this?"

"Since about 4:00 p.m. this afternoon." I told her.

"Mitch, aren't you suppose to keep him calm?"

"He doesn't want to be calm. Let him go. He's fine." That evening he even jumped up on our bed. So much for following doctor's orders.

Two weeks later Einstein and I went to see the vet to have his sutures removed. I was surprised to find a sign on the door that read, "We are closed today attending an all-day seminar."

"Okay, Einstein, I guess I'll have to break another rule today and play veterinarian." Einstein and I went back home, and I got out my trusty pocketknife, opened the small scissors and cut the sutures and pulled them out. Einstein didn't even move, just stood there and wagged his tail.

In June 2001, we were having rabbit problems for the second year in a row. The rabbits loved to feast on the flowers and grass in our back yard. We tried everything to keep them at bay. Fox piss, bobcat piss, coyote piss, hot pepper spray, live traps—everything humane, but nothing deterred them. Finally, with all my options exhausted, I felt the last resort was to try poisoning the critters. I found where they had eaten the grass almost to the roots and put the blue-green-colored pellets in and around the feeding area.

It was a Saturday afternoon, and we were being extremely careful when we opened and closed the screen door, making sure Einstein stayed in the house. It was Brenda who went back outside first. I waited approximately two to three minutes before following her. As I walked back towards the area where Brenda was working, I was talking to her about some trivial subject, when I abruptly stopped what I was saying in the middle of my sentence. Out of my peripheral vision, I spotted this little white head bobbing up and down. I turned to see what my mind said couldn't be true, and my heart sunk. There was Einstein gulping the poison down as fast as he could. I freaked out. "Oh, my God!" I yelled as I was running to stop him. "How did he get out of the house?" I now had him in my grasp but my last question was directed right at Brenda, as if it was her fault.

"I don't know," she said in a voice telling me *Don't you try and blame this on me.*

I rushed him into the laundry room, which is located next to the kitchen, put him into the large wash basin, forced his mouth open and started wiping as much of the blue-green-colored poison from his tongue as I could.

"Call a veterinarian!" I yelled at Brenda.

"Who should I call?"

"Open the yellow pages and see who has emergency care," I said as I was trying to remain calm, but I knew I was failing. "I'll do the same thing," I said to her.

I left Einstein in the tub basin and ran to my office located in the basement. I used the yellow pages to find a number for Twenty-Four-Hour Emergency Care and dialed the number. The person who answered the phone sounded very young, so I asked her if she was a vet. She said she was an assistant but could "try" and help me if I would tell her what the problem was. I was persistent with wanting to speak directly to a vet, and finally she put her on the phone. I explained the situation as fast as I could, and she told me I needed to force him to swallow one tablespoon of hydrogen peroxide, and wait ten minutes to see if he threw up any of the poison. If not, I was to try it again.

"If you can't get him to throw up either time, you need to bring him in," she told me.

Still in a state of panic, I bolted to the master bathroom and found the hydrogen peroxide, grabbed a tablespoon from the kitchen drawer and followed the vet's instructions. Einstein didn't fight the idea of having a funny tasting liquid forced down his throat; it was just the opposite. With his mouth foaming white from the peroxide mixing with the leftover poison, he looked at me and wagged his tail as if he was fine. But he looked like he was rabid.

"Brenda, he seems to be okay," I told her in a much calmer voice.

"I don't know, Mitch. You might want to take him to the vet just in case."

I waited the ten minutes as instructed, and Einstein didn't throw up. I proceeded with another tablespoon, waited ten minutes, and he still didn't do anything except act like he was enjoying all the attention. "I think he's fine, but I'll take him in anyway."

"I think it's a good idea." Brenda never did panic. She remained calm throughout the whole ordeal.

Einstein was still in the wash basin, dripping wet with peroxide. I opened the cabinet above the washing machine and dryer and grabbed a couple of towels, did a quick wipe of his face with one of them and brought the extra one along for the ride in case he threw up on the way. The emergency room was located in Apple Valley, Minnesota, approximately twenty to twenty-five minutes away. We arrived in fifteen minutes. I couldn't bear the thought that I might have just poisoned our dog. I was greeted by a young woman who couldn't have been more than twenty years old. My brain told me she wasn't the vet, so I didn't give her a chance to ask any questions. I told her what she needed to do. "You need to get the vet immediately. I'm the guy who called about my dog eating the poison."

She actually started laughing at me. "Your wife called a few minutes ago to tell us you might be a little excited, but don't worry," she said as she reached for Einstein, "we'll take good care of him."

The two of them disappeared into the infamous "back room." I was left to fill out the paperwork and play the waiting game. Almost an hour later, I finally met the doctor who I spoke to on the phone. She explained to me the procedure for an animal that is brought to them who is suspected of swallowing poison. "We induced vomiting by having Einstein smell a chemical. The chemical reaction causes him to heave everything in his stomach. When Einstein finally did let her go, a wad of blue-green poison the size of an orange came out of him."

"Is he going to be all right" I wanted to know.

"We don't know yet. You're going to have to take him to your regular vet tomorrow and have them do a blood analysis to see if there are any traces of poison in his blood. If they do find traces of poison, you will need to put him on Vitamin K. But I have to tell you, it's really expensive. I believe it's sixty dollars a week and he will need to be on the pills for four weeks."

That was her explanation. I didn't say it to her, but I sure thought it, *What's my alternative? Pay the sixty bucks a week for four weeks or have a dead dog! Look, lady, we spent over $1,200 bucks on replacing our Great Room carpeting after he peed on it. I don't think another $240 is going to matter at this point in time. God, I wanted to yell that out loud.*

When it came to Einstein, we always thought of him as the child we never had. For a vet to make it sound like it was easier to let him die than give him Vitamin K wasn't very funny at the time . . . now I think it's hilarious. Can you imagine me coming home and saying, "Ah, Brenda, now let's think about this sixty bucks a week thing. You know it sure is a lot of money!"

She would have killed me first then paid the sixty bucks.

I took Einstein to our regular vet on Monday, and the results came back that he was fine.

On Monday September 3rd, 2001, the day after Brenda died, a large group of my friends and family were sitting with me outside on the deck. Brenda's oldest brother, Bernie, noticed Einstein was sticking his head between the rocks, which bordered the bottom portion of the east deck, eating something. When he investigated what Einstein was eating, it was apparent to Bernie that Einstein had found a way to reach the mouse poison I thought I had put in a safe place. None of us knew how long Einstein had been there or how much poison he ate, but at least I knew what to do. I calmly asked my other brother-in-law Wayne "Cowboy" Webster if he could give the damn dog and me a ride to the emergency room. "No problem. Let's go," he said. This time around I didn't call ahead to the emergency room, and I didn't use hydrogen peroxide to see if I could get him to throw up. I remained calm but kept thinking, *I'm not going to lose you, buddy, not after yesterday, one death in the family is enough for this week.*

Wayne's occupation as a cattle buyer/auctioneer/fishing guide meant his transportation needs were a little different than mine. Wayne drove a big; black, dually truck made by Chevrolet. When we arrived at the emergency room, we didn't say anything to each other, but I know we both thought if anyone saw us it would've looked awfully funny seeing two big boys climb out of this big truck with this little tiny dog.

We walked inside, and I handed Einstein to the girl at the front desk and said, "Would you please take him and have the vet induce vomiting. This is the second time he's tried to commit suicide," I told her.

"What happened?" she asked.

"He got into the mouse poison again. We don't think he actually ate that much, but I'm not taking any chances."

Just like the time before, we had to wait for an hour before they were done with him. Wayne, who's the type of guy that couldn't sit still very long, was extremely patient, and I really appreciated it. If it weren't for Brenda passing away the day before, I think he would have told me to get a cab.

During our hour wait for the vet to make sure Einstein was okay, a lady walked in with her daughter and their cat. It was difficult for the two of us not to notice the daughter. What was funny as hell, when I look back on this story, was the fact that neither of us said a single word to each other. We just sat there staring at her, the daughter that is. She was only fifteen or sixteen years old, and was dressed like a hooker. I mean head to toe, total call-girl material, and she had the boobs, legs, looks, ass, hair, make up, shoes—she had it all, but I didn't really notice! Her mother, on the other hand, and I'll be kind, was a little on the larger side. They didn't look like they even belonged together. Enough said about "Big Mama."

If it weren't for the passing of Brenda the day before, I guarantee Wayne and I would have at least said something to each other, we would have at least smiled at each other, you know the look two guys give each other when they see a hooker, I mean a hottie. But we didn't. I thought, *It must be wrong to think she's a hottie when my wife died less than twenty-four hours ago.* But she was drawing so much attention to herself, I had to look. Even Brenda would have laughed at the situation.

It was a good thing the vet came out of the back room with Einstein, as Wayne and I couldn't take it anymore.

The vet told us, "We didn't find any poison in his system, but we could smell it when he threw up." This time they recommended I give Einstein Vitamin K as a precaution. "Vitamin K will act like a blood thinner, and I'd rather be on the safe side since you just had him in here a few months ago," the vet said.

I paid the bill, another one hundred sixty bucks, picked up Einstein, and out the door we went. We both got in the truck and looked at each other, and I couldn't hold back. "Wayne, can you believe how the young girls are dressing today? If she was my daughter, there's no way she'd be allowed to leave the house lookin' like that." I kept my serious edge about me, no smiling I told myself, for Brenda's sake. For some dumb reason, we both knew the situation was hilarious, but neither one of us could break into laughter, and believe me we wanted to. One of us did cap off the moment with a final comment, "She sure was *damn* good lookin' though!"

I won't divulge which one of us made the final comment regarding our little floozy encounter. I knew we'd laugh our asses off about her the next time we went fishin'. It's amazing to me, all the times we've been fishin' together since Brenda died, neither one of us has ever talked about what happened that day in the emergency room.

Einstein never showed any signs of being poisoned. Although he tried to commit suicide to be with his mama, I needed him more than he needed to be with her.

The three weeks that followed Brenda's death were extremely hard for Einstein. He was depressed, lonely and lost. When people asked, "How's Einstein doing?" my general response was, "He's still in a funk."

It was true for both of us those first few weeks. Most of the day, he spent laying on the white rug up against the back door that lead to the garage—the same door his mama would use to leave in the morning, and the same door he would stand by and wag his tail when she returned home from work. It was strange to see him stay there all day long because he had never done that in the seven and a half years we'd lived in the house. It was really hard for him between 9:00 and 9:45 p.m., the time when Brenda usually arrived home from work. I'd pick him up and hold him for half an hour or so during those "tough times," at least until he got antsy and wanted to go lay back by the door again. I guess we were holding each other, and it helped us make it to the next day. That was how we functioned, day to day.

Taking Einstein to my brother Todd's house that third week in September did seem to help. When we got home on Sunday night, Einstein was actually starting to come out of his funk. By the fifth week, Einstein was sleeping in his own bed in the laundry room. It's true what they say; everyone grieves in different ways, even animals.

Chapter 15

Our Wedding

rom the moment I put the engagement ring on her finger, December 23rd, 1996, Brenda started planning our wedding. She felt we should wait a year or more before getting married, which was fine with me. As a matter of fact, I was staying completely out of her way, as this woman was on a mission.

"No sense in me putting in my two cents worth about this wedding, you'd just give me change," I always told her.

"You're right about that, honey," she'd shoot back at me.

Brenda and I agreed the summer of 1998 would be the perfect time to tie the knot.

"We need to go to the club and reserve a Saturday for our reception," she said in the spring of 1997.

"What month are you thinking about?" I inquired.

"Either July or August."

"That's over a year away. What's the rush?" I didn't know any better.

"Mitch, trust me. People reserve their dates over a year in advance. I'm hoping we can still find an open Saturday in one of those months."

"I'm sure we won't have any problems." I thought I was so smart. "I'll call Perry, and we can meet with him today if you want to."

"That would be a good idea. Why don't you call him right now?" Brenda knew me too well. She knew I'd procrastinate and forget to call him if I didn't do it while I was thinking about it.

Perry Johnson, who is the Director of Catering at Mendakota Country Club, answered his phone when I called, and he said to come on over.

Perry greeted us with a large black "events" calendar sitting on the counter next to him. "So, it's always nice to see you. When are you two thinking about getting married?" he asked.

"July or August," I said to him.

"Of this year?" he said as his eyes got wide, and the expression on his face said, You've got to be kidding.

"No, he means next year." Brenda took over from there. I was just yanking Perry's chain.

"You had me worried there for a minute." A little out of breath but composing himself, Perry said, "I know I don't have any dates available this year, and I know," he turned the pages of the events calendar to July 1998, "I only have a few dates left next summer. We can do the weekend after the Fourth of July or August 1st. Those are the only two dates we have for you to choose from. Otherwise, late September is the next available."

"What about August 1st?" Brenda asked me.

"That's fine by me. It's whatever you want, dear."

"Put us down for August 1st," I stated so proudly. It would now be up to Brenda to work with Perry on the decorations and food. I was done helping her plan this wedding, or so I thought.

With the reservation confirmed at the club, Brenda had everything under control. There was still one unresolved issue, and it was a biggie. "Who is going to marry us?" She left this loose end undone until spring 1998 when she finally called her client Rev. George Martin to ask him if he would be available to marry us on August 1st, 1998.

As luck would have it, George was available, his church was available, and he said he was honored to be asked to give the ceremony. He only had one request, to which we both agreed. He asked us to meet with him to take a "marriage compatibility test." "I know you two have been together for eight years, but we have all our couples take this test, and you might be surprised with the results." George had been a client of Brenda's for a long time, but I had only heard about George. I'd never met him. Before hanging up, they set the meeting time and test for mid June.

George was a very nice man, just as Brenda had described him to me. We visited with him for about half an hour. Then he asked us to take the compatibility test. Before the test began, I turned to Brenda and whispered, "The wedding is only a month and a half away. What if he tells us we're not compatible?"

"Stop it!" she said to me.

"Well, what are we going to do if we find out we're not supposed to get married?"

"Will you knock it off? You know that's not the case."

"Yeah, but what if?"

"We'll still get married. Now leave me alone and take your test." And with that statement, she ended all the fun I was having with her. She wasn't willing to stop her test and ask George, "What if?" because she knew after eight years we had it right.

Here's what we did know about our wedding. We did not want to have a traditional church wedding or a traditional wedding reception. My mother, Barb, her husband, Don Martin (no relation to George), Brenda's mother, Donna Voss, my brother Todd Freimark (pronounced Frymark), and his friend Trixie, Brenda's sister Becky and her husband, Wayne Webster, and two of our closest friends, Jim Prante and Peggy Garven, would attend the wedding ceremony. The word "reception" would be substituted by the word "party." The party following the ceremony would take place at Mendakota Country Club. We only invited two hundred of our closest friends. One hundred seventy made it.

There was only "one thing," as she put it, that Brenda asked me to do for her that first week of January 1998. She put me in charge of hiring the band for the party. By the time the fourth week of January 1998 rolled around, I hadn't even inquired about a band, when Brenda told me, "You better get going on getting a band, or we're going to be in trouble."

"No way. I won't have any problems getting a band." So I thought. My first call was to Perry at the club to ask for a few phone numbers regarding bands he hired for club events. I called the first number he gave me, and they were already booked but referred me to another group. When I called the referral, I was told the same story but once again was referred, this time to a talent agency. I was starting to realize why Brenda put me in charge of hiring the entertainment. She played me like a pawn, knowing my ego would get in the way when she said I better get going on hiring a band or I'd be in trouble. This was going to be a lot harder than I first thought. I knew she was right, but I was now determined more than ever to hire a great band but not let her know how difficult the process had been. The biggest surprise for me was the cost. In my mind I thought I could hire a great band for a grand or maybe less. "Brenda, I can't believe the prices the agencies want for a wedding band. If we want a good dance band, it will cost us two thousand dollars!"

"I told you, you should have been looking into this a long time ago."

"Yes Dear," I responded. "Well what do you think we should do," I asked her.

"I think you need to hire a band for the two thousand dollars and learn to listen to me because I know what I'm doing."

"Yes Dear." Those two words seemed to be working, at least I wasn't being confrontational, and she wasn't lecturing me about being so stubborn, always having to do things my way. I'd been using the, "Yes Dear," for a while, not realizing how much power those two words actually had. It was my way of telling her she was right. I never used "Yes Dear" in a patronizing manner.

I finally found a band called "Bob and the Beachcombers." Bob, "The Captain" as Mark Nelson nicknamed him, wanted twenty-five hundred dollars for the night. I negotiated the deal for two thousand the last week of January 1998. With my end of the bargain completed, I had an idea, which I thought would be cool if I could pull it off. "Brenda, I'd like Mark and Jeff (The Cartwright Brothers) to play at the party. You know how entertaining they are, and people will love them. They could play for thirty or forty minutes while people are mingling before dinner, and then we can have them play for an hour while Bob and the Beachcombers are on break. What do you think?"

"I think it's a great idea. You better call Mark and Jeff and find out if they would be willing to do it."

Mark and Jeff were coming to the "party" anyway, so when I called to ask them if they would be interested in entertaining us before dinner and during a break, they said it would be an honor.

Mark Nelson and Jeff Schwebach are two of our best friends from Sioux Falls, South Dakota. Jeff and I played in rock bands together while we attended the University of South Dakota in the early 1980s. We were both in Business School or B-School as we called it, getting our degrees in business management. The funny part of it was, we were trying our hardest to look like a couple of rock stars who only knew how to party. Not the clean-cut college boys who went to class everyday and studied. We really stood out in B-School as "the guys from FLITE," the name of our band.

Here's what we looked like back then, Brenda hung this photo on our "wall of shame" as we called it, and she told everyone who saw me in this photo, "I'd never have gone out with him back then." *I wonder why, dear.*

FLITE promo shot back in 1983. Trying to look cool for the chicks! Left to right: Kelly, Brad, Russ, Jeff, and Mitch.

Jeff was definitely the smarter of the two of us . . . he always knew how to get the answers to the exams for our marketing class. Not that he needed the answers; we just never had time to study due to our playing schedule. There's a million stories to tell about Jeff . . . but that's another book.

Mark used to hang out with us and, as he put it, "I wanted to be just like you guys." After college, I gave up the music business, but Mark and Jeff, now known as "The Cartwright Brothers," have become two of the best entertainers I know. (You can purchase all The Cartwright Brothers CDs by visiting their website: www.cartwrightbrothers.com.) Just the idea of getting our friends, The Cartwright Brothers, to perform would be icing on the cake, so to speak. When they agreed to play, both Brenda and I knew they would be responsible for helping make our day one to remember.

I had one more idea that would really make people talk. "I'd like to play and sing at the party, honey."

"You can't sing."

"I know, but I can fake it okay. I want to do it. I haven't been on stage playing guitar in fifteen years, but if Jimmy [his stage name is Jimi B. Loude] and Troy are willing, I think we can pull it off."

"Hey, if you three want to do it, do it," she said.

Jim Prante, or my other "brotha" as I call him, is one of the best drummers I've had the privilege of being on stage with. Jim and I met in 1995 while playing golf at Mendakota and have been best friends ever since.

We couldn't believe we never met each other during our rock & roll days. Now we were amazed how two former "long hairs" could even get accepted into a Country Club. Then we'd remind each other it was our wives who were responsible for us being able to play golf.

Troy Harms is married to Diana (formerly Voss), who is Brenda's first cousin. Troy stands six-foot-three-plus and let's just say he weighs more than I do. I knew who Troy was back in the 1980s when he played bass in a rock band, but I had never met him during our playing days. We nicknamed Troy "Big Daddy Harms" when Diana became pregnant in 1999.

When I called Jim and Troy and asked them if they would do this for Brenda and me, they both agreed without hesitating. The gig was on, and the format was to have The Cartwright Brothers play a variety of music while people were arriving for dinner. After dinner and dessert, Bob and the Beachcombers would be our main dance band. During the first break, Jimi, Troy, and I would perform five to seven songs we had rehearsed, with vocal assistance from Mark and Jeff, of course. The Cartwright Brothers would perform their comedy act after "The Three Amigos," so look out, this part was going to rock!

Brenda kept telling everyone who would listen, "I want people to walk away remembering this night as the best time they've ever had at a wedding reception, I mean party." I bet I heard her tell the story twenty times before we got married.

Jimi, Big Daddy Harms, and I practiced a few times during the summer. We knew we could pull the gig off, especially since I had recruited Mark and Jeff to back us up on three songs. The songs I picked to play and sing were: "Blue on Black," by the Kenny Wayne Shepherd Band; "Premonition" and "Who'll Stop the Rain," by John Fogerty; and "Tube Snake Boogie," by ZZ Top. Jimi would be singing "Susie Q," by Fogerty, and "What I Like about You," by the Romantics.

Since Brenda had taken charge of making all the arrangements except the music, I felt I needed to do something for her in honor of our day. I decided to rent a limo to pick us up at the house, drop us off at the church and then bring the wedding party back to the club. I felt it would be a nice touch of class having all of us together in one vehicle. She didn't quite see it my way, though.

A week before the wedding, I informed her I had hired a limo. Her only question was, "How much was the limo?" She didn't thank me or tell me how romantic it sounded. No, she was more concerned about the money.

"The rate is two hundred fifty dollars for the afternoon." I tried to explain to her "why" I did it, that I wanted to do it for her, for us, but she was blinded by the dollars I spent.

"That's too much, Mitch. You shouldn't have done that."

I thought she was going to tell me to cancel the limo by the way she was acting.

I'd already made the reservation, so I put my foot down on this argument. "Look, you need to quit worrying about the money all the time and let me do this . . . I want to do it for you!"

"But you know you don't need to."

She knew I wasn't going to back off and give in to her. I was mad and she knew this argument wasn't going anywhere. I walked a few feet away from her and turned around and left her with this final comment, "I know I don't have to do anything, but it's our day, and we deserve it."

I turned and walked into the garage, leaving her to either follow me and continue the argument or forget it and let me have my way. She didn't follow me into the garage, and I didn't hear another word about the cost of the limo. I think what bothered her more than the money, because, let's face it, two hundred fifty dollars was nothing compared to what we were spending on the party and the band. I believe it all had to do with the fact that I didn't talk to her about renting the limo before I went ahead and did it.

Even though she thought it was a waste of money hiring a limo to take us to the church and back to the club, I believe there are times in everyone's life when you will look back and say, "I'm so glad we did it your way," and I am so thankful I held my ground and did it my way. I have several pictures of us in the limo drinking champagne and having a good time with our family and friends, memories I will always cherish.

By the time August 1st, 1998, finally rolled around, Brenda was so exhausted from all the planning, I wasn't sure if she could hold up for one more day. I think she just wanted to get the ceremony over with and get a cocktail in her hand and start partying. Her facial expression told it all as she patiently waited for Todd and me to finish getting ready before the limo arrived.

I'll never forget seeing her in her wedding dress for the first time. She never let me see her wearing it until that afternoon . . . and she looked stunning, I couldn't take my eyes off her. She had her hair done in a way I had never seen, and she gave me chills every time I looked at her. She was so beautiful that day, just awesome to look at. My memory is etched with the

Brenda, Todd, and Mitch in the kitchen before the limo arrived.

Left to right: Brenda, Todd, Wayne Webster, Barb & Don Martin, and Mitch.

image of her standing in front of me looking me in the eyes and telling me she loved me, and how much she wanted to be my wife. All I could tell her was that she made me the happiest man on earth and how beautiful she looked.

We were starting a new journey together, almost like we were starting over from the very beginning, and the feeling we each had we shared with one another in a private moment before we left the house.

"I can't believe how much more I love you today than I did yesterday," I told her.

"I feel the same way, hon," and we embraced and kissed each other like we had never done before.

People always asked us after we were married whether or not we felt different towards each other. After eight years living with Brenda, I couldn't imagine feeling any more love for her than I already did. I can honestly say our feelings towards each other did change the day we were married, and it was all for the better. I don't know why—neither one of us tried to explain it when people asked—but when someone did ask, we both told them the same thing. "Yes, we do feel different now that we're married. We love each other more today than we did yesterday, and we don't know why, but it's the most wonderful feeling in

The limo.

Gathering next to the limo.

Ladies First.

Wayne "Cowboy" Webster, Becky, and Jimi in limo.

the world."

Our life together as a married couple was so awesome; I just never thought I'd be living without her.

Mitch signing the book while Brenda watches.

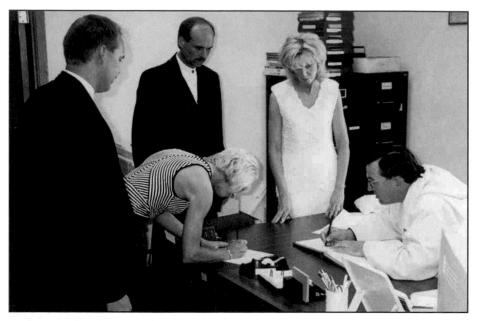

Becky signing the register.

Mitch and Brenda, with tears, saying vows.

"The limo's here," someone yelled out.

The first thing we needed to do after arriving at the church was sign the Church Register and sign the marriage certificate.

It was very unusual for Brenda to allow anyone but me to see her emotions, but on our wedding day, she wore her emotions for everyone to see. I remember looking into her eyes when we said our vows and seeing tears running down her face—tears of joy, love, and happiness. She was so happy to finally be married and be my wife. I was actually surprised to see her cry because I can only remember seeing Brenda cry five or six times in the eleven plus years

158

Our wedding vows. This is one of Brenda's favorite pictures from the wedding. Her mother Donna is in the background looking on as I am saying my vows.

Reverend George Martin, Brenda, and Mitch.

Mitch and Brenda kneeling during the ceremony.

Peggy Garven read the first reading, the second reading, and the reading from John.

we were together. She was always the strong one in our family, but this time she wasn't able to hold back her tears. Over the next three years, now as a married couple, I always made it a point to tell her not to hold her emotions inside, and as hard as it was for her, she managed to make an effort to let them out.

Peggy Garven read the First Reading, the Second Reading, and the Reading from John.

The First Reading:
The Song of Songs by Solomon, Chapter 8, verses 6-7.
True Love.

Set me as a seal on your heart, as a seal on your arm; For stern as death is love, relentless as the nether world is devotion; Its flames are a blazing fire.

Deep waters cannot quench love, nor floods sweep it away. Were one to offer all he owns to purchase love, he would be roundly mocked.

The Second Reading:
Mark, Chapter 10 verses 6-9.

But from the beginning of creation, God made them male and female. For this reason a man shall leave his father and mother and be joined to his wife, and the two shall become one

The wedding kiss.

Todd, Brenda, Mitch and Becky trying not to cry.

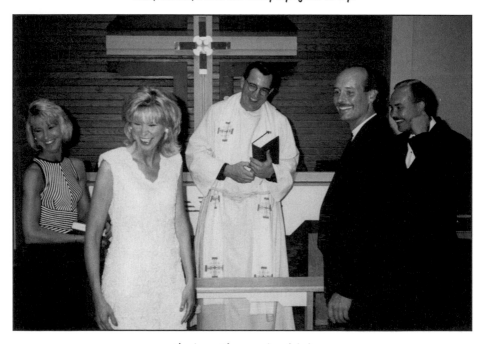

You know Wayne made a Joke!

"Jimi," Brenda, Mitch, and Peg Garven, Jimi's wife.

Brenda's mother, Donna, Brenda, Mitch, and Mitch's mother, Barb.

Don Martin, Brenda, Mitch, and Barb Martin.

Donna and Brenda embracing at church.

The moms take turns with congratulatory hugs!

flesh. So they are no longer two but one flesh. Therefore what God has joined together, no human being must separate.

Finally Married!

The Reading from John:
Chapter 15 verses 9-12.

As the Father loves me, so I also love you. Remain in my love. If you keep my commandments, You will remain in my love, just as I have kept my Father's commandments and remain in his love.

I have told you this so that my joy might be in you and your joy might be complete. This is my commandment: Love one another as I love you.

Mitch and Brenda sipping champagne in the limo.

On our way to the "party."

After the ceremony we had the limo driver take us the long way back to our house. We all sipped champagne, and a toast was made, "To Mitch and Brenda, for finally tying the knot." *Yes Dear, we finally did it, and it really felt good!*

Once we were back at the house, it seemed like everything went into hyper speed. I was busy getting my guitars and music together, and I had no idea what Brenda was doing until she said, "Mitch, we need to get over to the club." That pretty much made everyone move in the direction she wanted.

When we arrived at the front entrance, by limo of course, Brenda was off making sure everything was in its right place, and as far as I could tell everything was perfect. I spoke to Mark and Jeff and to Bob and The Beachcombers to make sure we had the entertainment coordinated. As planned, The Cartwright Brothers started playing as people were being seated for dinner.

One of the bigger surprises during the evening came from Brenda as a gift to me. She had arranged for Carla Kuyper and

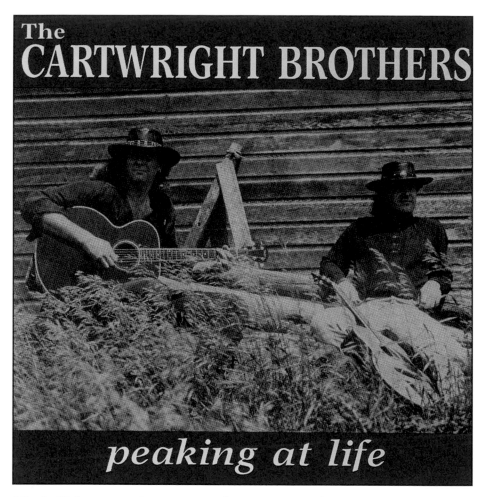

The CARTWRIGHT BROTHERS

peaking at life

Mark Nelson to sing a song that expressed exactly how she felt about me in her life. She also made sure we would be the only ones allowed on the dance floor. Of course this was extremely appropriate considering it was our wedding reception, yet completely against Brenda's way of doing things. She didn't like the limelight nor did she like to show public displays of affection towards me. When she told me it was her idea to have Carla and Mark sing to us, and she was the one who picked out the song, I was so deeply touched, I almost cried. I saw a side of her she rarely showed.

The words to "All My Life" meant so much to Brenda and mean so much to me. I literally broke down when I played the

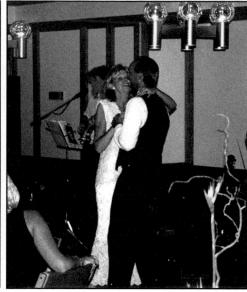

Mark and Carla singing, "All My Life," by Linda Ronstadt and Aaron Neville while Mitch and Brenda dance.

The wedding dance.

song for the first time after three years. Just reading the words describes how much we loved each other. When Carla was singing, Brenda was singing the words to me from her heart . . . even now it's difficult for me to hear the words.

All My Life

Carla   Am I really here in your arms?
This is just like I dreamed it would be.
I feel like I'm frozen in time.
You're the only one I can see.

Chorus   Hey, I've looked All My Life, for You,
Now you're here
Hey, I'll spend All My Life with You . . .
All My Life!

Mark   And I really never knew how to love
I just hoped somehow I'd see
Oh, I, asked for a little help from above
Send that Angel down to me . . .

Chorus   Hey, I've looked All My Life, for You,
Now you're here
Hey, I'll spend All My Life with You . . .
All My Life!

Carla   Never thought I could feel love so tender.
Never thought I could let those feelings show.

Mark   But now my heart is on my sleeve
And this love will never leave I know, I know . . .

Chorus   Hey, I've looked All My Life, for You,
And Now You're Here!!
Hey, I'll spend All My Life with You . . .
All My Life!

I'm so thankful Brenda's life was filled with so much happiness. I am the luckiest man on earth to have known her, loved her, and to have been her husband.

Bob and the Beachcombers played a few more songs after Mark and Carla sang "All My Life." During their break, Jimi, Troy, and I, along with Mark and Jeff, took the stage.

As we were about to finish the song "What I Like About You," Mark leaned back from his microphone and yelled out "fol-

Here we are, "The Three Amigos" on August 1st, 1998. Mitch playing the guitar, Jimi B. Loude on the drums, and Troy "Big Daddy Harms" on the bass.

Mitch rockin' in the band Flite at age twenty-one. I've lost the hair and clothes, but I still have the guitar.

Mitch and Jeff singing at the wedding reception.

Marianne Larsen and Brenda. Marianne was a very dear friend of Brenda's.

Brenda was so happy all her friends and family were with us.

My sister Shelly and her husband Jamie. Notice the Birds of Paradise on the table.

Our "adopted son," Dustin, dancing with Brenda.

Louise Huston, Marge Cuddy, and Marianne Larsen were three of Brenda's closest friends.

Brenda taking a break and relaxing.

low me" and we went right into "R.O.C.K. in the U.S.A." by John Mellencamp, which Mark sang. From my personal standpoint, I had a great time doing something I hadn't done in fifteen years. It never really occurred to me what our family and friends thought about our performance until people starting telling me they couldn't believe the groom got up and performed; most of them didn't even know I played guitar.

One of the greatest compliments came from Mark Nelson who told me this was the best wedding reception he had ever attended. For Mark to tell us our party was "the best" meant more to Brenda and me because Mark has played/sang/attended more parties during the past twenty years than most people will attend in a lifetime. As we had said before, we wanted this to be a party people would remember forever.

With the wedding and party finally over with, we could now settle into a new chapter of our lives as husband and wife. The one difference between our marriage and the majority of married couples was my request for Brenda to keep her last name Voss. When we first discussed the issue, she was all set to change her name to Freimark.

"I'm not so sure it's a wise idea," I told her. "Let's think about a few things first, Voss is easier to pronounce than Freimark (pronounced Frymark). Nobody gets my last name correct. They all say Freemark. When we go to restaurants, we always use your name because they never pronounce mine right. Another reason is your business. For twenty-five years, your clients have known you as Brenda Sue Voss." I was hoping she was listening to me.

"Maybe you have a point," she said. "What about Voss-Freimark?" she wanted to know.

"Only if you want it that way, I'm leaving the decision completely up to you." I said to her.

Brenda's decision was to leave her name as is, "Voss," which was what I was hoping she would do from the very beginning.

Chapter 16

The Baker Boys and Our Very Own "Martha Stewart"

uring the spring of 1999, Jim Prante and I decided we wanted to be more involved in the social events our club was holding. We requested, and it was granted for us to start a Social Committee with Jim and I as co-chairs. Our goal was to help promote the events the club was hosting and encourage others to get involved. Out of all the major events the club held during the year, the one on which we focused was the New Year's Eve party. Jim and I, along with most everyone with whom we spoke, agreed that the attendance over the past five years had fallen so low that the club should consider canceling any ideas of having future New Year's Eve parties.

"This year will be different," we promised. "It's the millennium party, and we shouldn't have any problems getting people to attend." We said that in April. Our committee met once a month, so we waited until our next meeting in May to bring up the need to start planning for New Year's. The first thing we needed to do was hire a band. Not a wedding band like Brenda and I had. We needed something different. Since Jimi had more music connections in the Twin Cities than Perry, it was appropriate for him to lead the way. It didn't take long for Jimi to find out that the bands worth hiring were either already booked or asking five to six thousand dollars for the one night.

"Bad news, dude. I can't find a band for under five g's," but Jimi had another idea. "What about you, me, 'Big Daddy Harms' (Troy Harms), and Donald Baker (Steve Alm) put a band together and do the gig?"

"If you want to do it, Jimi, then call Donald, and I'll call Troy. Let's see what they say," I told him.

When we spoke later that evening, we both had good news, "Baker's up for it," Jimi said.

"So is Big Daddy."

"I guess the gig's on!" we both said to one another.

"How much should we charge them?" Jimi wanted to know.

"I'm thinking half of what the other bands are charging will get their attention, so how about $2,500.00?"

"Sounds like a lot of money to me," Jimi said.

"It sounds like a bargain to me. Besides, we'll make a whole production out of it and give 'em something to remember."

The next meeting our Social Committee had scheduled was the third week of June. The very first order of business was to have the minutes from the previous meeting read. When the subject of hiring a band was read, everyone immediately wanted to know what Jimi had found out.

"Well, I have good news and bad news," he stated. "The bad news is, all the bands who are any good at all are either already booked, or they are charging five to six thousand dollars. The good news is Mitch and I, along with two of our buddies, can do the gig if you're interested."

Jimi's last statement raised a few eyebrows along with a few interesting faces. Now that we had everyone's attention, our General Manager, Steve Watson, chimed in with the fifty-question drill. The bottom line to Steve's questions was, One: Can you do it? Two: How much? We both assured Steve and the rest of the committee we could handle the job.

"As far as the price goes, we'd be charging twenty-five hundred," I said without blinking an eye.

After several more long conversations between the committee members, it was decided to go ahead with our proposal with one stipulation: "You need to have one hundred twenty-five people signed up before November 15th, or I'm canceling the party," Steve stated.

Jimi and I looked at each other, and we both knew what our answer was. "We don't see a problem with getting that many people, after all it is the Millennium."

During our September Social Committee meeting it was decided an all-out campaign would be waged to get our one hundred twenty-five guests before November 15th. Table tents in the grill, posters throughout the club, full-page advertisement in our monthly newsletter to the members, and word of mouth, were all going to be used to make sure we secured the New Year's Eve party.

The "band" started rehearsals in October, moving all the equipment into our basement. The four of us: Jimi, Troy, Steve, and I would meet once a week and rehearse or party whichever we felt like doing at the time. We really had no idea whether or not there would be 125 people signed up by November 15th but we couldn't take a chance and not start rehearsing—just in case we actually had to work on New Year's.

Steve Alm was always the first to arrive for rehearsal. Steve is our keyboard, harmonica, and guitar player when needed, lead singer and tequila connoisseur. I guess Steve could just about do the gig himself. Steve's nickname is Donald Baker and it became customary for us to call each other Baker or just Donald. When it came time for us to get "serious" and decide on a name for the band, I suggested The Baker Boys and it stuck. We started having all kinds of fun with the name: The Baker Boys, "Men Who Like to Bake," or as on our first practice CD, "Half Baked." It was so funny when Brenda couldn't figure out why we called ourselves The Baker Boys.

"Honey, you have to go all the way back to our college days," that's when she finally understood.

Troy Harms, or Big Daddy Harms, as we called him. I can't talk or write about Troy without making reference to his nickname. Troy was our bass player. He always showed up for practice with a new brand of beer or a new type of tequila for us to try. Talk about some fun rehearsals.

Jim Prante or Jimi B. Loude or Baker or Donald or Brotha (brother) or whatever we'd call him, he'd answer. Jimi and I have agreed we must be brothas. This crazy notion comes from the stories we've told each other about our fathers and the only conclusion we can come up with is we must have the same father.

Since October 1st, Jimi and I were keeping a close eye on the New Year's Eve sign up sheet. By the end of October we only had eighty people with confirmed reservations and two weeks left to hit our deadline of one hundred twenty-five.

"Jimi, it's time we start making some phone calls," I told him. He agreed if this party was going to happen, it was up to us. On November 15th around 7:00 p.m., we were taking a small break from rehearsals, so I walked over to the Club to see if the show was a go or not. When I looked at the sign-up sheet, I counted 115 people, only ten short of our minimum goal. I could see Steve Watson's light on in his office, so I walked in, said hello and stated, "Steve, we have 115 people signed up for the party. There are more people signed up this year than in the last five New Year's Eve parties. What's your verdict?"

Steve didn't even hesitate, "The party is on!" He said smiling. "You guys better be good."

With good news to report, I walked back home to tell the boys.

How does all this pertain to Brenda? It's very simple. For three months the band rehearsed in the basement of our home. We only practiced once a week in October, and twice a week in November, on Monday and Tuesday or Monday and Friday. Brenda had Mondays off, and she loved to cook and bake for company. On Mondays we always got the royal treatment. She would feed us at 5:00 p.m. before rehearsal started, and at 10:00 p.m. we'd make our way upstairs to the delicious smells of her latest experiment. "Tonight I want you boys to try a new hot dip recipe," she'd tell us as she removed the large deep dish from the oven. Her Mexican dip and her artichoke dip became our two favorites. I guess she used us as her guinea pigs whenever she needed to try something new, and the boys had no problem helping her with the taste test. By the time December rolled around, the boys had dubbed Brenda "Our Martha Stewart." Even on the days she worked and would get home at 9:30 p.m. she'd come downstairs to listen to us for ten or fifteen minutes, then announce, "I put something in the oven for you guys, and it will be ready at 10:00. Don't forget about it or it'll burn."

"Time to quit," Jimi or Troy would say right at 9:55 p.m.

"She's unbelievable," the guys always told me. "She gets up at five, gets home at nine-thirty, and then cooks for us. She's a saint, dude," Jimi said as he slapped me on the shoulder. "She *is* Martha Stewart!" And we'd raise our glasses to make a toast in honor of Brenda.

During the last week of December 1999, we were rehearsing every other night and actually starting to sound pretty good. Brenda made it home early during one of our practice sessions and listened to us for over an hour. "You guys are really good!" she told us during those last few rehearsals.

"Thanks, hon. Everyone has worked really hard these last three months to get ready for this."

"It's paid off because you guys are great!"

Brenda didn't hand out compliments unless she meant them, so we were flattered she took the time to listen to us and to give us her honest opinion.

On December 28th, Jimi, Peggy Garven (Jim's wife), Brenda, and I went to the club to hang the black backdrop for our staging. On the backdrop, we attached both large and small 2000 signs Brenda had made by using fishing string. We also came up with the idea to have an official clock on stage so everyone in the room would celebrate New Year's based on "band time." Brenda was also instrumental in coming up with the official Baker Boys outfit. In early November, she found a silky black fabric with gold 2000s and asked her mother, Donna, to make each of us a vest. The boys thought it was great because we got out of having to wear tuxes.

On December 31, 1999, we opened our show with a tune by Van Morrison, "Brown Eyed Girl." The members and guests packed the dance floor from that first song to end of our show at 1:00 a.m. During our first break, Steve Watson caught up to me and told me, "You guys are great. I'd like to book you again next year, and I'll pay you $500.00 more to do it."

After the show ended, Brenda and I invited anyone who wanted to stop by the house for a late-night snack, to do so, as Brenda had prepared ham sandwiches, potato salad, chocolate chip cookies, and coffee. What amazed me more than anything about her that night, was her stamina.

She had enough energy to be an excellent

Peggy Garven and Jim Prante. Jimi showing off his 2000 vest.

The O'fishul clock, the backdrop with the 2000s hanging below it, and us on stage wearing our "2000 vests." Four minutes before midnight and the dance floor is still going strong. The head count for the party hit an amazing 170-plus people, the biggest New Year's Eve to be held at Mendakota, and Brenda played a major role in the success.

Susan and Brian Weedman, Brenda, and Todd.

Brenda with her friends from work.

hostess for thirty people . . . she really was our Martha Stewart. Our second year playing New Year's Eve at Mendakota was as much fun for The Baker Boys as the first. We only had 150 people compared to the year before, but this group knew how to party. "Big Daddy Harms" decided he wouldn't be playing with us, and we couldn't blame him with the new addition of his son Jake the year before. Our good friend Scott Entenman was anointed a "Baker" and joined the group, playing all the bass lines on his keyboard. We also hired a female singer to add that "pretty" voice and give us some more flexibility with our song list. Her name is Carole Kline, and we called her Kiki. We renamed the band Kiki and The Baker Boys for New Year's Eve 2000.

I'm not sure when Brenda started feeling uncomfortable about me playing in the band on New Year's, but her body language during the evening of December 31, 2000, told me she wasn't a happy camper. I finally confronted her about my interpretation of how she was feeling during one of our breaks. She just looked at me and said, "This will be the last New Year's Eve party I'm going to without you being with me."

She didn't like the idea of sitting alone without her husband beside her. I couldn't blame her for the way she felt.

Kiki and Mitch.

"This is the last time we'll be playing, hon. Next year I want to take you to Hawaii for New Year's." Those words were magic to her ears.

"Hawaii!" she shouted while smiling her beautiful smile. "Thank you, Mitch," she said as she hugged me. "Please don't invite anyone over to the house this year. I just want to go home, relax and go to bed."

With our third set left to play it was easy for me to tell her "I won't invite anyone over. You go on home after the show and don't wait up. It'll be awhile before I get out of here."

The party ended at 1:00 a.m., and I didn't get home for another forty-five minutes. Brenda had left with my mother, Barb, and her husband, Don Martin, who had made a special trip from Arizona to be with us for the big bash. My brother Todd, who also attended the party, stayed with me to help load

Kiki, Scott Entenman, and Mitch.

all my gear. When Todd and I got home, Brenda was already in bed, so we stayed up and visited with Barb and Don.

In the morning, Brenda woke up at her usual time and woke me up to ask me if I was serious about taking her to Hawaii. "I told I wouldn't joke about something that made you happy. Now let me go back to sleep. It's 5:00 a.m. for God's sake."

Every month for the next eight months, I had this constant reminder about my promise to take her to Hawaii. I had every intention of taking her; I just hadn't bought the tickets. Two weeks before she died she asked me "When are you going to buy those tickets to Hawaii?"

"I'm going to wait until there's a big sale by the airlines, probably later in September." I told her.

Brenda with her arms crossed—just look at her body language.

Jimi, Kiki, and Steve Alm.

Steve Alm.

"I can't wait to get over there," she said. "Let's leave right after Christmas on the 26th, and stay until January 3rd."

"It's whatever you want to do, dear." I told her. That was the last conversation we had about our trip to the islands, the last time she mentioned I needed to buy those tickets.

Chapter 17

Secrets to Our Loving Relationship

I'll never forget sitting with Brenda in a restaurant and discussing what it will be like when we get old, in our seventies and eighties. "Would we still be as interested in each other as we are now? Or will we just sit across the table from one another, never looking or speaking to each other?" We always seemed to notice those "certain" couples, whether they were young or old, the ones who sat across from one another never saying a word, never making eye contact with each other. We felt sorry for them because they seemed so unhappy.

"Can you imagine not having anything to say to your significant other?" I'd ask her.

"No, I couldn't just sit across from you and never say anything."

"But look at all the couples we see when we go out who look so unhappy with each other, I don't want that to ever happen to us."

I can look back on our eleven years together and can't recall either one of us not having something interesting to say to the other. I now know how important it is to be able to sit with someone I care about and talk for minutes or hours about "nothing," you're just talking, making eye contact, showing them you care. I felt a sense of security knowing Brenda was genuinely interested in what I had to say and the same went for her.

I'm not qualified to tell others how to live their lives, nor do I think Brenda and I had a perfect marriage, but after eleven years of living together, three of which we were married, I'd have to say our relationship was as close to perfect for us as we could make it. We had accomplished something in our relationship that made it really great . . . we learned "how" to live with each other. I believe for us, the secret to our relationship was when we finally learned the "how" part, how to get along through the tough times, which only made the good years that much better. I know it's human nature to get on each other's nerves once in a while, so it was only by trial and error (some would call them love spats or arguments or fighting) how we managed to get along with each other no matter how mad, upset, or pissed off we were at each other. Those incidents were few and far between, thank goodness, but when they did happen, I'd have to admit to being the one who caused the majority of them. Not on purpose, mind you, but it was just my nature for so many years to be combative, judgmental, cynical or argumentative. What I finally learned from Brenda was how to listen without interrupting or responding in a negative way. I learned these skills the hard way, mainly from watching her completely shut down when I upset her. This brings me to our next secret, learning "how" to communicate without upsetting each other. After we figured out how to communicate, everything else became easy.

The road to learning "how" to communicate with Brenda had a few bumps along the way—okay, some were large potholes—but after five or six years of beating my head against the wall, I finally figured out we had three levels of insanity in our relationship. Not truly insane, of course, but times when one person allowed emotions to rule behavior. The feeling I've had is like I'd lost my mind, and I'd wonder "who was that person who just said those stupid things to her?" I felt like I must have had a moment of "insanity."

My definition of the first level was when I would get "mad" at her. What normally caused this emotion to rear its ugly head were the times when we were having a heated debate, and I felt I was right and she was wrong. I'd get "mad" because she wouldn't agree with me. I'd argue my point as if it were the most important issue in the world. I'd forget there were times when I should be "listening" with both ears and keeping my mouth shut. "God gave us two ears and one mouth for a reason—to listen twice as much as we're talkin'." I wonder who said that.

Staying mad at her would only last for a short amount of time while I went through my "cooling down period," which gave me enough time to find my brain and realize what an idiot I'd been. Once I regained my sanity, I'd draw the conclusion that she was right and I was wrong (but hated to admit it). When I would finally admit to my inadequate way of handling the situation, it was amazing how quickly she either did see it my way or we found that mutual solution to our debate. The reality check was this: between the two of us, we had a better solution together than arguing our separate opinions, although she was probably right ninety-nine percent of the time (which took me years to figure out), and the other one percent of the time when I was right, I'd start to doubt my own instincts and forget to push the issue, which of course helped us to get along that much better.

The "mad" level of insanity couldn't hurt our relationship as long as we put our egos into our back pockets and realized we were not the only one with an opinion that counts.

The second level of insanity I called "hurtful." Sticks and stones can break bones, but words can cut deeper and hurt a whole hell of a lot more. Saying something we didn't mean to say or the way we said it usually caused one of us to become upset. Saying something "hurtful" could be done intentionally but normally "I didn't mean it that way!" were the words coming out of my mouth as she turned and walked away. Again it was back to "think before you speak, you moron." I'd eventually apologize, and we'd makeup the same day. I can only remember Brenda saying something that hurt me once in eleven years.

The third level of insanity I called "pissed off." Being pissed off at someone doesn't sound that bad, but for us it was the worst kind of feeling in the world. We only hit level three two times in eleven years, and either time we could have split up. Luckily for me, she was too stubborn to leave. Both occurrences happened during the first six years we were together. I know for a fact, I really pissed her off during my gambling days, 1992 to 1993, as she worked hard for her money and couldn't stand to see me throwing mine away. She finally snapped one night, and it was either her or the casino. Of course, it was an easy decision for me; had she not put her foot down I probably would've bankrupted us both.

The second time we hit level three took a few years to build up inside me before I blew my top. I had finally had it with her taking all the credit for "why" we had what we had. She pushed the issue in my face, acting like I didn't contribute anything to our financial success but only found ways to spend, spend, and spend. She was the only one who worked hard, and she wished she could just lie around and do nothing on weekends. It wasn't true, and she knew it, but it was too late, and I let her have it with both barrels. Like I said, sometimes a person goes insane during one of these instances. I remember we said some really dumb things to each other, and, of course, I made her cry, but in the end we apologized to each other. We never had a problem after that fight and that was back in 1996.

We managed to get through both of those ugly incidents but only because we were willing to sit down and openly communicate all the issues and concerns without the other person walking away. Sooner or later we would both let our guard down and stop trying to be "right."

One of the biggest adjustments for Brenda was learning that she might not be right all the time—not that she was wrong very often—but when she was she had learn to admit it and eventually she did, which was really a big stride forward for her.

Thinking about her having to learn she's not always right reminds me of the following story. We had been debating about some trivial issue, when Brenda said some things to me that really "hurt." I walked away from her, and I believe I called her a nasty name, something that started with a B which I would never do, but I knew it would hurt her right back. Not exactly the way two adults should act, but it happened. It was hours later and several tears shed on her part, when Brenda walked up to me put her arms around me and told me how sorry she was for hurting me. It's amazing how just a few words like "I'm sorry," "I apologize," or "Please forgive me," along with human touch, can mend hurt feelings and restore a relationship right back to where it once was. Of course I returned the apology and hugged her with so much meaning, she had to tell me, "Mitch, let go. You're hurting me." But she was smiling.

From 1996 until her death on September 2, 2001, we never went to bed mad, hurt, or pissed off at each other. I always told her if she wanted to have one of her heated debates with me we first had to take all our clothes off. We tried it once and never did get to the arguing part; although we did manage the heated discussion. (Maybe the real secret to a relationship is to always have your heated debates naked.)

For our relationship to grow, really grow, I needed to learn to let her do what she wanted to do without always putting in my two cents worth of advice. What always got me into trouble was how I gave her advice, which determined whether or not she would listen to me. If I said, "Let me tell you . . ." then I never got anywhere with her. But, if I said to her, "Can I give you my opinion?" She always said yes . . . whether or not it did any good is another issue, but at least we were communicating. Once I learned to take the words "tell you" out of my vocabulary and replace them with questions like, "Could you use some advice?" "Can I help you?" "It's only my opinion, I'm not trying to tell you what to do," and the killer phrase "Brenda, you're probably *right,* but have you considered," I made huge strides in our communicating once I learned "how" to phrase my responses.

The "no compromise" attitude or the "I'm right and he/she is wrong" attitude never accomplished anything except to build walls between us. I know it took me five years to bring those walls down, and it was with those two little words that I started to say to her that made all the difference in the world and of course they were "YES DEAR." At first she didn't believe I was being sincere, especially since my normal response was to argue or have a heated discussion. But it was the way I said "Yes Dear" that told her I agreed with her and I loved her.

Money has always played a critical role in our relationship. Mainly because we never had any for the first six years we were together. I wouldn't have thought money would be at the top of the list as to why couples have problems, but in our case it ranked right up there. I know Brenda had a right to be concerned about how I spent my money. After all, she was only trying to build a future for us. When I came into the relationship, I didn't have a dime, but I sure had a boatload of debt. My credit was good, but my percentage of debt to equity sucked. I had too many credit cards and always found a way to max them out. Two years into our relationship, Brenda made the decision it would be best if she handled all the finances in our household. I never saw my paycheck after that, and it was probably a good thing because she was the master at making ends meet each month and only spent the little extra we had when we needed something important.

In 1997, we were financially in a position to save more and spend less. Brenda's attitude about work also started to change as she contemplated her manager's position at Regis. "I don't know why you continue to manage when the extra money isn't worth the aggravation you put up with. Why don't you step down as the manager and just do what you love to do? Which is your clients. Forget about all the rest of the bullshit you're putting up with. You know I'm making enough money to pay the bills, so just do it!" I pushed hard for her to quit managing in 1997, as she was complaining more and more about the long hours she was putting in. She finally made up her mind to quit managing and focus on her clients. Over the next several years, Brenda cut back on the number of hours she was working, especially in the summer, as she enjoyed more time at home and in her gardens. After her first year on her own at ShearMadness, she told me at least a dozen times during the summer of 2001 that "Next year I won't be working Saturdays."

I believe the reason money was so important to Brenda stemmed from an incident with her brother. I didn't know why she felt so strongly about the subject until she told me what happened.

Between 1983 and 1987, she had lent over $25,000 to one of her brothers who never made an attempt to pay her back. I always wondered why she got uptight in those early years we were together whenever money issues came up. I still remember watching her cry her eyes out in the early 1990s when this same brother filed bankruptcy and named his sister, Brenda, first on the list of creditors he wasn't going to pay back.

After reading the court papers, she started crying. She was sobbing so hard trying to speak at the same time. "Mitch, I can't believe he'd do this to me. If he'd only have tried to pay me back, even a dollar a week would have been okay. But he's never made an attempt, and now he names me first on the list."

"Listen, we don't need his money, and one day we'll be in a position that you will forget all about it." I tried to make her feel better but she was really hurt that day. I finally understood why she acted the way she did when it came to money matters. From that day forward I totally respected her decisions when it came to finances. I know Brenda would want her brother to know she did finally let go of those angry feelings she had toward him, and I was really proud of her for doing so. I, on the other hand, can't say the same thing. I've always had a very hard time dealing with the fact that someone could take advantage her, let alone one of her brothers. On top of it all, the mere fact he never made an attempt to do the right thing really bothers me, even to this day. I have never figured out how he lives with himself knowing he will never be able to make it right with Brenda now that she is gone.

It didn't take more than six or eight months after we received the bankruptcy notice when another brother of hers called us wanting to know if we would give him money so he could buy a fishing boat . . . I almost started laughing at him because I already knew her answer. I went ahead and told him, "No, I'm sorry we're not going to give you money so you can buy a boat." I didn't even own one; I sure as hell wasn't going to give him money to buy one.

When it came to spending her money, Brenda had no problem splurging on good food and good service. Brenda loved to go out to eat, to be waited on and pampered. It was her way to relax and visit with me about a variety of subjects without having to worry about cleaning up a big mess after dinner. One of her biggest issues with me, though, was how I treated people in the service industry. I was a real tightwad when it came to tipping, and it really bothered her. Brenda's persistence changed my attitude and my outlook on life. She helped strengthen our relationship in many ways. She never had to walk on eggshells whenever a "situation" occurred in public; she knew I would remain calm and handle the manner in a way that made her proud.

"The way you treat waiters, waitresses, bartenders, and of course your cosmetologists is a direct reflection of your overall personality," She'd always tell me. "The amount you tip also tells a lot about who you are. Mitch, if you don't believe me, watch yourself and your friends the next time you guys tip." Brenda explained it to me like this, "Having to deal with the general public can be the best and worst experience of your life, all in the same minute, hour, or day. People in the service industry put up with a lot of crap from people like you who think you are so much better than we are. You need to learn to treat us with respect and you need to show your appreciation with more than ten or fifteen percent."

Brenda never spent time figuring ten or fifteen percent, she tipped very well no matter what the bill totaled. She taught me to be very generous, a trait I've always had but never showed when it came to tipping.

Here are a couple of good examples of how Brenda tipped: If our total bill came to $12.00 for breakfast she'd give them $3.00 to $5.00 depending on the service. "You tell me what someone is going to do with $1.80?" she'd say. Her philosophy was simple, "I give great tips, and, therefore, I will receive great tips."

She was right, and it showed in the tips she received. For a $30.00 check she'd give an $8.00 tip without blinking an eye. Brenda told me this once, and I never forgot it, "I can always tell when someone sits in my chair to have their hair done whether or not they are in the service industry by how much tip they give me. Those people are the best tippers because they understand what I'm going through each and every day."

I still follow her advice and tip well as long as the service is good. If I receive mediocre or lousy service, I still tip fifteen percent and figure my servers had a bad day. I remember tipping my hygienist two years ago because she got me in when she didn't have to. I gave her five dollars, and I thought she was going to cry when she told me no one had ever given her a tip before.

"You deserve it," I told her.

When it comes to bartenders and servers, I always give them an extra couple of bucks when I buy a beer because, when the place gets crowded and I'm thirsty, guess who gets served first . . .

Chapter 18

Forty Rules I Learned the Hard Way

My rules aren't in any particular order except for the first one. It's from my perspective as a man, meant to benefit women.

Rule number 1: When in a new relationship with a woman, always remember to *lower* the toilet seat after going to the bathroom. I'll never forget the first time I stayed at Brenda's place and got up in the middle of the night to use the can. A few hours later, I heard a scream come from the bathroom that could have shattered glass.

Rule number 2: If you get lazy and leave the toilet seat down when you go, make sure to wipe up any splash marks you left behind. Otherwise, a wet hen is an angry hen.

Rule number 3: Be good at household chores—vacuuming, cleaning, laundry, etc. You'll be amazed at the brownie points you will earn if you can help do these chores around the house.

Rule number 4: Always put dirty clothes in the laundry basket vs. leaving them lay exactly where they came off, and reusing underwear and socks isn't a good thing.

Rule number 5: Don't try to fool her by putting the clothes you've worn that day back on their hangers. She'll sense you've done this, find them and pull them off the hangers one at a time, telling you to "never do this again!"

Rule number 6: If you don't know how to iron your clothes, at least make an attempt, but be really slow at it, so it bugs her until she tells you to "get out of her way." At least you made the attempt.

Rule number 7: Learn how to make the bed, then make this agreement with her, "The last one out of bed makes it." Then try to beat her out of bed at 5:00 a.m. Like I said, learn how to make the bed.

Rule number 8: Understand that when she gets home from work she needs to *talk*. All you need to do is learn to listen or be good at appearing you're listening. Nodding your head in agreement is a good thing; "Yes Dear" is a good thing. This all stems from the fact a woman needs to say 25,000 words a day, and, depending how much talk time she had before she saw you will depend on how much time of yours she needs.

Rule number 9: If you have something really important to say to her, and she just got home from work, always let her talk first. See Rule number 8. And, don't forget to ask her, "How was your day, honey?" But don't get mad if she forgets to ask you how yours was.

Rule number 10: Her ideas are usually the best.

Rule number 11: You're wrong ninety percent of the time, and the other ten percent she's right.

Rule number 12: If she wants to, let her handle the finances.

Rule number 13: Tell her everyday how much you love her.

Rule number 14: Prove how much you love her by doing the little things for her. See Rule number 3.

Rule number 15: When you do the laundry, make sure you really know what you're doing.

Rule number 16: Don't dry her favorite tops on high.

Rule number 17: After doing the laundry, learn where all her clothes belong. It makes it easier for her to find them.

Rule number 18: After she's fixed you a wonderful dinner, don't get up from the table and leave the dirty dishes for her to put away. Tell her to sit down and relax because you'll take care of it.

Rule number 19: Learn to cook for her.

Rule number 20: Know when she needs her space.

Rule number 21: You don't have to do everything together.

Rule number 22: Talk to each other about death.

Rule number 23: Trust her better judgment.

Rule number 24: Be honest at all times, even when it may hurt.

Rule number 25: Never go to bed mad at each other.

Rule number 26: If you've had an argument, tell her you're sorry. See Rule number 11.

Rule number 27: When she asks you what you think about the outfit she's wearing—See Rule number 24.

Rule number 28: Never look at other women when she's with you. If you do get busted, tell her, "Honey, she's really good looking isn't she, but nothing compared to you."

Rule number 29: If she's talking to you while you're watching TV, make sure you hear the important stuff.

Rule number 30: Take the trash out.

Rule number 31: Take her on vacation.

Rule number 32: If given the chance, praise her in public.

Rule number 33: Make major decisions together.

Rule number 34: She's more important than golf or fishing.

Rule number 35: Tell her, "Thank you," and, "I appreciate you." Don't ever take her for granted.

Rule number 36: If you don't know her definition of "doing the little things," you need to ask her what they are.

Rule number 37: Buying her flowers or taking her to dinner doesn't go as far as "DOING THE LITTLE THINGS!!"

Rule number 38: Take her out to eat once a week (don't make it fancy!).

Rule number 39: Open doors for her and help her with her coat.

Rule number 40: If she wants to own 35 pairs of shoes . . . let her!

I know I've probably missed 40 more rules that could be in print, but these forty I had to learn over eleven years. I hope you found the humor in between the seriousness.

Chapter 19

Back to Sunday Night and the Days That Followed

was completely exhausted from all the phone calls I had made after Brenda died. I didn't even notice one of Brenda's brothers, his wife, and their daughter standing in the kitchen by the center island. I heard someone in the background say they were still at the state fair when they received the call and rushed over to the house. This was the same brother to whom Brenda had lent the money. For a split second when I looked at him, I became really angry to see him standing in "our house." *Sure, now you show up,* I thought, but I didn't say it. He and his family had never been to our house while Brenda was alive, yet there he was, standing right in front of me. I don't even remember if I acknowledged their presence or not. I hope I was kind enough to say hello to them because the next thing I do remember is yelling at him, "You'll never know how much she loved you!" My tone said it all, and he knew he wasn't welcome.

"Yes I do!" he yelled back at me.

I left it at that. *Let him think about what I just said for a while,* I told myself. That was when Brenda intervened.

"Knock it off, Mitch."

And as quick as you can snap your fingers, the anger I felt toward him left me. The real reason he was there was to take Kim, our niece, who had witnessed Brenda die, home. At age thirteen, I only pray Kim is doing okay. But how can a thirteen-year old really be okay on the inside after this? I asked her mother how she was doing, and she told me fine . . .

"Did you get her any outside help?" I wanted to know.

"No, she's fine," was her mother's answer. I only hope she is.

Jackie Chase had left around 10:30 p.m., and Mike agreed to stay with me until my brother Todd arrived. I knew I'd need my family and friends to surround me during the next few days, weeks, and months. There would be a lot of tag-team efforts needed on their part to get me through the ordeal. Donna had gone upstairs around 11:00 p.m. to try and get some rest. She'd stay with us the rest of the week until the funeral on Thursday, September 6th.

It was after midnight when the phone rang. It was someone so very dear to me, someone I've always thought of as my friend, my confidant, mentor, father figure, someone I cared about and loved; it was Doc.

Irvin Cleveland Holtz, D.C. To his close friends, he's known as Jack or Doctor, or Doc, or "the healer." It was Doc on the phone, but I knew Mike Swor, another close friend was with him. These two are my fishing buddies, the guys I was suppose to meet in Nester Falls, Ontario, on Monday afternoon, September 3rd, 2001.

"Mitch, this is Doc. I can't believe what we just found out. What happened?"

I immediately started to cry. "Doc, I don't know what happened. She died in my arms at the house."

"Oh, my God. We couldn't believe it when we first got the call. We want you to know we're thinking about you and care about you."

"Thanks, Doc. It's so good to hear your voice."

"Mitch, we know you're going through hell right now, and we want to come back to be with you. Have you had time to decide when the funeral services will be? Because were coming back for the funeral."

"I'm pretty sure Thursday morning, but Doc, you guys don't need to come back. You know Brenda wouldn't want to be the cause of cutting your vacation short."

"Forget it. We wouldn't even think of staying. We'll be there on Thursday. Mitch, you take care, and we'll see you soon."

We both hung up, and he was right. I really needed them to come back and be with me.

It was close to 1:00 a.m. when Mike asked me if it would be okay if he went home. Mike put his arms around me and gave me a reassurance hug and told me he'd always be there for me no matter what. I knew he would, and he always has.

I left the garage door open after Mike left, knowing my brother Todd would arrive soon. It was Monday morning, 1:10

Mike Swor, Mitch, Joan and Dr. Jack Holtz.

a.m., and I was sitting on the couch in the hearth, still believing the front door was going to open and Brenda would walk in and tell me, "Hi, hon. It's only a joke. I'm really not dead. I'm okay, see?" That's when I heard the door in our kitchen, the one that leads to the garage, open, and I was brought back to reality. She was gone and would never be coming home.

I knew it was Todd who was walking through the garage door; he was the one person I needed at that moment to be with me, to help me start to make some sense of all the emotions I was feeling. I was up and running to him before the door even closed. I didn't even give him a chance to make it to the kitchen. We embraced in the hallway. Todd, who always kept his emotions tucked way down deep inside, lowered his head, starting crying on my shoulder and gave me a hug I will never forget. With both of us sobbing, hugging each other so hard, I felt a feeling of closeness to my brother I had never experienced in my life. It was the love we'd always had for each other but never had verbalized. We never said, "I love you," to each other, nor had we ever really embraced in a way that I could feel his heart beating against mine. Just thinking about those few moments we shared still makes me feel close to him. I know it was Brenda weaving her magic through the two of us. Our embrace lasted for several minutes before I could speak. When I finally caught my breath, I put my hand on the back of his head and pulled him closer to me and told him, "Todd, you know she loved you so very much."

With tears falling from his face onto my shirt, all he could tell me was, "I know."

We made our way into the kitchen, and I asked him if he wanted something to drink. I knew it was going to be a long night, and I was ready to talk to him about the events that took place earlier in the day.

"I still can't believe she's gone. Do you know how crazy all this is?"

Todd was so emotionally drained and tired from the four hour drive, all he was able to do was nod his head in agreement.

"One minute she's smiling at me and telling me she'll take care of baking those chocolate chip cookies, and the next minute I'm giving her mouth to mouth trying to save her life!" I recounted the story verbatim, with Todd not saying anything but absorbing the details one word at a time. I'm sure it was hard for him to sit and listen to me, but at that moment it was exactly what I needed him to do.

"Todd, I'm really upset at myself. It's almost as if I have two personalities talking to each other. One is greiving for Brenda, while at the same time the other wants to know whether or not I'll be able to handle the finances without her. These feelings, these voices, are making me sick. I can't help myself. I need the answers tonight."

As I was talking to him, I opened the drawer where we kept our checkbooks and starting looking for the last time she paid our life insurance premiums. "I found the entries in our joint account for my premiums, but I can't find were she has been paying on hers. This is really starting to scare me, Todd." The look on my face, the sound of my voice, told him I was panicking and he needed to help calm me down.

"Why are you so focused on knowing all this tonight?" he asked me. Todd, who has been selling life, health, and disability insurance for over fifteen years, was our insurance agent, and I knew he would be able to answer my questions.

"I don't know. I wish I had an answer for you. I just can't stop my brain from thinking about Brenda, and I can't stop thinking about whether or not we had enough life insurance on her. I'm sorry, Todd, I know this probably sounds really sick to you, but I need to know the answers now! Do you remember how much life insurance we had on her?"

I didn't even give Todd a chance to answer as I turned and walked downstairs to the basement. Todd followed me probably not knowing what I was doing. "I'm going to find our policies," I said, "and I want you to help me figure this out." After I searched in the filing cabinet and finally located the polices, I turned to Todd and said, "Thank God for Scott Kass. Todd, you'll really like Scott and his wife Marlene."

Brenda had introduced me to Scott and Marlene Cass in 1993, and we instantly liked one another. Scott, who had always been Brenda's insurance agent, had converted a small life insurance policy she owned into a larger one. It was never really any of my business when it came to the insurance dealings between Scott and Brenda. Since my background included seven years in the business, Brenda would ask me my opinion, and I always gave her solid advice but told her she needed to make the final decision.

"Todd, here's the policy we bought from you six years ago. I remember Transamerica writing to us after Brenda's exam and telling us we could double the face amount for only a few more dollars a month. What's bothering me so much is whether or not we did it."

I opened the policy, and, printed on the first page in big bold letters was the face amount. I was relieved to see we had taken advantage of the offer, but I still didn't know if she had kept the policy in force. "I need to know if she has been paying the premiums," I stated, looking up at Todd while sitting on the basement floor holding the policy in my hand.

"I'm telling you, Mitch, if she wouldn't have paid the premiums, I would have been notified." Todd was right about the premiums being paid. I knew from my own years of experience in the insurance business that the agent of record is notified immediately when a premium is overdue. But I wanted to see it for myself, to see her handwriting in the checkbook journal proving the premiums had been paid. It was the only way I was going to get rid of the "voices" inside my head.

"Then why is it I can only find the quarterly premiums being paid on my policy and not hers?

"I can't answer that question, Mitch."

"The only place I haven't looked is in her personal checkbook."

We went back upstairs and I retrieved Brenda's purse. When I went to open her purse a scent hit my nose. It was her scent, a smell only I would recognize after eleven years of living with this woman. It was beautiful and stopped me dead in my tracks. I lifted the purse to my nose and took a deep breath, inhaling her inside me.

"Here's her personal checkbook," I said as I put her purse on the kitchen island. It only took a few seconds, and I started to see a pattern of entries every three months payable to Transamerica. "I can't believe her. Here she was paying for her own life insurance out of her personal checking account. I told her not to do that, but when did she ever really listen to me when it came to money issues."

We looked at each other knowing Brenda would never have allowed her policy or mine to lapse.

It was only one month prior to her death when Brenda and I were discussing life and death issues and whether or not I should increase the amount of life insurance I owned. I gave her the same old song and dance I had given her for eleven years. "I know between the two of us, I'll be the one who goes first, but if you decide to kick the bucket before I do, you know I'm going to find three young blondes to move in and take care of me."

Then she'd give me that look, the same one she'd always given me when we talked about the "what if something happened to you" scenario, the one that told me I was so full of shit. The next thing she'd do is tell me, "If something ever does happen to me, I want you to go on, and, Mitch, remember I want you to be happy."

There was always something reassuring about hearing her say those words, but I never wanted to believe anything would ever happen to her first. "You know if anything ever happens to me, hon, you need to move on and you need to be happy." I always told her how I felt, but she never wanted to discuss the issue if I died first. "You're so much stronger than me. I don't know what I'd do without you," I'd tell her.

The reality of losing my spouse is this: neither one of us

really knew what the other would do if put into the situation I'm now faced with. All we knew was to tell each other to be happy and live life to the fullest. "Don't be sorry for yourself and make sure you find a way to be happy." Even while she was alive, we agreed that we shouldn't listen to those who thought they knew what we should and shouldn't be doing because we were not here to live our lives for the "know-it-alls." Unless someone has lived through what I've lived through they really have *no* idea when it comes to giving me advice. I was very fortunate to have Brenda, who was willing to openly discuss life and death issues. Over the eleven years we were together, we had prepared each other to deal with these events if they were to ever unfold. By talking about life and death and the reality of the "what if's," we had prepared each other to face the next chapter in our life, no matter how difficult it would be.

During our discussion regarding life and death, I wanted her to feel she would be able to financially "make it" without my income if I were to go first. In early August 2001, I decided to add an additional half million dollars of life insurance on myself, "that way you can do whatever you want to do without any worries." I told her.

She didn't say a word as I called my brother Todd that evening to take care of setting up the paperwork. So here I was one month later with an additional half million on me to protect her and now she was gone.

"Todd, you look really tired. Do want to lie down?"

"Yes, I do."

It was close to 2:30 a.m., but I knew I wouldn't be able to sleep in our bed that night.

"I'm going to sleep on the couch, Todd. Why don't you sleep on the chaise lounge."

It was only a matter of minutes, and he was asleep. I, on the other hand, couldn't sleep nor would my brain allow me to quit thinking about her. The re-run that I kept seeing that night and still see once in a while to this very day is her face, so still, her eyes staring straight ahead and she's not breathing. I laid there staring outside the back window. The moon was lighting the sky, and the stars were as bright as could be. Every time I thought I could fall asleep, the re-run would hit me, and I'd start crying. It was too real, and for once in my life there was nothing I could do to help her. The thought of not being able to help someone who needs you is a very gut-wrenching feeling.

"You're never coming home. What in the world am I going to do now?" I'd whisper those words out loud, not to wake Todd, but hoping Brenda would hear me and say something to make me feel better. "Honey, I hope you're okay. I know you didn't suffer, but I need to hear your voice."

She never answered me, and it really scared me. I went looking for Einstein and found him lying in the hallway next to the garage door, still waiting for Brenda to come home. "Come on, little buddy. Daddy needs you now more than ever." I took Einstein back to the couch and laid him next to me and started to pet him and talk to him about his mama. I told him how much she loved him, and how she would never want us to be sad without her.

The clock on the VCR in the Great Room told me it was 5:00 a.m., and since I still couldn't fall asleep I decided to get up and use the bathroom. I was pacing the kitchen floor for a few minutes afterwards when out of the blue I completely lost my sense of connection to Brenda. I was hit with an overwhelming emotional sensation of loss. The pain and the emptiness I felt in my gut and my heart was so overwhelming, I started to tremble. I looked at my hands and they wouldn't stop shaking. The only thing I could think of to do was to try and find a way to regain the connection I'd had with her in order to rid myself of these horrible feelings. Out of pure instinct I opened the cabinet above the desk in the kitchen and on the third shelf was her purse, exactly where I had put it earlier. I had given her that purse for Christmas in 1992, and she always took it with her wherever she went. Because she loved it so much, she had it re-stitched three separate times. I was hoping her scent would help to settle me down so I reached to the third shelf and grabbed it, opened it up and inhaled as deeply as I could. Her scent was there, and for a moment I was okay, but I still couldn't shake the feeling that I had not only lost her, but I'd lost my spiritual connection to her. I started to weep uncontrollably as I was looking skyward and asking Brenda to speak to me. Since I didn't want to wake Todd or Donna, I walked into the hallway that leads to the garage and sat down on the white rug. I curled up in the fetal position holding her purse tightly in my arms.

It was 8:00 a.m. when Donna put her hand on my shoulder. Three hours of non-stop tears, and I was still clutching Brenda's purse with both arms, hugging it as if it were her.

"Mitch, come with me." Donna said.

"I'm sorry, Donna, but I can't stop crying."

"It's okay, Mitch. You have to let it out." We sat in the kitchen hearth area on the couch, Donna with her arm around me. There aren't any words that can take the pain away and Donna knew it. Only human touch and time heals wounds this deep. After ten minutes or so, I was starting to feel like I could at least control my emotions, but I knew it was going to be a long day.

It was only Monday September third, yet it felt like Brenda had been gone forever. I hadn't slept since I woke up Sunday morning and asked her if it would be okay if I played golf with the boys. Now I had to face the reality of planning my wife's funeral and deal with all the unseen waves of emotion that would hit me one by one. It was Monday September third, the day Jim and Peg would be back from helping his mother in North Dakota; it was the day we would have to meet with the funeral home and start making arrangements for Thursday's services. Monday was going to be a long day, and I really needed to reconnect with Brenda, or I might not make it through the morning without constantly breaking down.

"Donna I'm going upstairs to take a shower." I needed some alone time in case I broke down again. I could use the sound of the shower to drown out my sobbing. It was important to me to try and keep myself as composed as possible around my family and friends.

Once I was in the shower I couldn't help but start to cry, it was an occurrence I would face every time I showered for the next two weeks. To my surprise, I also found my connection to Brenda standing in the shower with both my hands covering my face talking to her as if I would never hear from her again. She came back into my heart and told me how strong I needed to be for her.

"Thank you, honey. I thought I'd lost you."

"You'll never lose me, Mitch. I'll always be here for you."

The strength she gave me with those words was unbelievable.

Later that morning, Todd, Donna, and I climbed into Todd's truck, and he drove us to the funeral home to make the arrangements for Thursday. I was composed but feeling very numb as we entered the funeral home. The first thing that hit me was the smell. It was the smell I remembered as a child that overwhelmed me that morning. My father, Del Freimark, is a mortician, and over the years I'd been in and out of enough funeral homes to know how much I despised that smell they all had.

We were greeted by Larry Willwerscheid of Willwerscheid & Peters. He brought the three of us into a room, and we sat at a small round table, Donna on my right and Todd sitting across from me. I can remember thinking, *This isn't happening. I'm being asked to look at a menu as if I'm ordering a hamburger at a sit-down restaurant.* This thought had nothing to do with the professionalism of Mr. Willwerscheid, but it was how I felt. We had to make several decisions, the minor ones Todd and Donna handled. The major decision would be picking out the casket, a decision I would have to make. The casket showroom was conveniently located in a room adjacent to us. I entered the room first and immediately noticed a gold-and-silver-toned casket but walked by to take a look around. There were no "blue light specials," and I didn't want to ask what the deal of the day was. Negotiating was my forte, but how do you negotiate with a funeral director? The answer was simple, you don't.

I kept my eye on the gold-and-silver casket as Donna and Todd were looking around. I knew that casket was perfect for Brenda and within five minutes I made up my mind. "This is the one I want for her. Gold and silver were two of her favorite colors." It was that easy for me to make up my mind, and a little help from above didn't hurt.

The next decision we had to make was the type of vault the casket would go into. I didn't know what Larry meant, so I asked him why there was a choice.

"Some people prefer the very inexpensive vaults, but they are not waterproof; others prefer to make sure the vault is waterproof," he explained.

"That's an easy decision; I want to make sure the vault is waterproof." I told him. Again, how do you negotiate with these people? I really didn't care about the money, but I felt a little uncomfortable not being able to say something like, "Hey, the competition down the street is offering a better price." It was my nature to always try and get a better deal. But, as Brenda taught me, sometimes you're better off not saying anything.

We gathered back around the small round table in the meeting room, and Larry asked us to select a card and to estimate the number we would need for the services. I thought it would be simple to find a card and be done with it, but I was having difficulty finding something that represented Brenda's life until I came across a small card called Nature's Seasons. On the front and back cover it showed a shoreline, the wind obviously still as the water was silently soaking up the crimson sky reflecting off its beauty. One large tree branch hanging over the rocky shoreline told me this was the one for her. On the inside it read:

God hath not promised
Skies always blue,
Flower-strewn pathways
All our lives through;
God hath not promised
Sun without rain,
Joy without sorrow,
Peace without pain.

But God hath promised
Strength for the day,
Rest for the labor,
Light for the way
Grace for the trials,
Help from above,
Unfailing sympathy,
Undying love.

One of the issues that Larry brought up which I hadn't even considered was whether or not the church would be available for Thursday, September 6th.

"I'll contact them and call you once they let me know," he told us. "Now we should think about the time you want to start the services and the amount of time we need to drive to Sioux Valley, Minnesota, for the burial," Larry said.

"It's about a three-hour drive from my house, and the church is a half-hour closer, so if we use three hours we should be okay," I told him.

"Okay, I'll estimate leaving Risen Savior by 11:30 a.m. arriving in Sioux Valley no later than 2:30 p.m." Larry explained.

Donna had already told him the name of the cemetery was Sioux Valley Cemetery; where her husband, Brenda's father, John Voss, Sr., was buried.

"I'll wait to hear from you regarding whether or not the church will be available," I said.

One of the last requests I made prior to leaving the funeral home was to ask if it would be okay if I brought Brenda's make-up and a picture of how I wanted her hair to look. Larry told me it would not be a problem. "Also, any jewelry you would like for her to wear," he kindly reminded me.

"I'll drop everything off on Tuesday morning," I told him.

On the way home, Todd told me he needed to head back to Watertown to get some clothes and his suit. "I left the house in such a hurry, I didn't pack anything," he told Donna and me. His plan was to be back to my house on Wednesday afternoon.

Around 2:00 p.m. on Monday it was verified that the church would be available at 10:30 a.m. on Thursday, September 6th for the funeral services. Larry Willwerscheid also made all the arrangements for the burial service in Sioux Valley. He then informed me that I needed to call and speak to Fr. James Gorman to set up a time to meet with him on Tuesday to arrange the church service. When I called Risen Savior, Fr. Jim was extremely pleasant on the phone, which gave me a really good feeling about him, and we set the meeting time for 3:00 p.m. on Tuesday.

I was keeping myself busy on Monday, mainly answering the phone and speaking to those I had left messages for on Sunday night. Around 4:00 p.m. my golfing buddies started to show up one by one. Mitch Wylie, Mark Luers, Mike Chase, Rodney West, Mark Agranoff along with Brenda's family: Becky and Wayne Webster, Bernie, Linda, and their daughter Jennifer Voss. We all sat outside on the deck visiting. That's when my brother-in-law Bernie found Einstein trying to get at the rat poison under the deck.

Jim and Peg arrived Monday evening, and, of course, it was extremely difficult for all three of us to try and comprehend the events of Sunday night. I knew all too well how much Brenda meant to them, especially Jimi. Brenda was his hair stylist, his friend, his best friend's wife, and, most of all, she was his Martha Stewart. Jimi was responsible for giving her the nickname, and Brenda loved to cook and bake for him.

James and I had always called each other Brother or "Brotha" as Jimi would say. We always teased each other that we really were brothers because our fathers were so much alike that we must be "brothas." Jimi being from North Dakota, and me from South Dakota, we'd grown so close during those last seven years that Jimi was considered part of our family; even Einstein called him "Uncle Jimi." Now we were missing Brenda, and I could see it in his eyes as the tears fell from his face, hear it in his voice as he tried to speak, and feel it in his heart as we embraced, he knew exactly what I was going through.

"She loved you, Jimi. She loved you so much," was all I could tell him. There weren't any words to help ease the pain we felt that evening. We'd have to rely on each other for support to make it from day to day.

Once we were settled down enough to converse without crying, Peg began making a list of items I would need for the remainder of the week. I needed Peg to take charge of our situation, and she knew exactly what to do. It was only two years prior to Brenda's death that Peggy and Jimi had gone through a tragic loss when her brother-in-law Kurt, who was married to her sister Renee, died unexpectedly. "We'll bring over pop, water, and beer and keep most of it in coolers in the garage," she said.

She was also concerned about me. "Mitch, have you gotten any sleep?"

"No, I haven't slept at all."

"You need to get some rest tonight."

By the way she said it, I knew I didn't have a choice, but it was 10:30 p.m., and I wasn't even close to being tired. "Jimi, why don't you and I go to the drugstore and pick up some Unisom, some detergent, some hand soap, and whatever else I can think of that Mitch might need." Peg said.

"Thanks you guys I really appreciate all the help."

By 11:30 p.m. they returned from their shopping spree and told me to take a Unisom. Jimi would be staying the night, which was a huge comfort to me. Mike Chase had also stopped by to make sure I was doing okay. When Mike saw I was in good hands, he only stayed for a few minutes, then went home. Although Donna was staying at the house until Thursday, I needed my close friends with me at this point in time. I took the Unisom not knowing what to expect as I had never taken a sleeping pill before. I still couldn't sleep in my bed so the couch was my only option. Jimi made himself comfortable on the chaise lounge, and the next thing I knew it was 5:00 a.m. in the morning. I tried to get up off the couch but the Unisom still had me feeling really groggy. I forced myself to get up as I hate the feeling of being out of control. I told myself that would be that last time I took a sleeping pill.

Once I was up, I kept myself busy cleaning the kitchen, doing the laundry, organizing all the food that people had dropped off on Monday, and, of course, my mind was always on Brenda. I don't believe more than thirty seconds ever went by without a thought or vision of her in my head. I also needed Einstein close to me Tuesday morning. When I held him, he would push himself against my chest as hard as he could, look up at me and ask a million questions with his eyes. We really needed each other during those first few days. He needed to be picked up and held as much as I needed him close to me.

By 8:00 a.m. Jimi and Donna were up and moving around. It was a new day, another day without Brenda. It was Tuesday, September 4th.

I had made coffee and offered the two of them breakfast. My mind was focused on what I needed to get done during the day. "Jimi, can you and Peg pick up Barb, Don, Jamie, and Shelly from the airport this afternoon? Barb and Don arrive on NWA at 1:30 p.m.. Jamie and Shelly come in around 1:45 p.m. I don't think I'll be able to handle picking them up. I know seeing them will definitely be too hard for me and I'm not sure if any of us would be able to drive back," I explained.

"No problem, brotha. Is there anything else you need us to do?"

"No, you've done enough already. Just staying with me means so much. Thank you. I love you, Jimi."

Jimi has a heart of gold; he and Peg would do anything for their friends.

"I'm going upstairs to shower, and then I'm going to take her dress, makeup, and jewelry to the funeral home," I told him.

213

After I showered and got dressed, I found myself standing in front of the mirror in the master bathroom staring into space. I must have been spending too much time upstairs because Jimi came looking for me.

"How ya doing?" he asked me as he walked into the master bathroom. I looked at him, and the tears started to flow from both our eyes. As we stood there holding each other, I told him, "Jimi, I miss her so much. I can't stand it."

"I know. I miss her, too." As we stepped back to catch our breath, I said to him, "I think I've already cried a river of tears."

"Come on, let's go downstairs," he said to me.

"Let me first make sure I have everything for the funeral home, and I'll be right down." I had managed to pick out one of her beautiful black dresses, the only one that had sheer sleeves. The jewelry I selected was her wedding ring, a diamond bangle bracelet I bought her in Arizona, her gold bangle bracelet she wore to work everyday, her marquee diamond necklace, and those twenty-five dollar, "priceless," fake, marquee diamond earrings.

When I got back from the funeral home, I was feeling very calm and peaceful, but the pain of losing Brenda would soon hit me all over again. As I walked into the kitchen, there was Carrie talking and smiling her beautiful smile. As she looked over to see who was entering the kitchen, our eyes met and we both started to cry. I really wanted to be strong for her, but I knew how painful Brenda's death was for me, and I also knew her death would be equally as painful for Carrie. As I walked over to her, I didn't even notice who else was in the kitchen; I just made my way to her. She got up from her chair, and, as we embraced, we both started to cry uncontrollably. I held her in my arms for several minutes before we both calmed down.

"I can't believe she's gone, Mitch."

"I know. It doesn't make any sense to me either."

"What happened?" she wanted to know. I told her the same story I'd been telling everyone else, "Except we don't know what caused her death. The autopsy is going to take several weeks according to the hospital."

"How are you doing?" she asked.

"I'm holding up the best I can. It's one minute at a time for me."

It was past one fifteen in the afternoon, and Jimi had just left to get everyone from the airport, when I heard a knock at the front door. When I opened it, there stood my neighbors, Phil Keeney, and his wife, Sue McLean-Keeney. "Mitch, we're so sorry. We had no idea what happened. We were out of town on Sunday, and we just found out."

The three of us stood on the front porch and held each other. There wasn't a dry eye to be found. "Mitch, if there's anything you need us to do please ask."

Chapter 20

Meeting with Father Jim and Sister Martha

uesday afternoon at 3:00 p.m. was our scheduled appointment with Fr. James Gorman and Sr. Martha Alken, O.P. at the Church of the Risen Savior in Burnsville, Minnesota. I asked my brother-in-law Wayne Webster, my niece Carrie Webster and Brenda's mother, Donna, to accompany me.

Fr. Jim led us into a room that reminded me of a Sunday school classroom, complete with a large green chalkboard but missing the chairs and teacher's desk. Instead, they had been replaced with a large, rectangular table that sat in the middle of the room. Fr. Jim told us Sr. Martha would be joining us, and, about the time he said it, she entered the room.

I had never met Fr. Jim, but my first impression told me he was an inspiring priest. Just shaking his hand made me feel very comfortable he was giving the services. We could see it in his mannerisms and hear it in his voice that he loved helping people, and we would need his help. We quickly learned he's an extremely intelligent man with the ability to think and see way beyond the conversation at hand. I almost started laughing as I watched his facial expression change as his brain raced forward a million miles an hour while the words coming out of his mouth tried to catch up to his next thought.

Neither Fr. Jim nor Sr. Martha knew Brenda, but they both were anxious to have us describe her to them.

"Please tell us about Brenda. What was she like? What did she love to do? What are some of the adjectives you would use to describe her?" Sr. Martha and Fr. Jim wanted to know all the details we could give to them. It didn't take long and the four of us were giving the two of them stories about her, adjectives to describe her, and Fr. Jim wrote them all down:

She loved life and people loved her, she was kind, generous to a fault, compassionate. She always said, "Go for it." She always encouraged others, she was passionate about life and her work, she was friendly to everyone she met. She could remember anything someone told her, she was a great communicator, she had such a big heart, she loved music, she loved to dance, she loved art. "Fun" was her middle name. She always had a "let's do it" attitude. The aura that surrounded her was awesome. People admired her and wanted to emulate her. She was always positive, and she had charisma. She was vibrant and humorous, she was a laborer, she loved to garden, she loved to cook, she was faithful to her friends, she was smart and she was very beautiful.

The next step was to pick the music for the service. Fr. Jim had graduated from college with a music degree and told us "music has been my passion since I was a child." He could literally think of a song appropriate for the service then tell us what page it was on, hum or sing a few lines, never looking in the hymnal; it was truly amazing to witness.

"I believe I am beginning to know who Brenda was, and I wish I would have met her. It sounds to me like music was a large part of her life, so we should have as many songs as possible throughout the service." He looked at the four of us, looking for reassurance that he was on the right path. We were all nodding our heads in agreement as he continued. "For the Prelude I'm thinking 'I Know That My Redeemer Lives' would be a very good choice." Then he hummed or sang a few lines for us.

Wayne added, "What about 'In the Garden'?"

"Excellent choice. 'In the Garden' would be perfect after the Prelude," Fr. Jim said. "I have another one in mind. 'Joyful, Joyful We Adore You' for the Gathering Hymn. Another great song would be 'On Eagles Wings' and 'Sing With All the Saints in Glory' and for the Recessional, 'Jesus Christ Is Risen Today.'" Fr. Jim was now standing at the chalkboard writing all the songs down in order. He was filled with so much energy and devotion.

While all this discussion with Fr. Jim was going on, Sr. Martha was busy finding scripture readings and looking for examples of writings we could use in the bulletin to be handed out on Thursday. That was when the higher power above took over. Out of Sr. Martha's hands, which were stuffed with examples of bulletins, fell a small, white bulletin onto the middle of the table. On the one side was a picture of Butterflies and on the back a picture of a woman gardening. I almost started to cry as it looked like Brenda's hands were in those gloves as she was busy gardening in her flower garden.

With her mouth hanging open and not able to say a word, the look on Sr. Martha's face was contagious. We all sat silent for a brief moment, all thinking the same thing.

The next act from above was when the Scripture reading was pulled like magic from a stack of readings Fr. Jim was sorting. "This is truly appropriate for the first reading!" he said as he started to read Proverbs 31: 25-31, I couldn't help but start to cry. Fr. Jim continued reading, as I reached across the table for another tissue.

> "She is clothed with strength and dignity,
>> And she laughs at the days to come.
>>> She opens her mouth in wisdom,
>> And on her tongue is kindly counsel.
> She watches the conduct of her household,
>> And eats not her food in idleness.
>>> Her loved ones rise up and praise her;
>> Her husband, too, extols her.
> "Many are the women of proven worth,
>> But you have excelled them all."
>>> Charm is deceptive and beauty fleeting;
>> The woman who fears the lord is to be praised.
> Give her a reward for her labors,
>> And let her works praise her at the city gate.

This is the word of the Lord

"Father, I want to read that on Thursday." I said as I wiped the tears from my eyes and my face.

"There's no way you will be able to hold up," he said as if he had experienced this before. My voice and my strength were back, and I looked him straight in the eyes and said, "Yes,

Father, I will be able to hold up, and I am going to read the first reading on Thursday!" In my mind, I knew I could handle it and would be fine. I also felt it would be an honor to read at my wife's funeral.

Reading at mass was not something new for me. When I lived in Sioux Falls, South Dakota, it wasn't unusual for me to read the first reading at Mass on Sundays.

"Okay. It's fine with me." Fr. Jim seemed convinced, and we moved on to the next item.

"All right, I think we're about done. Let me outline the service on the board for all of us to see." He started at the far left of the chalkboard and began:

Prelude:	"I Know That My Redeemer Lives" (followed by: "In the Garden")
Gathering Hymn:	"Joyful, Joyful We Adore You
Scripture Readings:	Proverbs 31:25-31 Response
	Matthew 5:1-12
Teaching:	"I Heard the Voice of Jesus Say"
Prayers of the Faithful:	(to be read by Wayne) "On Eagle's Wings
Closing Hymn:	"Sing With All the Saints in Glory"
Recessional:	"Jesus Christ is Risen Today"

Our meeting had lasted an hour, and the only thing left to do was pick the color for the bulletin. The choices were endless, but we decided on purple, another favorite color of Brenda's.

As we left the church to go back to the house, I was still in awe at how everything fell into place during the meeting. "It's still amazing to me how on Sunday night when we were at the hospital and I was asked "Where do we want the services held?" I immediately saw a picture of a white Catholic church, and I knew we had to take her to Risen Savior. I'm really impressed with Fr. Jim; he'll do an exceptional job on Thursday."

I don't know if I was reassuring myself that I had made the right decision, but we all were in agreement.

On our way home, we had to take a detour as traffic was backed up on Interstate 35E. As I approached a four-way stop and signaled to take a left, I had to pause for a few seconds to gather myself. To my amazement, the church Brenda and I were married in, Saints Martha and Mary Episcopal Church, was right in front of me. "Does everyone remember this church?" I asked. No one had to say anything, we all knew. As I made the left turn staring at the church, I blurted out, "Wow, this has been some sort of day!"

Funeral Service
for
Brenda Voss

February 2, 1955 - September 2, 2001

Front of bulletin.

LITANY OF REMEMBRANCE

In the rising of the sun and its going down,
  We remember her.
In the opening of the buds and in the rebirth of spring,
  We remember her.
In the blueness of the sky and in the warmth of summer,
  We remember her.
In the rustling of the leaves and in the beauty of autumn,
  We remember her.
In the beginning of the year and when it ends,
  We remember her.
When we are lost and sick at heart,
  We remember her.
So long as we live, she too shall live, for she is part of us,
  We remember her.

Back of bulletin.

Chapter 21

Wednesday, September 5, 2001
Day Four

uesday night was pretty laid back with nothing much going on. Wednesday morning, I woke up at 3:00 a.m. and found myself checking e-mail, cleaning the kitchen, doing the dishes and thinking about all the issues I now had to face without Brenda. "Stay busy doing something, anything," I kept telling myself.

By 9:00 a.m., Barb and Don were up along with Carrie and Donna. It was 11:00 a.m. when Brenda's sisters had arrived along with several nieces and nephews. By mid-afternoon, Peggy and Jimi had stopped by with backer board to put pictures on showing all the years of our lives together. Peggy, my niece Kelsey, my sister Shelly, and I sorted through all the pictures. It's funny how the smallest things would set me off and make me cry. As I was digging through the pictures, I came across a picture of Kevin Malecha, at four years old. Kevin is the son of Dan and Penny Malecha, two of our friends. I guess what caught me off guard was the fact that Brenda had thought so much of Kevin. When The Baker Boys played the New Year's Eve party in 1999, it was Brenda who helped make sure Dan and Penny had a babysitter at our house for Kevin. She also made sure Kevin had a Christmas present to open when he arrived. It was just Brenda's way of helping Kevin feel more comfortable about staying at our house. She gave him a toy milk cow that could walk and "mooo'd." Kevin was also infatuated with the fish ponds in our back yard and the fact I took him and his dad ice-fishing added to the memories of seeing Kevin in that picture. Penny told me that Kevin, even at four years old, couldn't get over the fact that Brenda was gone. I held the picture in my hand and cried for only a few seconds, "This one has to go on the board."

Our neighbor, Keith and Linda Hall's son Dustin, stopped by while we were sorting the pictures and asked if he could help

Kevin Malecha.

us. Dustin was nine years old the first time I met him. He lives only four houses down the street and loves to visit with the grown-ups. Dustin would ride his bike to our house and sit and visit with Brenda for as long as she would let him. We trusted Dustin to the point we gave him one of our house keys and whenever I was gone traveling for work, it was Dustin who would stop by after school and let Einstein out and feed him. The relationship has grown over the years as Brenda always left him $5.00 for

Dustin Hall.

his efforts. They would write notes to each other, Brenda telling him thank you, and Dustin telling her how everything went with Einstein. Now at age thirteen with his fourteenth birthday coming up in November, I couldn't tell him no. "Dustin, can you do me a really big favor?" I asked him. "Can you print some of the digital pictures I have stored on disk?"

"No problem." And he took the disks and returned within a half hour with eight-by-ten-inch color pictures to be used on one of the backer boards.

There were so many phone calls each day, but one in particular that Wednesday afternoon made me smile. It was Mary Ann O'Dougherty, Steve Alm's wife. "Mitch, I am so sorry about Brenda. I want to do something for you and for her. Would it be okay if I sang "Ave Verum Corpus" tomorrow at the funeral?"

I almost broke down when she asked me because Mary Ann has such a beautiful voice and such a big heart. "Mary Ann, I apologize for not asking you in the first place. I know Brenda and I would be honored if you sang. I'll call the church and make sure you're added as one of the soloists."

By late afternoon my brother Todd was back from Watertown, South Dakota. Two of my closest friends had also arrived, Jeff Doran, from Ft. Collins, Colorado, who was my college roommate my freshman year at the University of South Dakota, and John Green, a customer who had become a close friend, from Memphis, Tennessee. Most of Brenda's family arrived by 7:00 p.m., and all my friends from Mendakota Country Club were stopping by to give their condolences and show their support.

It was close to 11:00 p.m., and I had a house full of company with Carrie, Jeff, Donna, my mother, Barb, and her husband Don. John Green would be staying at a hotel to help out with the space issues. My neighbors Phil and Sue were kind enough to let my brother-in-law Jamie McDonald and my sister Shelly sleep at their house. Todd would sleep at Jimi and Peg's. Jeff would sleep in the chaise lounge, I was still on the couch, Carrie was in one guest room, Donna in another, and Barb and Don slept in the master bedroom.

We were all sitting around the hearth area when I asked Jeff if he had called his wife, Brenda, to tell her he had made it.

"No, she'll be all right," he said to me.

"Jeff, listen to me. Here's the phone. Call her, now!" I wasn't going to give him a choice.

Jeff dialed the number and spoke to her for ten minutes, then he gave me the phone. Brenda Doran and I spoke for several minutes as she reassured me they would always be there for me.

"You take care, Mitch," she said, "and you know we love you."

I gave the phone back to Jeff, and they told each other "I love you."

"Don't you feel better for calling her?" I asked him.

"You're right, I do feel better."

Wednesday night I tried to sleep, but the thought of having to bury my wife the next day was too much to bear. *Burying you will be one of the hardest things I have to do, honey, I'll need all the strength you can give me to make it through this.*

Chapter 22

The Funeral Service: She Gave Me the Strength of Superman!

Thursday, September 6th, I was up moving around the house at my usual time, 3:00 a.m. I started out my day by checking my e-mail, doing some laundry, doing the dishes and cleaning the house. All the things Brenda did, I now found myself doing. I made coffee but couldn't drink any. I knew I should eat something, but I wasn't hungry. I spent hours just sitting and thinking. To my surprise, I was feeling emotionally stable for someone about to bury his wife.

By 7:00 a.m. people were starting to move around the house. We had to leave no later than 8:30 a.m. to be at the church by 9:00 a.m. The time set aside for the family was from 9:00 to 9:30 a.m. The public showing would start at 9:30 a.m., and the services would begin at 10:30 a.m.

I was in the shower around 7:30 a.m. I thought this would be the day I'd cry the most, but to my surprise I was still feeling really good. I actually felt great. Standing in the shower I asked Brenda, "Honey, I'm going to say a few words before I give the first reading. Is that okay with you?"

"Just don't embarrass me." It was all she said.

"Don't worry. I won't." In my mind I envisioned getting up in front of everyone and saying a few words about our life together, why it took so long before we got married and maybe some advice for the guys, but I really wanted to give her something she always deserved.

"Now what am I going to wear?" I had no idea what I should wear to her funeral. She was the one who always helped me pick out my clothes. I decided I'd let her figure it out and she'd be the one who would let me know. "Okay, you need to give me a 'yes' or 'no' on this one. What if I wore the black sport coat and black pants you bought me before we went to Puerto Rico? And I'll wear the white shirt, the one with the bandit collar, with the black-and-gold button cover, black socks, and black shoes."

I got dressed and a very warm feeling came over me as she said, "You look very handsome."

We arrived at the church around 9:00 a.m., and I was feeling so strong, so confident, and I was smiling. I was wondering what was wrong with me. Shouldn't I be the worst-looking person here today? The first thing I did was go to the coffin to spend some time with Brenda. I wasn't sure why I was feeling so good, so I asked her, "Honey, how come I look and feel so happy on the day I'm about to bury you?"

Her response came in a voice that made me even stronger, "You need to be strong for our family and our friends."

"I will. I'll do it for you." I left the main area of the church and went out into the commons where we had placed the pictures. I greeted some of Brenda's family who had not made it up the night before. I also had Einstein with me, and he needed to go outside, which gave me a good excuse to get some fresh air.

Einstein, who doesn't need a leash, stayed next to me as I walked around the church to the back side talking to him the whole time. I wasn't moving very fast, and by the time we made the complete lap, it was close to 10:00 a.m. I found Keith, Linda, and Dustin Hall, as Dustin had agreed to take care of Einstein during and after the services.

Not knowing what I should or shouldn't be doing, I stood around in the commons area sipping on a bottle of water and talking to friends and family.

I remember everyone from that morning, but a few in particular still stick out in my mind:

Tony Potami, who was on the fishing trip with Doc Holtz and Mike Swor, the same trip I was leaving for on Monday, walked in and at first he didn't see me. My heart went out to Tony and his wife Toni (It really is Tony with a "y" and Toni with an "i"). Tony was diagnosed with cancer a few years ago, although he was doing well. I had to go to him and give him a hug.

Bob and Rita Meyers. Bob turned eighty-two years old on February 3rd, 2002; Brenda would have been forty-seven on February 5th. I can still remember Bob and Brenda sitting next to each other on Bob's eightieth birthday. I never knew what he was saying to her, but he sure had her laughing. I've played a lot of golf with Bob over the last seven years, and I can still remember telling a buddy of mine, "How would you like to get your ass beat by a seventy-five-year old that can shoot his age . . . or better?" During 2001, Bob fell not once but twice and hurt his right hand, keeping him from playing golf. Then his dog, his companion for the past fourteen years died. During the six months after Brenda's death, Bob and Rita have asked if they could take care of Einstein when I'm traveling. It's been nice to know Einstein and Bob are looking after one another.

There were so many people that it made me think, "If you count your friends by the number of people who show up at your funeral, then we were truly blessed!"

The next thing I knew, I had set my water bottle down, and I was standing at the front door shaking hands and hugging everyone who entered. I know I was standing there for at least twenty-five minutes when an attractive lady with a name badge on her left shoulder, which I never read, asked me to follow her. "Okay, sister. I'm right behind you,"

"I'm not a nun," she responded.

I looked at her name tag and it read "Barbara Stapleton." I wouldn't pick up on the fact she was married to Marty Stapleton, a member at Mendakota, until Sunday evening, September 9th, 2001, during the open house held for those who couldn't make it to the funeral services. Barbara asked me to follow her. "They're ready to start the services, and you need to do a mike check before we can seat the family."

There were so many people in the commons that when I tried to follow her I could only make it a few feet before someone would stop me and hug me or start talking to me. Barbara finally grabbed me by the elbow and said I'd better hang on to her so I don't get stopped every three feet, or we'll never get the services started on time.

"The reason I want you to do a mike check is because the acoustics in this building are a little tricky, and I want you to be comfortable speaking."

I pulled the first reading from my pocket and read a few lines.

"Make sure you read slowly and pause." Barbara gave me some good advice.

We were ready to get started. People were now being told to be seated so the services could begin.

With "I Know That My Redeemer Lives" playing, the families were asked to gather in the back of the church before being seated. I was holding onto Donna as I could see she was having a very difficult time. We were ushered to the front of the church in pairs with Donna and I being the last two to sit down. Fr. Jim asked me to make sure and sit at the end of the pew to make it easier for me to get in and out for the first reading. I wasn't paying much attention to what was going on around me when Larry Willwerscheid tapped me on the shoulder and asked me if there was anything I wanted to put into her casket before they closed it. That's when I remembered Dustin Hall had given me a letter he wrote to Brenda and asked me to put it in her casket for him.

"Yes there is, Larry," I reached into my wallet and handed him the letter.

Dear Brenda,

This will be the last letter that I will ever be able to write to you. You and Mitch were like close relatives to me. I know that I will see you in heaven some day. Don't worry about Mitch, because I'll take care of him.

Please, when you get to heaven, look up Heather Renee Hall. She was my aunt who died in a car crash. I know that she will show you around, and if you could tell her that I love her, I would be grateful.

I'm really going to miss getting your letters when I let out Einstein. This letter is getting harder and harder to end because I know this will be my last. Don't forget to look up Heather.

Love,

Dustin K. Hall

"Mitch, do you want us to remove the jewelry?" Larry asked.
"Yes I do."

With everyone seated and "In the Garden" being played, they brought the casket down the aisle and put her in front of the left podium, the one Wayne and I would use. They draped the coffin in white linen, which had a large gold cross down the center. In my head I was telling her I loved her, and I knew she was in a very good place today.

Father then asked us to turn to page 525 in the hymnal to sing "Joyful, Joyful We Adore You." At the end of the song, there was a brief moment of silence, and, of course, I didn't realize that was my cue. I didn't have a bulletin, so I wasn't really paying much attention. I just happened to look at Father Jim, and he nodded his head, telling me with his body language that I was the one they were waiting for.

I got up to start making my way to the podium, but when I passed by her coffin, I could hear Brenda saying, "Don't you embarrass me!"

"Oh, just calm down. Everything will be fine," I told her as I was waving my hands at her. I didn't realize how many people saw me gesturing towards her coffin, but it was Peggy, who later told me she knew Brenda must have said something to me.

I had left the first reading on the podium so once I was standing in front of everyone I first glanced around the room. I couldn't believe how many people were present. I started the eulogy, which no one knew I was going to do except for Brenda and myself. Here is what I said:

"My wife is a non-traditionalist, and today we are going to have a non-traditional funeral. People always asked us, 'Why did you wait eight years before you got married?' Her standard answer was always the same; 'It took me that long just to whip him into shape." Brenda taught me so much about life and how to love others. I loved her so much. This next message is for all the men who are here today. I want to give you the gift that she gave me. This is for all you men who are married or have a significant other in your life and want a relationship like we had because our relationship was so close to perfect. There are two words you need to learn:

"Yes Dear. Yes Dear."

(As I said that first "Yes Dear," I looked directly into Jimi's eyes, and he was smiling the biggest smile, and when I said the second "Yes Dear" he was saying it right along with me.)

I went on to read Proverbs 31: 25-31 just as Barbara instructed me to read it, nice and slow. When I was finished the reading, I stepped back from the podium and started walking back to my seat, when I realized I wasn't finished. There was one last thing that I needed to do. I turned around and walked back to the podium, looked at everyone in the church and smiled.

"You know, people receive awards during their lifetime, sometimes people get awards that are so meaningless. If there is anyone who deserves recognition, it is you, honey. You deserve a standing ovation!" I stepped out from behind the podium and began clapping, everyone in the church stood, and together we gave her a standing ovation. It was the one thing during her life that she always deserved.

It felt really good to do that for her. I knew Brenda never liked being in the spotlight; she always preferred to work her magic one on one. And magic was what she possessed.

I walked back to my seat and sat down. I still had not shed one single tear, not in the shower, not when I spent time alone with her at the casket, not walking Einstein around the church, not even when I greeted all the people who were present. "She had given me the strength of Superman." I looked up at Father Jim as he read Matthew 5: 1-12.

"A reading from the holy Gospel according to Matthew."

"When Jesus saw the crowds, he went up on the mountainside. After he had sat down his disciples gathered around him, and Jesus began to teach them:

"How blest are the poor in spirit: the Kingdom of God is theirs.

Blest, too, are the sorrowing; they shall be consoled.

Blest are the lowly, they shall inherit the land.

Blest are they who hunger and thirst for holiness; they shall have their fill.

Blest are they who show mercy;
mercy shall be theirs.

Blest are the single-hearted
for they shall see God.

Blest, too, are the peacemakers;
they shall be called children of God.

Blest are those persecuted for holiness' sake;
the Kingdom of God is theirs.

Blest are you when they insult you and persecute you and
utter every kind of slander against you because of me.
Be glad and rejoice, for your reward in heaven is great."

    As Father finished reading the holy gospel according to
Matthew, he paused before starting to tell Brenda's story, and I
happened to turn my head to my left and looked up to find Jimi.
The moment I saw him, we locked eyes, and I felt a sensation in
the pit of my stomach I knew was going to tear me to pieces. I
stood up from my seat, and, as fast as I could, I made my way
to where Jimi and Peggy were seated. I remember crawling over
Scott Entenman to get to Jimi. I was crying so hard, I couldn't
even breathe. I wrapped both arms around him and sat there
with Jimi holding me as if I were a young child who was lost and
finally found. I couldn't move. I just hugged Jimi as hard as I
could. Peggy was stroking my head, trying to comfort me, and
we were all in tears.

    By the end of Father's message, I was ready to go back to
my own seat, I hadn't heard a single word he said. Luckily I was
given a copy, which I've enclosed:

Brenda Voss Funeral
Risen Savior, Burnsville
September 6, 2001

Proverbs 31: 25-31   Matthew 5: 1-12

The words of the Scriptures from Proverbs and from the
Gospel of Matthew sum up beautifully and succinctly
what the life and legacy of Brenda Voss was all about.

Her life and legacy were poignant examples of those words of Scripture lived in their fullness.

Brenda was an exemplary human being. She loved life and she loved every person who came into her life, her husband, her parents, her brothers and sisters, her nephews and nieces, her many friends. And people loved Brenda—and it was natural, for what was there not to love with her? Brenda was a beautiful person, inside and out, a person who was kind and generous to a fault, and compassionate, a person who loved life and helped others to exalt in it. "Go for it!" Brenda said so often to others, and her courage helped and encouraged others to have faith and to be passionate about their lives and work and other people.

Brenda was a cosmetologist. for over 25 years, and she excelled in it, both in her craft and in the way she knew and treated her clients, who became more than just her clients—they became her friends and part of her extended family. Everyone from young to old could relate to Brenda and she to them. Brenda had a lot of information about people and could remember well the details about others' lives and could stay in touch so well. Brenda had the gift of a listening heart, and also the communicative skills to go along with that big heart of hers. Brenda love music, art, dancing, having fun, and a "let' s do it" attitude—no wonder there was such a wonderful aura about Brenda, and everyone looked up and admired her and wanted to emulate her good example and positive, exuberant charisma.

So why did she have to die now, in the prime of her life? What's that all about? Why did this happen to this vibrant, humorous, generous, compassionate woman that everyone that knew her loved her, who was the center of her family and friends, this woman who was such a mainstay of the community? Why did death touch her, and affect us so deeply? Why, why, why, we ask today, and will continue to ask for a long time. There are no answers, except possibly that—it was her time. It was her time to be in the fullness of life with God. September, 2001, is the time of her Sacred Autumn. This may be a source of only measured comfort for us today, but it does bring a measure of that and also some "perspective," at least, as we deal with this loss in our lives. In so many beautiful ways, we know that Brenda followed Jesus' footsteps, and so we can take comfort that now it is her time to be with the Lord. And because it is her time to be with the Lord, we know that Brenda's spirit will continue to be with us even until it is our time to join her with all the saints in the heavenly kingdom. Our faith that our God is with us and with her is at the center of our being a community of believers, and this faith will help us.

Today Brenda wants us to know that she is OK, that she is more than OK with the Lord, she is thriving and happy, and she wants us to rejoice in her new life and to be at peace.

I Heard the Voice of Jesus Say

1. I heard the voice of Jesus say,
    "Come unto me and rest.
    Lay down, O weary One, lay down
    Your head upon my breast."

    I looked to Jesus as I was,
    All weary, worn and sad.
    I found in him a resting place,
    And he has made me glad.

2. I heard the voice of Jesus say,
    "Behold, I freely give
    The 'Living Water';
    Thirsty one, stoop down
    And drink and live."

    I came to Jesus
    and I drank of that life-giving stream;

235

My thirst was quenched, my soul revived,
And now I live in him.

3. I heard the voice of Jesus say,
    "I am this dark world's light;
    Look unto me, your morn shall rise,
    And all your day be bright."

    I looked to Jesus, and I found him
    My star, my sun;
    And in that light of life I'll walk
    Till trav'ling days are done.

Prayers of the Faithful were read by my brother-in-law, Wayne Webster:

1. In Baptism, Brenda received the light of Christ. May God now welcome her into eternal life.
    We pray to the Lord
    Lord, hear our prayer

2. That in these days of mourning Brenda's loss and rejoicing in her life, her husband, Mitch, their dog, Einstein, her mother, Donna, and all of Brenda's family may be comforted with God's peace and strength.
    We pray to the Lord
    Lord, hear our prayer

3. In thanksgiving for Brenda's loyalty to her family, friends, and devoted clients.
    We pray to the Lord
    Lord, hear our prayer

4. To all those whose lives *we touch*, may we pass on the gifts that Brenda possessed so abundantly: love of life, compassion, humor, generosity, creativity, and courage.
    We pray to the Lord
    Lord, hear our prayer

5. That we remember our friends and family members who have gone before us, especially Brenda's father, John Voss, Sr., and her grandparents.
    We pray to the Lord
    Lord, hear our prayer.

The Lord's Prayer was followed by the Hymn of Praise: "Ave Verum Corpus," which was sung by Mary Ann O'Dougherty, a cappella! Her voice stirred something inside me that made me want to get up and hug her at the end of the song, but I knew I needed to sit still.

The final commendation was: "On Eagle's Wings," the closing hymn was "Sing With All the Saints in Glory," and the recessional was "Jesus Christ is Risen Today."

Inside the bulletin on the bottom left inside page was the following:

Thank you for joining us today to celebrate Brenda's life. The support, love and prayers you have shared with us have been truly overwhelming—we know Brenda is looking down from heaven with a smile. Your support in our time of grief will never be forgotten.
Mitch Freimark, Donna Voss & Family

Mary Ann O'Dougherty and Steve Alm Sunday evening September 9th.

"Yes Dear"

We departed for Sioux Valley, Minnesota, to bury Brenda next to her father, John Voss, Sr., who passed away on Wednesday afternoon, May 3, 1995. On the back of the bulletin they handed out at Johnny's funeral were the words to "I'm Free." A week after Brenda died, Lynn Schardt, who had bartended at our wedding reception gave me the same poem, which really sums up how Brenda and I would want each other to live the rest of our lives.

"I'm Free"

Don't grieve for me for now I'm free
I'm following the path God laid for me
I took his hand when I heard him call
I turned my back and left it all
I could not stay another day
To laugh, to love, to work or play
Tasks left undone must stay that way
I found that peace at close of day
If my parting has left a void
Then fill it with remembered joy
A friendship shared, a laugh, a kiss
Ah yes, these things I too will miss
Be not burdened with times of sorrow
I wish you the sunshine of tomorrow.
My life's been full, I've savored much
Good friends, good times, a loved one's touch
Perhaps my time seemed all too brief
Don't lengthen it now with undue grief
Lift up your hearts and share with me
God wanted me now
He Set Me Free.

I drove the two and a half hours to Sioux Valley feeling a little numb but strong enough to safely make the journey. It was cloudy and rained on and off the whole trip. I was wondering whether or not the rain would stop for the burial or if we would be subjected to the elements without coats or umbrellas. We arrived around 2:30 p.m., and Larry Willwerscheid from the funeral home asked that we start the services right away.

As soon as Pastor Steege started to speak, the wind calmed down, and any chance of rain would definitely be delayed. My sister Shelly told me the Hawaiians have a saying:

"The rains stop for Royalty"

Chapter 23

Her Clients, Our Friends and Family, the Letters They Sent Me

J decided early on, during the first few chapters of writing this book, that my view of Brenda was probably too biased for anyone who has never met her to truly appreciate the person she was on the inside. Therefore, I selected several letters that were sent to me from Brenda's clients, a few from our friends, and a beautiful letter I received from my mother. Their words pay such a tribute to this wonderful woman, and I thank you all for your support.

It's rather funny to me when I started to read what her clients wrote about her, funny in the sense that Brenda had duped me into believing "I never talk to my clients about our personal life." She had me convinced for eleven years that no one knew Einstein and I existed, so I was a little surprised when letter after letter after letter . . . well, you be the judge.

Dear Mitch,
My name is Sheila Bruce. I know we've never met, but I feel that I know you. My husband, Dave, our daughter Jennifer and I had been getting our hair cut from Brenda for the past several years. Brenda talked of you often. She and I would talk about everything. My appointment would last for over two hours, but it felt like I had been in the chair for only ten minutes—the time would go so fast! We had so much fun talking. Sometimes we would laugh so hard that we would start crying.

I miss Brenda so very much. She was a very special person—as I am sure you know. She had that gift that she could make others feel so wonderful about themselves. Jenny got her hair cut the last time we were in. On the way home, she said, "Mom, I sure like Brenda—she talks to me like you do—she makes me feel like a grown-up." Brenda always talked to Jenny when Jenny was at the shop. When Jenny was in the chair—it was just Brenda and Jenny.

I had a hard time explaining to Jenny that Brenda had died. She had so many questions I couldn't answer. She wants you and Einstein to know that she is sorry Brenda had to die.

I wanted to talk to you at the funeral, but I'm afraid I couldn't pull myself together enough to approach you. I was supposed to have seen Brenda that morning—I had an 8:45 appointment. I had been looking forward to getting together— our "talk" time. But, instead I was at her funeral. Our hearts are breaking for you, Mitch, and the rest of Brenda's family. I just wanted you to know that Dave, Jenny, and I loved Brenda very much and we pray for you that you will find comfort and the strength to go on.

Love,
Sheila Bruce

Dear Mitch,

You don't know me, but I just needed to write you to let you know how sorry I am over the loss of Brenda. I was Brenda's customer for 8 years. After 8 years of fun conversation and many confidences, I feel that I have not only lost my hair dresser but one of my best friends.

My heart goes out to you and Brenda's family. I know how much she loved you all and can only imagine how much she was and still is loved by all of you.

I recall our last conversation. I will be married 25 years this October 2001, and we talked about how important it is to have things in common with your spouse. We talked about your fishing trips and love of golf (that Brenda didn't share with you) but she said that she was OK with that. What the two of you shared was your home, and you liked doing "projects" together. Every time she talked about you Mitch, it was obvious how much you two were in love.

We also talked about family throughout the years. I come from a family of 9 brothers and sisters and I shared many stories with Brenda. In return I learned much about her family —I remember her concern about her young brother when he was going through his divorce, and she loved her mother so much. I remember her telling me about a niece that was getting married last summer and how she was looking forward to seeing everyone. I'm so glad she was able to see everyone before God took her at such a young age.

At this time when our nation is grieving so many, I wanted you to know that Brenda has not been forgotten.

I had made an appointment with Brenda a few weeks ago, which was scheduled for Tuesday, September 11, at 3:00 p.m. Hardly a day has gone by that I haven't thought of her (since I got that shocking call at the end of my first day back to teaching high school), but that Tuesday morning she was especially on my mind. I was thinking about how precious life is and that we must live each day to its fullest.

Brenda was so full of life and such a joy, and she also loved life! To be taken so suddenly is something none of us ever imagine. I know that I will live my life differently and be thankful for every day.

Take care Mitch—you are in my heart & prayers

Nancy Dahlin

September 3rd, 2001

Dear Mitch,

I'm thinking we never met, Mitch, but we shared love in Brenda Sue. Bonnie called last evening; of course I was shocked at such tragic news. I am so very sorry . . . these written words are totally inadequate to express my sadness of your great loss. Please know I carry loving thoughts of you close to my heart . . . and accept this old friend's support and encouragement at such a difficult time. I pray God's all encompassing love will hold you tight, comfort you . . . sustain you.

Brenda Sue and I were really "close" (thanks so much for suggesting Bonnie call me). I recall John Blair telling me of this new beautician I would really like, and so began fifteen years in Spencer, Iowa . . . then Sioux Falls, South Dakota (my husband adored her, too) and then Minneapolis, Minnesota . . . of precious continued friendship. I'm certain I was one of her loyalest "boosters," and I loved her a lot. I am so sorry, Mitch.

Gretchen Evans

Dear Mitch,

Please accept our sympathy in your loss.

Brenda was a very special person, and she will be missed by many. She was a classy lady, but she was very down to earth and friendly. I don't think she realized how beautiful she was—inside and out.

I've never met you, but I feel like I know you. Brenda always seemed happy when she spoke of you. You meant the world to her.

We often talked about our flower gardens, and I will think of her whenever I look at the beautiful colors outside my window.

I'm proud to have known her and to have called her "friend." I will miss her very much.

Sue Martin

Dear Mitch,

It is so hard to express my feelings, but I'll try—Brenda was one of my very best friends. We shared our thoughts and hopes with each other. Despite the differences in our ages we were friends from the day we met.

Brenda was a *very, very* special person and I was so happy when she found you and elated when you were married. I knew when she told me you were getting married that you also had to be a special person.

I am so, so sorry, and I don't know the words to give you comfort. I also do not understand the "why" of these things—all I know to do is to embrace your faith and your family. She will always be in my heart, and if I can do anything to help please call.

Marianne Larsen

Dear Mitch,

I apologize this is coming so late. We wanted to send our deep sympathy and a few words if we may, about our relationship with Brenda.

We will miss her greatly. We have wonderful memories—she was more than just a stylist to us.

We are a family of five. Steve, Rita, Garret, Austin and Heather. We were clients of hers starting at Regis, when she was manager there. (over five years) So, after many years of all our appointments, we really got to know each other. She knew us by name, of course, but also personally.

We could always count on her with our hair. She was a great stylist—we never had a problem with our hair. She would get us hair products, new ones to try, for myself and the kids.

Then last year, when my son's 11th birthday came up, Brenda knew he enjoyed dirt biking, so she arranged a day we could meet with Heath Voss. It was so nice of her! My son was thrilled! The day before his birthday, we made it a surprise and took him out to meet Heath. Brenda got the boys Heaths T-shirts, they got autographs, and we were able to watch him practice on his track out back and saw his semi-truck. It was a great day—we will never forget!

Just like Brenda. We will never forget. We were so shocked and saddened and still are, of her passing away. We will miss her . . .

With Sincere Sympathy,
Rita Jensen

Dear Mitch,

I am extremely saddened to hear of Brenda's death. I knew Brenda for over six years and considered her a friend—someone I respected, enjoyed and cared about.

Words cannot express how much I will miss her. We talked about all the things we loved—family, decorating our homes, dogs, gardening, eating, exercise, work . . . oh, and hair!

Brenda hired my daughter, Haley, for her first job. She was also very kind and special to my mother, Dolores. My whole family knew about Brenda and are all saddened.

It is hard to find words to offer you encouragement since this is a big loss in your life. You are in my thoughts and prayers, Mitch. The good times and happy memories will always be with you.

I will always remember and miss Brenda. She was a very special person.

Nancy Jurgensen

Dear Mitch,

There are no words to express the sadness and sorrow for Brenda's passing. I pray that you find comfort from your family and friends and maybe a little from this from someone who only knew a tiny bit of the person Brenda was.

I want you to know how much I enjoyed her and how wonderful I thought she was. We had many common interests, especially gardening, and she never failed to ask about my daughters.

Brenda always had a special treat for them and would just laugh when they asked for one even before she cut their hair. They always knew she would have one. There is not a time we don't drive up 35E and the two of them say—"That's where Brenda lives!" I still have the beautiful clothes she gave them and have never forgotten her thoughtfulness.

I spent more time with her than my own family, and it was always more fun. I loved hearing about her niece's wedding, playing peek-a-boo with her nephew, and how he would only dance with her. I will miss her.

May God watch over you and your family. You are in my thoughts and prayers.

Kathie Brownrigg

Dear Mitch,

Beautiful, vibrant and so happy with her life is how I always recall Brenda.

As a customer, also a friend of hers for 7 years, I always looked forward to seeing her. Brenda and I would laugh at the stories of my 4, 16, 19 & 23 year old kids. Brenda shared many stories of her family, which we would also laugh about.

The bottom line was always how special each of her family members were to her and how much she loved you.

Our thoughts and prayers are with you at this time.

Jim & Sally Oss

Thursday September 6th, 2001

Dear Mitch,

God bless you and keep you safe and secure in his loving everlasting arms.

I would like to express my thoughts about your beautiful wife's influence on clients she cared for like me, my 92-year-old mother, Hilma Mudek, daughters etc.

Brenda was a very sweet, caring, talented woman, the kind of girl every mom would like for a daughter or daughter-in-law. When my mom, Hilma, came to get her hair fixed, she was so kind and gentle to her. Brenda knew everyone in our family by name and would ask about them when I came there.

Brenda talked about you and her family, too, and we frequently talked about the Lord. She is so deeply missed by us, and we send our love and prayers for you.

God bless you,
Marlene Hoover & Hilma

Mitch and Brenda's Family,

As a longtime client, Brenda and I shared all the news of our lives each time she performed her magic on my hair. She had an incredible memory, always asking for updates on events or problems we talked of weeks before. I will forever remember her kindness in helping with my search for new employment. Brenda recommended me for a job with another client and got me in the door for an interview. That she gave of her time and effort, I will always be grateful and carry the memory.

As a stylist, Brenda was in a position to affect so many lives—one's self-esteem and how we feel about our looks. I often wondered if she was aware of the important role she played in my life.

I will miss her.
Reneé Anderson

Mitch,

My prayers are with you.

I will miss Brenda terribly. Remember all the great times!

Brenda was always smiling, always happy, always laughing. We talked about flowers & decorating and family.

My life has been enriched because of knowing her—Thank You.

Love,
Kathy Walker—She made me beautiful for 10+ years.

Mitch,

As a client of Brenda's for the past 8 years, I always looked forward to visiting with her as she cut and styled my hair. She was such a delight . . . always happy and friendly, intelligent on a wide variety of subjects, beautiful and kind . . .

she never had an unkind word to say about anyone. Her family was the top priority in her life. She loved you all very much. Brenda was such a special person. It was a privilege to have known her, and I'll miss her too.

May knowing she's surrounded by God's love give you comfort, and may happy memories of her warm your heart in the days ahead.

With Sorrow,
Jo Ann Le Clair

Dear Mitch,

Not a day has passed these last four weeks that I have not thought of you, Brenda, and Einstein. The thousands of people who lost their lives on 9/11 also reminded me of how one as healthy and vibrant as Brenda can so quickly be gone. I do hope that by now you have an answer to why it happened.

Mitch, my heart goes out to you because I know how lost you are feeling without Brenda. I loved her, too, and miss her so much. I've shared a lot over the last many years, some silly and some sad. And we especially shared our love for our Shih Tzus, Einstein and Molly.

Please know that Lee and I are praying for you that you will be comforted by our Lord. Brenda will always have a special place in my heart.

Pat Wyman

Dear Mitch,

We think about you every day, and our hearts are broken with the thought of Brenda's loss. We feel helpless knowing that there is nothing we can do to make your pain lessen.

I'm thankful for that evening we had together recently at the golf course. She looked so beautiful, as always—her hair, her jewelry, her clothes—but most notably her smile! I don't think I ever saw her without that pretty smile. She always seemed so upbeat and chipper, and she was always so kind and friendly to me. Another part of Brenda that stays strong in my memory is how much she loved you and her family. You could tell by the way she talked how much she cared and how very important you all were in her life.

I hope that as you reflect upon your lives together, you are filled with good memories of times you spent together.

You were right, she deserves a standing ovation.

Our hearts are with you,
Becky & Marcus Gernes

Dear Mitch & Brenda's Family,

It is with great sadness and shock that I write this letter.

I was a regular client of Brenda's for 9 years. I saw her every 4-5 weeks for a 9-year period. Just recently (last year) I got an unlisted phone number, and I always made my appointments each time I left. So, as a result of that, I was not able to be contacted when Brenda died. I just found out last week at a school function. I was stunned, to say the least, and left the school function and went to Shear Madness. The manager, Jody, was there and told me the details of Brenda's death.

I have been mourning her loss all week, as I'm sure all of you are.

Brenda was just so very very special to me. She knew all the details of my life, which I gladly shared with her. She was always so interested. She did my daughters' hair when they were in high school. She came to their graduation Open Houses. I knew about her loving husband, Mitch, who she always spoke so fondly of and her loving large family that she was so fond of also.

The last time I saw her was Saturday Sept. 1st as I had a noon-appointment that day. I guess (and thru no one's fault) because I never got to say good bye to her—I just find it so hard to realize she's gone.

I would like to share this story with all of you: On the Saturday September 1st that she did my hair: we were talking about what we would do if we ever won the lottery (as you know there had been a $285M lottery a few weeks before) anyhow, we talked about if we would quit work and Brenda said, "No, I wouldn't quit work right away—I'd go in and give everybody free haircuts for a month and then I'd quit." Yes that was Brenda!

I will always remember what a classy, classy lady she was. Her beautiful blonde hair and beautiful smile.

You are all in my thoughts and prayers as you grieve over the loss of your wife, daughter, sister, and aunt and sister-in-law and daughter-in-law.

The card that I am sending describes Brenda so accurately.

> She had a special way
> That warmed the hearts
> Of everyone who knew her—
> and the qualities
> that made her
> the wonderful person she was
> have left us all
> with many beautiful memories . . .

I just wanted you all to know how much I cared for Brenda, how fond I was of her and how deeply I will miss her. I extend my sincere sympathy to all of you, and I will continue to keep you in my prayers.

May God Bless All of You and Keep You Strong.

Mary Bengtson

Mitch,

I was blessed to be one of Brenda's customers. It was a joy to spend time with her every month. Brenda was a woman of integrity and sharing with her about everything was fun. She was always positive and upbeat. One of our favorite places we had in common was Gertens Greenhouse—always sharing ideas about flowers/plants.

I am so sorry for your loss. I will miss Brenda—I really looked forward to seeing her.

Nancy Thunselle

To Brenda's Family,

Over the past 8 years or so, my daughter and I have, on a number of occasions, enjoyed driving from Austin (Minnesota, of course) up to Burnsville to have Brenda Sue style and/or highlight our hair. I could always count on Brenda for a meticulous cut and color. We would share "dog stories," as we are both owners of Shih Tzu's—Einstein and Leesa.

Brenda had a soft and pleasant personality and always a smile. Even though our times were few and far between, she left a lasting impression on me, and I will miss her *very much.*

My deepest Sympathies,
Kathy Bjorge

Dear Mitch,

Although our sympathy expression has been slow in coming, we miss Brenda more each day. It was quite a shock to hear because we always think of Brenda as so alive and vivacious. She took care of us for nearly 11 years. She was always warm and caring—and always such a happy breath of fresh air. It still is very unreal.

It is impossible for us to know how you feel—but even at a distance please know that everyone Brenda knew thought she was wonderful.

Our deepest sympathy and prayers are with you.

Sincerely,
Russ, Dee and Sophia Sampson

Mitch,

I just wanted to write a note and let you know how sorry I am about Brenda. I was a client of Brenda's; I had met her through Therese (Manzer) Crosby. I only knew Brenda for one year, but she became a friend in that short time. She was a true gem in this world, and she will be missed by all who knew her. I hope in time your pain will ease, and the memories of her will comfort you.

Kristi Scalzo

Dear Mitch,

I'm a friend of Brenda Sue's from Spencer days. Brenda Sue would cut my hair when I came to Minneapolis. I always felt like I had had the royal treatment. Brenda Sue had a real talent, a gift from God for doing hair.

I just want you to know you have our sincere sympathy with Brenda Sue's death. May God give you comfort, joy and peace.

Pat & Steve Baumgarten

Mitch,

You don't know me, but Brenda did my hair for many years. She was a wonderful person and one that will be truly missed by everyone she ever came into contact with.

She was always cheerful when I saw her. My sympathy goes out to you and all of her family and your family.

Anne Thoresen

Dear Mitch,

I was deeply saddened to hear of Brenda's death. She has cut my hair for the past 10 years, and not only did she do a great job with my hair, but she gave of herself! She also had such a beautiful smile and laugh! I can't even imagine what you must be going through, but please know that Brenda will be missed by many!

My thoughts and prayers are with you.

Sincerely,
Lisa Morris

Dear Mitch,

We were so shocked and deeply saddened to hear of Brenda's sudden passing. I'm thankful we were all together recently at that fun evening at Mike and Jackie's home. I was glad to know they were with you at the hospital.

Mitch, what a huge loss. Our hearts genuinely go out to you during this grief filled time. You and your family are in our prayers.

With Love,
Brad & Kay Englund

Mitch,

The memories—always hold on to the memories. We, too, have wonderful memories of Brenda. She was always someone I looked for, to talk with, at MCC gatherings. She was always so open and kind to me.

And for me, seeing her in the black, shiny beemer, wind blowing her hair and a wave to me!

We will *both* always remember Brenda's beautiful smile . . .

Becca & Peter Wong

Mitch,

We would like you to know that we are thinking of you every day. There is no way for us to understand all that you are going through right now, although we do know that every day will get just a "little bit" easier. Stay as strong as you have always been, and take advantage of all the friendships that you and Brenda have developed (without effort . . . meaning that you and Brenda are such easy people to like and to know). In some way, I have to believe this is your gift from Brenda in this whole extraordinary loss.

Call us anytime.

Randy, Jackie, Kyle & Chad Breckenkamp

Hey Mitch,

How have you been holding up?

I know the first couple of weeks are the hardest to handle. My dad died in a farming accident. It was also on a Sunday. He was loading round bales onto his semi. He must have hit a lever that dropped the round bale, and it rolled down the tractor and it rolled over him. Somehow he shut the tractor off, and he walked into my Grandparents' house. It happened on their farm. I know that my grandma stayed with us but I don't remember how many days it was until I got to go see my dad. The one thing that I will never forget was the first time I saw him he was in a coma, and my brother and I each took one of his hands and said, "Hi Dad," and he jumped. It was the only reaction that he had while he was in his coma. I was only seven when my dad died, so I thought that he would wake up and come home with us at any minute. After the funeral it felt like he was going to pop out of a closet laughing, saying it was all a joke. He will have been gone 8 years this February 2002. Every year it gets easier and easier. You pick yourself up and go on. You have your good days and your bad days. I know that I ask myself why me? Why my dad? I know that God has a plan for all of us and that we will be together again someday. Brenda too. I am just glad that we were blessed with her while she was still with us. I just wanted to let you know that I understand what you are going through and that we all love you very much and are praying for you.

Your Niece,
Kasey Wassenaar

DEAR MITCH,

I MET SUZIE IN 1978 AT THE SIOUX FALLS, SOUTH DAKOTA AIRPORT. WE WERE BOTH HEADING TO DENVER, COLORADO, FOR AN ANNUAL REGIS MANAGERS' MEETING. WE BOTH MANAGED SALONS FOR REGIS; SUZIE WAS IN SPENCER, IOWA, AND I MANAGED IN SIOUX FALLS, SOUTH DAKOTA.

I REMEMBER WE STAYED UP ALL NIGHT, HAD A FEW COCKTAILS, AND WERE BACK AT IT THE NEXT DAY FOR OUR MEETINGS. WE HAD SO MUCH FUN GETTING TO KNOW EACH OTHER. THIS WAS THE START OF OUR BUILDING THE MEMORIES OF OUR LIFELONG FRIENDSHIP.

SUZIE MANAGED THE SPENCER SALON FOR A FEW YEARS THEN DECIDED TO MOVE TO SIOUX FALLS AND WORK FOR REGIS. I OF COURSE WAS ECSTATIC! THIS GAVE SUZIE AND ME MORE OF A CHANCE TO GET INTO TROUBLE, THE ANGELS WE WERE ANYWAY!

EVERY WEDNESDAY NIGHT WE WOULD MEET AT CHI CHI'S FOR MARGARITAS, SALSA, AND CHIPS. THIS WAS WHERE WE WOULD SOLVE ALL THE WORLD'S PROBLEMS AND IN THE END REALIZED WE WERE JUST LIKE THE MAJORITY OF THE POPULATION. BUT IT STILL GAVE US A RELEASE OF OUR EMOTIONS, WHICH WE THOUGHT WE NEEDED. WE LAUGHED AND GIGGLED LIKE A COUPLE OF HIGH SCHOOLERS. WE LOVED IT. IT WAS OUR VENT SESSION; CHEAPER THAN ANY SHRINK WOULD HAVE CHARGED US AND GOD FORBID ANYTHING WOULD MESS UP OUR WEDNESDAY NIGHT PLANS, OR WE WOULDN'T BE ABLE TO FUNCTION TILL THE NEXT WEEK!

MITCH, SUZIE WAS ALWAYS THERE FOR ME. SHE WAS MY STRENGTH, MY ROCK, AND MOST OF ALL, MY IDOL. I ADMIRED HER FOR HER PATIENCE AND KINDNESS. SUZIE HELPED ME AND MY CHILDREN THROUGH A VERY DIFFICULT TIME IN OUR LIVES AFTER MY DIVORCE FROM THEIR FATHER. SHE WOULD PICK THEM UP FROM THE SITTERS, FEED THEM, ENTERTAIN THEM, NURTURED THEM, AND TREATED THEM AS THOUGH THEY WERE HER OWN. MY CHILDREN, ALYSHA (THREE YEARS OLD AT THE TIME) AND JUSTIN (TWO YEARS OLD AT THE TIME) LOOKED FORWARD TO SEEING SUZIE. THEY WOULD ASK ME IF SUZIE WAS

THEIR AUNT. WHY? HOW COME? WE LOVE HER? WHY DOESN'T GOD MAKE HER OUR AUNT? AND OF COURSE I HAD TO EXPLAIN TO ALYSHA AND JUSTIN THAT IT DOESN'T WORK THAT WAY. AT THAT POINT IT DIDN'T MATTER BECAUSE TO THEM SHE WAS THEIR AUNT.

IF YOU ARE WONDERING WHY I CALL HER SUZIE, WELL, WHEN I MET BRENDA BACK IN 1978 SHE INTRO-DUCED HERSELF AS SUE VOSS, AND OF COURSE I LIKE TO ADD MY OWN FLAIR TO THINGS SO I STARTED CALLING BRENDA, SUZIE OR SUZIE Q. I WOULD GET THE STRANGEST LOOKS, BUT THAT WAS OKAY BECAUSE I KNEW WHAT I WAS TALKING ABOUT WHETHER ANY ONE ELSE DID AT THAT POINT DIDN'T MATTER TO ME.

SHE REMINDED ME OF A CHINA DOLL: WELL PUT TOGETHER, HER GLOW OF BEAUTY, FRAGILE YET VERY STRONG, A WOMEN OF DIRECTION, STRENGTH, DIGNITY, HONESTY, A TOUCH OF CLASS AND DETERMINATION. SHE WOULD SET HER MIND TO WHAT SHE WANTED AND SHE WENT AFTER IT. SHE WORKED VERY HARD TO ACHIEVE HER GOALS IN ORDER TO BE SUCCESSFUL. HOW I ADMIRED HER, WHAT AN INSPIRATION!

SUZIE MET YOU, MITCH, AND THOUGHT SHE WAS IN LOVE. SHE CALLED ME AND TOLD ME, "I MET THIS NEAT GUY, WOW! HE IS HANDSOME, HE IS KIND, LOTS OF FUN, AND HE IS WHAT I'VE BEEN WAITING FOR." I TOLD HER IT SOUNDS LIKE YOU MET THE PERFECT MAN! I WAS SO HAPPY FOR HER, I KNOW IT WOULDN'T TAKE JUST ANYBODY TO SWEEP HER OFF HER FEET, SHE WAS PRETTY ANAL AND WHAT YOU WOULD CALL PICKY, PICKY, AND PICKY. I COULDN'T WAIT TO MEET THIS GUY. THE TIME FINALLY DID PRESENT ITSELF, AND I WAS IMPRESSED. SUZIE WAS RIGHT, I NEVER DOUBTED HER, AND YOU WERE AS CLOSE TO THE PERFECT MALE AS YOU COULD GET! IT WAS SO DELIGHTFUL TO SEE SUZIE'S HAPPINESS, SHE DESERVED SOMEONE LIKE YOU MITCH, AND YOU WERE HER KNIGHT IN SHINING ARMOR!

YOUR RELATIONSHIP LED TO YOU MOVING TO THE TWIN CITIES AND SUZIE HAD NO PROBLEM TRANSFERRING WITH REGIS, WHERE SHE ACCEPTED THE MANAGEMENT POSITION IN BURNSVILLE.

EVEN THOUGH SHE LIVED A FEW HOURS AWAY IT NEVER SEEMED TO STAND IN THE WAY OF OUR FRIENDSHIP.

SHE WAS SO MUCH BETTER AT KEEPING TRACK OF US THAN I WAS. SHE WAS ALWAYS ON TOP OF IT ALL! IT DIDN'T MATTER IF WE TALKED ONCE A MONTH OR ONCE EVERY SIX MONTHS. WE NEVER HAD A PROBLEM PICKING UP WHERE WE LEFT OFF. SHE AND I HAD A UNIQUE FRIENDSHIP. IT WAS LIKE WE COULD TELL SOMETHING WASN'T RIGHT OR WE WERE ABOUT TO MISS SOMETHING WHICH WOULD PROVOKE A PHONE CALL, IT WAS LIKE WE HAD MENTAL TELEPATHY.

SUZIE CALLED ME IN MAY OF 2001 AND ASKED ME WHAT I WAS DOING ON AUGUST 15TH. I SAID I DIDN'T KNOW WHAT I WAS DOING TOMORROW LET ALONE THAT FAR AHEAD, WHY? "BECAUSE I'M COMING TO SIOUX FALLS AND I WANT TO KNOW IF YOU ARE GOING TO BE AVAILABLE." WELL, IT DIDN'T TAKE LONG FOR ME TO FIGURE OUT WHAT MY PLANS WERE. SUZIE CALLED BACK IN JUNE OF 2001 AND ASKED IF WE COULD MEET ON THE 16TH VS. THE 15TH AS HER PLANS HAD CHANGED. OF COURSE IT WAS NO PROBLEM FOR ME.

SHE ARRIVED ON TIME, MEETING ME AT MY OFFICE. SHE WALKED IN LOOKING AS BEAUTIFUL AND GLAMOROUS AS ALWAYS. SHE HADN'T MISSED A BEAT FROM THE LAST TIME WE WERE TOGETHER. WE LEFT, AND, YES, OF COURSE, WE HAD TO GO FOR OUR USUAL MARGARITAS, SALSA, AND CHIPS. WE CHIT-CHATTED ABOUT OUR LIVES AND ABOUT HOW WE SOLVED ALL THE WORLD'S PROBLEMS, TALKED ABOUT THE GOOD-OLD DAYS, LAUGHED AND GIGGLED AND TALKED ABOUT OUR BELOVED HUSBANDS AND WHAT JOY THEY BRING TO OUR LIVES. WE ENJOYED THAT MOMENT OF RELAXATION, WHICH NEITHER OF US KNOWS WELL. WE DID REALIZE ONE THING, OUR AGE HAS CAUGHT UP TO US, WE COULDN'T STAY UP ALL NIGHT LIKE WE USED TO. WE TURNED IN EARLY THAT NIGHT, SUZIE HAD HER NIECE'S WEDDING TO GO TO THE NEXT DAY, AND I HAD TO BE AT WORK EARLY. WE PARTED OUR WAYS AND MADE PLANS TO GET TOGETHER SOMETIME IN SEPTEMBER, "BEFORE THE SNOW FLIES."

ON SEPTEMBER 2, 2001, I RECEIVED A PHONE CALL FROM YOU WITH THE DEVASTATING NEWS THAT SUZIE HAD PASSED ON. I COULD NOT BELIEVE IT; I DIDN'T WANT TO BELIEVE IT. A THOUSAND THOUGHTS RAN THROUGH MY MIND. IT GOES TO SHOW HOW PRECIOUS TIME REALLY IS, AND HOW WE TAKE MOMENTS OF TIME FOR GRANTED. WE NEVER

KNOW WHAT TOMORROW WILL BRING. SUZIE WILL ALWAYS BE TREASURED IN MY HEART AND MEMORIES. SHE IS A GREAT LOSS TO US ALL, SHE HAD SO MUCH TO GIVE AND OFFER.

GOD DOES HAVE A PLAN FOR EACH OF US. IT IS HARD FOR US TO UNDERSTAND AND ACCEPT AT TIMES. BUT, SUZIE MUST HAVE BEEN FINISHED WITH WHAT GOD HAD PLANNED FOR HER ON EARTH. WHAT A WONDERFUL BEAUTIFUL PERSON. THANK YOU, GOD, FOR GIVING US THE TIME WE HAD TOGETHER. I WILL CHERISH THE MEMORIES FOREVER.

GOD I MISS HER! MAY GOD BLESS YOU, MITCH, SUZIE'S FRIEND FOREVER,

KARLA KUYPER

Alysha, Justin, Dwight, and Karla Kuyper.

Dear Mitch,

I can not begin to tell you how sorry I am that you have to go through the pain of Brenda's passing on. As you said, she was an angel, and she still is!

The day we flew back home and our plane was in the sky, the sun burst forth for only a moment, and I felt it was Brenda shining through the clouds. She will always be a bright spot in all of our lives.

I loved to watch her confidence come forth whenever she needed to make decisions, how she handled herself and others in difficult situations, how she cared for herself and all those around her, how she could make things happen with just a decision to "get it done." Nothing stopped her from doing what she felt was important. She loved life, her husband, her family, her work, her home, her yard—everything she touched became beautiful.

I so appreciated her patience with you, Mitch. She weaved you into what you are today, and I loved her for that and all the wonderful things she stood for.

How many tears have been shed for this beautiful person? I feel they could fill an ocean! Your tribute to Brenda at her funeral service was absolutely touching. I was so proud of you! When my brother died, I could not understand why this tragedy came to such a great guy. A person who also loved life and all those he met. No matter how often I questioned this, I always knew that my faith in God was the only thing that could give me an inner peace. That is the one thing I could not live without, or want to live without. We must ask for it daily. You will receive comfort from those who truly love and care about you. Don and I are so thankful you have a wealth of *true* friends.

> "True friends are like diamonds
> Precious but rare
> False friends are like autumn leaves
> Found Everywhere."

I was so amazed when you said you have always remembered that saying. We just never know what will have an impact on our lives.

Know that we love and care about you.
Mom

Chapter 24

September 11th, the Day We Will Never Forget

After the burial on Thursday and the lunch that followed, it was time for us to head back to the Twin Cities. We agreed to caravan home, and I decided we should celebrate Brenda's life by making several stops along the way. "You know she wants us to have a good time tonight!" Who was going to argue with me? So, instead of taking the usual route, which was interstate the whole way home, we headed towards Mankato, Minnesota, taking the "back roads" and made three stops. Our caravan included my vehicle with my mother, Barb, and Don Martin, and my niece Carrie Webster. Jackie and Mike Chase took Jim (Jimi) Prante and Peggy Garven with them. Jackie was driving her vehicle, for safety reasons I imagined. Not that Mike's car isn't safe. I just don't believe Mike's car has ever been driven further than to his office and the golf course. Oh, and there is the one statement I recall Jackie making, "I won't ride in his car."

My brother Todd drove his truck and took my good buddy John Green, my sister, and her husband, Shelly, and Jamie Macdonald. The first two stops we made didn't last longer than one or two beers and we were on our way. Our third stop was Mankato, and, after driving through the maze of road construction the city of Mankato has set up, we finally found a Friday's to get something to eat.

My good friend John Green, "Little Elvis," as I call him, who can light up a room, had us all in stitches for over an hour. John's clean sense of humor along with his Southern accent was exactly what we all needed after such a grueling week. "You know he's funny when Jimi and Mikie can't get a word in edgewise!" I told the gang.

By the time we arrived back at the house, it was around 12:30 a.m. Rita Meyers had been kind enough to "house sit" while we were gone. She met us at the door and said she didn't have any problems.

I hadn't even thought about needing a house sitter until, earlier in the week, Jimi and Peg told me how people will actually read the obits, wait until everyone is at the services then steal everything. "When Kurt died, we had two people stop by the house during the services. Good thing we had a house sitter for Renee!" Peggy told me.

Friday and Saturday, the 7th and 8th are really vague to me; I can't even recall what I did on either one of those days. Sunday September 9th, my brother-in-law Jamie Macdonald flew back to New York, but his wife, my sister Shelly had decided to stay until Tuesday the 11th.

Sunday evening, Jimi and Peggy planned a gathering at the club for those who couldn't make the services on Thursday the 6th. It was very thoughtful on their part, and I really appreciated all their efforts.

I had to stop and realize it was Sunday the 9th, one week . . . it had been one week since Brenda had died, yet it seemed like an eternity. I was very happy to see all my friends on Sunday evening, but I was really searching for one person in particular. He didn't know I wanted to see him. I didn't know if seeing him would help me or not but I was hoping he would show up. It was around 7:00 p.m. and the room was full of friends and family. As I looked around the room, I spotted Tom. He had made it. Tom made eye contact with me as I was halfway across the room. The closer I got to him the more obvious it was his emotions had overwhelmed him. Tears were rolling down his face. "Mitch, I'm so sorry!" It was all he could say as he put both arms around me.

I whispered in his ear, "You're one of the few who truly understands."

My friend's name is Tom Splinter. I didn't ever want to share this bond with Tom, but fate had put me in a position that now drew me to want to see him, to have him tell me it will get better. Tom lost his first wife several years before to cancer, and I needed Tom to give me that look of reassurance that life does go on and time will help ease the pain. Tom's second wife, Leanne, was with him Sunday night, and seeing how happy and in love those two were made me feel really good inside. Tom's words of encouragement are still with me. "Mitch, you will grieve her forever, you'll never forget her, and in time you will find happiness." Thank you, Tom and Leanne, for being my friends and giving me hope.

Monday September 10th, Carrie was getting ready to go back to California, and I could tell she was apprehensive about her decision to move there. "Give it another month and see how you feel. If you decide you need to move back, you can stay with me until you know what you want to do."

I drove her to the airport Monday morning not realizing how difficult it was going to be for me to drop her off. We made our good-byes very short, otherwise neither one of us would have had a dry eye. Carrie is still living in California, and I'm so happy for her.

Monday night I asked Don and Barb if they wouldn't mind moving into one of the guest bedrooms. I wanted to see if I could sleep in my bed. I found myself very comfortable back in my own bed. It was surprising at first, but I knew I had to start putting my life back in order, and this was a good first step. The only problem with being back in my own bedroom was that we were all sharing the same guest shower. The shower door that Brenda and I ordered back in August still hadn't arrived. Now I know, good things come to those who wait, but why was it every damn time I bought something it took a minimum of two months to get here?

The glass shower door in the master bathroom was ordered in early August by Brenda and me. We spent a Monday afternoon at the glass company picking out exactly what we wanted, and since it would have to be custom made, the delivery and installation would be in approximately four weeks. I was contacted in mid-September, and we set the date for Monday, September twenty-fourth. When they showed up for the installation, I showed them where the shower was and just let them do their thing. When José told me to come upstairs to make the final inspection, I took one look at the hardware they used and asked him, "José, isn't the hardware suppose to be gold instead of silver?"

"Oh, Amigo, I am so sorry. You're right. We'll take it down and replace it right away."

Well, "right away" actually meant October eighteenth because the hardware wasn't available "back at the shop." On Thursday October eighteenth, José showed up with the header bar for the shower in his hand and a big smile on his face.

"Amigo, I have the right hardware today!" he announced holding the bar in his hand.

"So then tell me, José, why is the bar still silver?"

He said something in Spanish I couldn't interpret, but I could use my imagination. He later informed me the hardware was being "special ordered" out of California and would be in the next week. On Wednesday, October twenty-fourth José and his new helper arrived with the correct "gold" hardware and finished the job.

Anyway, I slept okay Monday night back in my own bed. Tuesday morning I awoke early, around 3:00 a.m. again. Don, Barb, and Shelly were all scheduled to leave for the airport around 10:00 a.m. By 7:30 a.m. they had brought their suitcases downstairs and had them ready to be loaded in my Yukon.

The TV was on, and only Don and I were in the kitchen. Shelly and Mom were both upstairs getting ready. I wasn't paying any attention to what was on the TV until I heard the breaking news that the World Trade Center was on fire. When I focused on what the TV was showing, it looked to me like only one floor was in flames.

"Look at that, Don; it looks like a small plane hit the building." I said it so nonchalantly because I've flown into New York so many times I couldn't figure out what else might have caused the hole in the building. As the news people tried to guess what had happened, I yelled upstairs to Shelly to come down to see what was happening in New York.

As we watched the flames burn from the first building, the second building suddenly burst into flames as well. The horror was unbearable. I asked Shelly, "Where would Jamie be on Tuesdays?"

As calm as she could be (she was seven and one-half months pregnant at the time), she answered me, "Well, it's Tuesday, and on Tuesdays he's probably not heading down to the towers."

"Maybe you should try and call him to make sure we know where he is." I handed her the phone and every attempt she made to contact him was unsuccessful due to the overwhelming call load being experienced in New York.

On our end, we sat on pins and needles waiting for Jamie to call us to let us know he was all right. Every time the phone rang, everyone held their breath, and every time I answered the phone it wasn't Jamie. The anxiety built in all of us as the first hour passed by with no information on his whereabouts. My only thoughts were, "We are not going to lose another family member!" Finally, about an hour and fifteen minutes after the second attack, the phone rang, and all I could say was "Hello Jamie."

On September 16th, my brother-in-law Jamie Macdonald sent the following e-mail recounting his experience the morning of 9/11 and the days that followed. Jamie is from Scotland and his dialect comes through in his story:

"Sorry if some of my e-mail replies have been a little brief over the last few days, but as you can imagine, life in NYC has been turned upside down.

"Shelly flew in from Minneapolis this afternoon (Saturday, September 15th) after her first flight was cancelled. She's pretty exhausted and looking forward to routine here—whatever that means for someone thirty-four weeks pregnant.

"Looking at the attack through my work's point of view, it was a disastrous week which could have been a great deal worse. On Tuesday morning, I was on the subway heading for a 9:30 a.m. meeting at our company office. Our office sits on the twelfth floor of 90 West Street with north facing windows opposite the South WTC. The window seats go to Mike, Bill, Jay, Tom, and Joyce. In total there are about twenty-four people based there, and I think most were in at 9:00 a.m.

"As my train sat at 59th Street, the announcer was saying trains were not stopping at the WTC due to an incident. Most didn't hear the faint message and those that did were doing the usual eye-rolling that precedes figuring out plan B.

"Something I didn't see the media spend a lot of time on was the commuter aspect of the WTC. After spending my London years seeing Waterloo and Liverpool Street stations at rush hour, I thought I was used to high volume. Then on my first commute to our company office I saw the terminals at WTC in full flow, and it's a whole different league. Besides five subway lines having stations there, the PATH terminus from Jersey was built under the towers to strategically dump tens of thousands of workers, and the effect is like a human Niagara Falls. And another thing . . . the pictures do no justice to the size of the plaza and the towers themselves. I had to trek through the atrium in the South Tower to reach the office and it's about sixty meters wide. Most skyscrapers are a short block at most which is more like forty meters max. And then it's sixty meters the other way too . . . just enormous. The atrium is about five stories high which is what's needed to give it a sense of proportion . . . in fact the charred pieces that are still nearly vertical are the walls of the atrium. I believe the total office space destroyed is not far off twenty million square feet . . . that's roughly a square mile.

"So . . . the subway train pulled into 42nd Street and a man got on clearly alarmed and declared a plane had hit the WTC. He got the sort of response a beggar gets. However, some who had heard the announcer at 59th Street started to get more info from the man, however, once another commuter got on at 33rd to say that a second plane had hit the towers, then people started looking over their newspapers and getting a little pale. Our train would go no further than Fourth Street which is in the Village and leaves Tribeca before you arrive at the Towers. So, once on the street—as there was no choice but to walk—everyone went to the corners to get a view. There was a continuous sound that was caused by scores of people getting their first glimpse of the view and either swearing or gasping. The flames were licking two or three stories high up the outside of both towers and there was a stream of burning desks, chairs, partitions, conference tables all cascading out of the gaping holes.

"At this point, I didn't go any closer but our company staff was evacuating the office. Their accounts were harrowing and described bodies and body parts landing on the highway and car park beside the office. One of our people was hit by flying debris but luckily was okay . . . in fact we lost no one so that was a huge relief. There was substantial danger from 'shards' of glass which were lethal after falling so far and typically being large parts of the windows.

"I must have stood on the street for forty minutes or so watching vans and cars coming north with dented roofs and smashed windows. By now the crowds were maybe thirty deep at the corners where you could get a view unobstructed by trees. All of a sudden the top of the south tower started to flake and there was the most awful wail that went up from the crowd as everyone realized what was happening. It was in such slow motion. People just burst into tears, others grabbed their heads and couldn't look, car drivers leapt out and screamed angrily at the sight . . . I just felt a strange numbness until it dawned on me that the towers were so big, it was unlikely the evacuation was complete. Then I just felt sick. The cloud of debris was like a huge rolling monster, and everyone staggered forward in some kind of instinctual way thinking we might pull it back. This thing just went *over* the tops of huge buildings and seemed to go on forever.

"The lines for pay phones were horrendous and cell phones were useless. My instinct was to find shelter and refuge as I was shaking and feeling like I should grab a rifle or a shovel on the way—all very strange. As Scott and Hallie live on 15th Street just north of the Village, I headed there, joining the exodus from the south. We all kept looking back, and there were still hundreds rooted to the street corners and spilling well into the traffic. Sirens were everywhere, and then the first fighter jet went overhead—sending us into momentary panic. I turned down 15th Street and made about twenty yards before there was a surge of crowd noise behind me. All I can say is it reminded me of being at a football game where you're looking the wrong way as some striker steals the winner with seconds left in the game. Of course instead of jubilation it was that awful wail again. Lots of us ran to the corner to see the second debris cloud, and I just had to turn and seek refuge, this one was even faster—it was awful.

"Hallie was just coming down from a neighbor's rooftop, so luckily I was able to stay there and use their phone. Others joined us, and we took it in turns to call family and work. Ironically, I thought only to call my boss' home line which meant he didn't get the message until 4:00 p.m. since he was walking all the way from the office to his daughter's apartment four miles north. Therefore, all my colleagues were anxious to find out if I was okay. I just didn't think work was so important at the time.

"Partial subway service got me home about 6:00 p.m., and then it became a communications nightmare. Too many phone lines and e-mail addresses with varying degrees of access . . . I needed an administrative assistant just to handle the call backs. The TV channels could not have sensationalized the story if they tried, and as you all know, it was hypnotic viewing.

"Mike and Lauren were one of the many Battery Park residents displaced, so Mike had apparently lost his home and business in one fell swoop—yet he was leading in such an admirable way. Just concentrating on seeing if the staff were okay and spending a long time talking to them all. He set up in the Plaza hotel and started to piece together a way ahead for the business. It was pretty clear the office was at best burnt out and at worst completely flattened . . . in fact we don't really know as yet and it may be weeks before we get near to the building. Meantime, I started checking out my sites to get a sense of what we had. The fourteen-year-old site at the World Financial Center (across the West Side Highway from the WTC) was full of debris and dust and we've since learned the roof caved in. The staff is pretty traumatized and stressed about their jobs. I managed to place the manager in an account where by chance I had a vacancy. Goodness knows what we'll do about the physical therapy business as it was a key source of profit for us.

"The Merrill Lynch site (which isn't one of mine) opened only this year and looks out of action. Part of the Merrill building partially collapsed and that held 5,000 workers. The Merrill account is important for us as we just signed a national agreement with them but now . . . who knows what their priorities are to be. So those staff members will need to be placed also.

"The only other of our twenty sites that was affected physically was Soho, which had to close due to the acrid smoke once the wind direction changed. I might be able to open that Monday judging by the way things are going.

"We attempted to call a senior management meeting at a borrowed office in midtown on Thursday; however, a bomb scare stopped us from even starting, so we ended up on the sidewalk having an impromptu huddle to straighten things out. Amazingly, the guys found space that day and starting buying computers, phones, and post-it pads like mad. By the end of today, I think the space is good to go—where there's a will there's a way, I guess. The new office is on Eighth Avenue and 26th Street, which is great for me and, importantly, in a very low key building as there is a lot of anxiety about future attacks.

"A man hole cover blew into the air under a blast of flame just up the street from the Starbucks I was in with Johnny. This was Friday evening and Kerry (Johnny's wife) was just coming in the door and looked horrified. We don't know what caused it but the passers by were so casual—amazing.

"Some of my team at the Waldorf didn't want to come to work on Friday as the president was due to stay over, and the atmosphere was tense. They really aren't paid to handle this sort of stuff, so it's been hard on them. A lot have lost people they know, so the mourning is becoming very real. Heather lost a friend who was one of the managers at the Windows on the World restaurant; Jacqui lost twelve firemen friends who she grew up with in Queens.

"I feel so sad for the communities in Jersey where a lot of the well-paid white-collar workers had settled with their families —ironically, to avoid the 'dangers' of the city.

"The hotels have seen huge cancellations in their banquets and rooms business. Occupancy is down to forty percent, and the Waldorf laid off 100 staff Friday—that's the side of capitalism I can't live with, to be honest. I expect the next few weeks will see more of the same.

"So, there's my rather disjointed story . . . it's good to relay it as it will take some time to work through this . . . and it's good to know there are friends out there."

Jamie Macdonald

Chapter 25

The Autopsy Report and the "Silver Lining"

hen do you think I will have the report sent to me?" It was the fourth week of September, and I was wondering why I hadn't heard anything regarding the autopsy report. I decided to call the coroner's office to find out what was holding up the final report. The one question the medical examiner couldn't answer was "when" they could get to the "case," as my wife was now being referred to, to finish the report. The best estimate was three to four months due to the high volume of cases they were experiencing.

I immediately called a friend of mine, who is an attorney, to seek counsel of the non-legal kind. "I can't believe it will take up to three months for them to find out 'why' she died. Is there anything you can do?"

"I know a few people, and I'll make some calls for you on Monday, but, Mitch, you have to remember three months is probably a normal time frame."

I called my buddy back on the following Tuesday, and he said he did speak with the examiners' office but no promises were made.

I'm not sure what he said, but I did receive a phone call from Susan J. Roe, M.D., assistant medical examiner, the first week in October. She called to inform me they found a large mass on Brenda's pelvis, and it is ovarian cancer.

"What are you talking about?" I was really confused. "She just had her annual exam in July, and I have the report showing everything was fine!"

"You mean you didn't know about the large mass on her pelvis?" Dr. Roe's voice told me someone screwed up. "Mitch, there is no way her doctor could have missed this."

"Well it's obvious she did miss it. Brenda's personal physician for the past ten years is female, so it bothers me that she wouldn't take the time or have the patience to find, what you're telling me is a large mass. I'll deal with her later. Please tell me the cancer had nothing to do with what killed her."

"It didn't. The mass on her pelvis and what Brenda died from are unrelated. The cause of her death is *Acute Dissection of the Left Main Coronary Artery.* It means her Left Main Coronary Artery tore."

"Did this have anything to do with her Heart?" I needed to know because the Red Cross said they couldn't use her heart for a transplant because she had been dead too long.

"No, her heart was in perfect shape."

"Is what she died of something that's very common?"

"Mitch, this is only the third case we've seen in Ramsey County."

"I need to let you know the real reason I called you. You need to inform Brenda's family about the ovarian cancer, and the female family members need to let their family doctors know it is in the family."

"I'll call her mother today."

I called Donna that afternoon and relayed the information exactly as Dr. Roe presented it to me.

On Saturday October 13th, I received the Final Autopsy Protocol from the Office of the Medical Examiner:

CASE TITLE: SPONTANEOUS ACUTE DISSECTION OF THE LEFT MAIN CORONARY ARTERY

Name Brenda S. Voss **Age** 46 **Sex** F **Race** Cauc
Date of Death 9/2/01 **Time** 1658 **Date of Exam** 9/3/01 **Time** 0935
Place of Death United Hospital ER, St. Paul (Ramsey County), MN
Pathologist Susan J. Roe, M.D., Assistant Medical Examiner
Place of Exam Ramsey County Medical Examiner's Office

FINAL ANATOMIC DIAGNOSIS

I. Cardiac findings
    A. Spontaneous acute dissection of the left main coronary artery with extension into the trifurcation.
    B. Local acute epicadial hemorrhage over dissected segment.
II. Minimally stenotic congenitally bicuspid aortic valve
III. Serous cystadenocarcinoma, ovarian primary.
    A. Large pelvic mass.
    B. Peritoneal studding.

     C. Metastases to serosal surface of bowel and capsular surface of liver.

IV.   S/P resuscitative efforts.

V.   Cerebral edema.

VI.   Pulmonary congestion.

VII. Laboratory results

     A. Toxicology

          1. Blood ethanol – negative.

Susan Roe M D

Susan J. Roe, M.D.

Assistant Medical Examiner

The "Silver Lining," if one can be found from such a tragedy, is the fact that Brenda didn't have to suffer a long drawn-out death, which would have been the case once the ovarian cancer was diagnosed. She might have lived another six months, but she would have gone through hell.

Right after I received the autopsy report, a friend of mine from Arizona, Bob Marshburn, called to see how I was doing. Brenda and I always enjoyed the times we were able to spend with Bob and is wife, Kim, mainly because they are so in love with each other and so much fun to be with. So, when Bob called to find out how I was getting along, I just had to ask him, "Bob, how did your first wife die?"

"It was Ovarian cancer."

"What was it like going through this with her?" I needed Bob to tell me, someone I knew wouldn't pull any punches or sugar coat it.

"It was horrible, Mitch. By the time they diagnose ovarian cancer, it's too late to do anything. She suffered a long and drawn-out death. In the very last days of her life, I couldn't even recognize her. You are so lucky Brenda was taken quickly."

"I know. There's no way Brenda would have been able to stand knowing she was going to die that way. Bob, I really believe a higher power decided to take her in a way she wouldn't suffer, yet leave her dignity, her beauty, and her love intact."

Thank you so much, Bob, for sharing part of your life with me and to help me put this whole ordeal into perspective.

When I look back on all the events that occurred on Sunday September 2nd, 2001, I have come to really appreciate the fact Brenda went quickly; helping to preserve my memories of her beauty and grace and escaping the memories that could be tarnished by some wicked disease, a disease that slowly sucks the life from a body, leaving nothing but an empty shell and a person even loved ones don't recognize.

Yes, we were truly blessed with the eleven years we had together, and I am blessed with such a wealth of friends whose love has carried me through the darkest of days. I was blessed with the way God decided to take Brenda. I've said it so many times during those first two weeks after she died, "She was an angel on this planet, now she has her wings."

Chapter 26

Planning for Death
The Last Thing We Think About

J sold life insurance for over seven years before completely changing careers. Out of the seven years I was in the insurance business, I had to deliver three death claims. There is one in particular, I'll never forget as long as I live.

I was twenty-five years old when my manager asked me to help a young lady whose husband had just committed suicide. She was twenty-three years old and had only been married for a few years when her husband went to the garage, and, with the garage door still closed, started his car and rolled the windows down.

I was working for Prudential, and Prudential's policy definitions regarding suicide said the policy had to be in force for two years or the claim would be denied. This guy must have made sure he waited the right amount of time because if he would have committed suicide a month earlier, his surviving spouse wouldn't have gotten a dime.

I delivered a check to the "widow," which is very difficult for me to say since the day after Brenda died I was labeled the "widower," just like Lori had to face the fact she now had a label of "widow" at twenty-three years of age. The death benefit was a meager $30,000, which was to be used to pay off the mortgage if something should ever happen to either of them. After the paper work was signed and I gave her the check, she thanked me for being so kind and then asked me for advice on what to do with the money.

"I know the money was supposed to be used to pay for the house, but if I pay off the mortgage I won't have any money left to live on, the funeral expenses and bills have wiped me out. Plus the banker has been calling me telling me I "have to" pay the mortgage off once I get the check."

I gave her the best advice I could, which was to tell her honestly what her options were and let her decide what to do.

"Lori, first of all you don't have to pay off the mortgage. That's totally up to you. Second, you need to write down what it costs you each month to live in this house. Include everything you can think of. I'll leave you this brochure to help you. Then you need to decide whether or not you can afford to stay here. During the next few months, use the money to pay the mortgage and pay your bills. You don't want to make any rash decisions right now, so my best advice is to do nothing for now. Remember the only way the bank can force your hand is if you stop paying them."

A few weeks later, I received a phone call from Lori. She was crying as she told me the banker had continued to harass her to pay off the mortgage. "Have you made your payments to them on time?"

"Yes, I have. Plus, I've never been late with the payment."

"Okay, I'll tell you what we're going to do. You meet me at your bank, and I'll have a little chat with your banker. How does that sound?"

"I'd really appreciate it, Mitch."

I met Lori at the Savings & Loan, and we requested to speak to the asshole that was causing her so much anxiety. We walked into his office, and I shut the door behind us and moved in on "his space" never allowing him to stand up from his high-back, leather chair. With one hand on his desk and the other on his chair, I leaned in really close and said, "Do you know who this is?" I was pointing right at Lori.

"Yes I do."

I was making him extremely uncomfortable, and I could hear it in his voice. My facial expression and body language told him I was pissed off. He wasn't sure whether or not I was going to knock the shit out of him.

"Let me make one thing really clear, buddy. If you ever call her again and ask for any money, you and I will be having this conversation alone. Do you understand what I'm telling you?"

"Are you a lawyer?" He snapped back at me deciding to be brave.

"No, I'm her friend. If I were a lawyer, I'd sue you for harassment. So what is it going to be, Mr. Banker man?"

Needless to say, he backed off and never called Lori again. I saw Lori at a nightclub about a year later, and she looked great. She gave me a hug and thanked me again for helping her. I'm not sure I was really helping her or whether I was sick of seeing people taken advantage of by scumbags who only care about what's in their best interest. Maybe I should have been a lawyer.

The only reason I would ever put this story in print is to illustrate that people who don't properly plan for a death of their spouse will be burdened by many unforeseen expenses. Not only are they grieving the loss of their loved one but they have to face the possible loss of a major income source or the main caretaker for their children. The bills, the mortgage, or rent don't stop just because someone's life was turned upside-down. Proper planning will eliminate the stress and anxiety associated with situations like Lori's.

I'm not an attorney, CPA, or Financial Advisor. I can only give you my opinion based on my life experiences. If you do not have a will, the state you live in will more than likely govern your estate when you die. If you do have a will, that won't eliminate the costs associated with probatable property if you or your spouse did not plan correctly. In my opinion, a will is nothing more than a road map that tells those left behind what the deceased's intentions were after death. Just because someone states in a will that he or she "leaves everything to my spouse" doesn't mean everything will end up going to that spouse. Let me use my situation to explain.

Brenda and I both had wills. Our wills helped explain our wishes in case one of us died or we both died at the same time. What neither one of us realized is property held in just one of our names is treated differently than property held in both our names by the State of Minnesota. In this case, property held in Brenda's name only was subject to probate if the value was $20,000 or more, again, this is according to the laws in the State of Minnesota. (Laws vary by state.) This includes "all" property: cars, stocks, bonds, checking accounts, land, homes, etc.

The biggest surprise to me was the checking account issues. Brenda was self-employed when she died. She had a business checking account, but it was unavailable for me to access. The reason was she did not designate anyone as her beneficiary in case she died. It wasn't her fault. She just didn't know any different, and neither did I. In our situation, fortunately, I didn't need the money to pay the bills during the sixty to ninety days it takes to settle a simple estate like ours. But what if the situation was in reverse and Brenda would have been a stay-at-home mom with three kids and needed the money to feed and clothe them, to pay the rent or mortgage?

My point is simple; people should stop thinking about planning and DO IT!

These were my rules of thumb when I sold insurance:

1. Life Insurance: When I figured how much life insurance someone needed, I took their annual income times ten plus I added any major debt. If you're the Executive of the Household (stay home mom or dad), decide what your full-time job is worth if you have to hire someone to take care of the kids, clean the house, do the laundry, cook, run errands, etc. So many of my friends told me after Brenda died "Mitch, I don't have any life insurance on my wife."

2. Disability Insurance: The chances of becoming disabled are much greater than dying. Therefore, I used to advise at least sixty to seventy percent income replacement, as disability claims are paid tax free if the premiums were paid with taxable dollars.

3. Health Insurance: Don't even think about not owning health insurance. The risk isn't worth it.

I stated previously that I'm not qualified to give financial advice nor would I attempt to in this book. Consult the professionals and allow them to help.

The remainder of this chapter is the information regarding the costs associated with Brenda's death. I believe it is important that I share the actual expenses associated with Brenda's death in order for people who are "just thinking about planning," actually do something, and it will be worth it.

The Funeral Service for Brenda S. Voss

Professional Services

Funeral director & staff	$995.00
Embalming	$495.00
Other preparation and care	$290.00
Visitation at other facility	$295.00
Funeral service at other facility	$295.00
Transfer of remains to funeral home	$350.00
Funeral coach for funeral	$425.00
Service vehicle	$50.00

FUNERAL HOME SERVICE CHARGES	**$3195.00**

0293 Gold Blend Gray01	$1795.00
Monticello	$850.00
White Guest	$32.86
400 Church Scene	$140.85

THE COST OF OUR SERVICES, EQUIPMENT, AND MERCHANDISE THAT YOU HAVE SELECTED	**$6013.71**

AT THE TIME FUNERAL ARRANGEMENTS WERE MADE, WE ADVANCED CERTAIN PAYMENTS TO OTHERS AS AN ACCOMMODATION. THE FOLLOWING IS AN ACCOUNTING FOR THOSE CHARGES.

Certified copies	$102.00
Hairdressing	$50.00
Clergy honorarium	$225.00
Flowers	$170.00
Cemetery charges	$300.00
Transportation	$286.00
Vault installation	$70.00
Medical examiner's fees	$14.00
Haulage	$20.00

TOTAL CASH ADVANCES AND SPECIAL CHARGES	**$1237.00**
SALES TAX	**$11.29**
CONTRACT PRICE	**$7244.00**

Here are the bills from the ambulance services, hospital charges, doctors.

HealthEast Care System

DATE	DESCRIPTION	AMOUNT
9/2/01	Advanced Life Support Level 2	$1,147.50
9/2/01	ALS Mileage Charge 6 @ 15.00 each	90.00
	PAY THIS AMOUNT	**$1,237.50**

ST PAUL HEART CLINIC

DATE	DESCRIPTION	AMOUNT
9/2/01	ECHO 2-D LMTD STUDY PROFESSIONAL	$ 96.48
9/2/01	DOPPLER PROFESSIONAL	$ 80.66
9/2/01	DOPPLER COLOR FLOW PROFESSIONAL	$ 64.78
9/2/01	PROVIDER TAX	$ 3.63
	PAY THIS AMOUNT	**$ 245.55**

UNITED HOSPITAL

DATE	DESCRIPTION	AMOUNT
9/2/01	PPO Emergency Room	**$3,230.35**

DR. JAMES T. HYNES

DATE	DESCRIPTION	AMOUNT
9/2/01	PPO Emergency Room	**$1,240.00**

Here is a short list of items that I needed to make sure was paid in order to live on my monthly income:

Funeral Services, Hospital, Ambulance, Doctors:	**$13,197.40**
Attorney's fees, Court Costs, Title Transfer, Newspaper	**$ 1,000.00**
Pay off Credit Cards	**$15,000.00**
Pay off Car Loan	**$18,000.00**
Pay off New Roof Installation	**$14,000.00**
Pay Quarterly Estimated Taxes	**$ 5,900.00**
Total	**$67,097.40**

Chapter 27

Take Hold of Every Moment

Jimi Prante sent me the following e-mail on Friday October 12, 2001:

"A friend of mine opened his wife's underwear drawer and picked up a silk-paper-wrapped package:

"'This,' he said, 'isn't any ordinary package.'

"He unwrapped the box and stared at both the silk paper and the box.

"'She got this the first time we went to New York, eight or nine years ago. She had never put it on. She was saving it for a special occasion. Well, I guess this is it.' He got near the bed and placed the gift box next to the other clothes he was taking to the funeral home. His wife had just died. He turned to me and said: 'Never save something for a special occasion. Every day in your life is a special occasion.'

"I still think those words changed my life. Now I read more and clean less. I sit on the porch without worrying about anything.

"I understood that life should be a source of experience to be lived up to, not survived through. I no longer keep anything. I use crystal glasses every day. I'll wear new clothes to go to the supermarket, if I feel like it.

"I don't save my special perfume for special occasions; I use it whenever I want to. The words 'Someday . . .' and 'One Day . . .' are fading from my dictionary.

"If it's worth seeing, listening or doing, I want to see, listen or do it *NOW*."

I don't know what my friend's wife would have done if she knew she wouldn't be there the next morning. This nobody can tell. I think she might have called her relatives and closest friends. She might call old friends to make peace over past quarrels. I'd like to think she would go out for Mexican, her favorite food. It's these small things that I would regret not doing, if I knew my time had come.

I would regret it, because I would no longer see the friends I would meet, letters . . . letters that I wanted to write "One of these days."

Now, I try not to delay, postpone or keep anything that could bring laughter and joy into our lives. And, on each morning, I say to myself that this will be a special day. Each day, each hour, each minute, is special.

Chapter 28

My Letter to Brenda

ear Brenda,

It was so unbelievably painful for me to watch you die in my arms on Sunday, September 2, 2001. You were not only my wife, you were my best friend, someone I could confide in, someone who never judged me but helped guide me through the ups and downs of life's rocky road.

I could always make you laugh, and you knew how important that was to me. You never complained about anything, even when you knew you only had moments to live. You left this physical world the same as the day I met you, with so much style and grace. Your beauty never left you.

My life will never be the same without you, but no one could expect it to be. I know you've always been there for me, because I wouldn't have been able to function day to day without your love and support.

Thank you for giving me the best eleven years anyone could ask for. I was so very fortunate you chose me to spend those years with. I wasn't always the easiest person to get along with but you managed to transform me into the person I am today. I'm a more considerate, kinder, gentler, patient and caring person, and it's all because of you.

My life will no doubt take on a new chapter, but I will promise you this. You will always be a very large part of it. Your legacy is my legacy, and I can't wait to tell your story to anyone who wishes to listen.

"Yes Dear"

You were truly a special person, a "diamond in the ruff."

Rest in peace, my darling, knowing your work is finally done. You helped change the lives of so many people, and for that I'm so proud of you.

I'll never forget your smile, your laugh, your warmth. You were one of the most creative people I have ever met, and only a few of us knew it. You were so modest, never wanting to stand out in the crowd. People were drawn to you whether you knew it or not.

I've never been a poet or songwriter, but I've written something for you.

I see you everywhere I look, you can't hide
I'm so proud to have been the man you loved inside.
You picked me to spend the past 10 and 1
Oh my sweet our lives had just begun.

The pain I was in you didn't see . . . but I guess you did,
You've always been there for me.

He must have really needed you . . . needed your smile
It was selfish of me to think I could have you all this while.
When there is so much pain from September 11th, Brenda I'm glad
You didn't see it . . . but I guess you did, yes, I know you did.

Now I know why God needed you with him
To help comfort and care for all the victims.
It's your smile and your charm that will warm
the hearts of all those we lost.

I know you're dancing with your dad,
For all the love that he had
Was passed on to someone special like you
And you've passed it on to me too.

I hope to touch a life like you did mine
It will be the ultimate compliment to you,
someone who was so divine.

All my love,

Chapter 29

Pictures

Mitch and Brenda

Brenda fly-fishing in Calgary. This 5½ pound rainbow trout was
the first fish she ever caught in her life.

Lake Tahoe, 1996, with the Belimo Girls: Brenda, Lisa O'Connor, Val Daniel, Jackie Breckenkamp,
and Edith Washington. That's our good friend Randy Breckenkamp making a play for the ladies!

Maryse and Werner Buck, Brenda, and Mitch. Calgary 1999.
"I worked for Werner at Belimo for over seven years."

Pre-party New Year's Eve, December 31, 2000. Left to right: Mary Ann O'Dougherty, Peggy Garven, Todd Freimark, Mitch, Brenda, Don Martin holding Einstein, Steve Alm, Kiki Kline, Scott Entenman, Kristy Clark, and Jimi Prante.

Marianne Larsen and Brenda at Barb and Don Martin's home,
Sun Lakes, Arizona, November 23, 2000

Mitch, Brenda, and Peter Schmidlin. Belimo's Puerto Rico cruise, April 2001.

Brenda's baby picture.

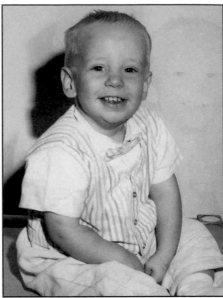

Mitch's baby picture.

Brenda with her Grandma "Gert" Ihnen.

Donna and John Voss, Sr., Brenda's parents.

Brenda, Mitch, Ric and Teddy Hagen, Ruth Martin, John and Shirley Lee, and Don Martin.
January 10, 1998, Sun Lakes, Arizona.

Jeff, Aubrey, Brenda, and Hannah Doran.

Diana, Jacob, and "Big Daddy" Troy Harms, Sunday September 9, 2001, Mendakota CC.

Henry "Mr. Embers" Kristal, Scott Entenman and Kristy Clark.
Sunday, September 9, 2001, Mendakota CC.

Todd, Don and Barb, Mitch and Brenda. November 26, 2000.

Brenda and Mitch at Brian and Susan Weedman's wedding reception.

Dustin Hall and Mitch, Sunday September 9, 2001.

Jimi and Peggy, Dan and Penny Malecha, and Mitch
after a round of golf on Labor Day weekend, 1999.

Brian and Susan Weedman.

Tara and Tasha Carlson,
Along with their mother, Martha, were longtime loyal clients.

The Boys Skiing at Whistler, British Columbia - January 18, 2002.
Left to right: front: Dr. Jack "Jackson" Holtz, Michael "Thirds" Swor, Dr. David "Deano" Zanick; back: Paul "Mr. Clean" Gatto, Gerald "Peppy" Pedlar, Jimmy "Smil 'n' Holtz, Dale "The Eagle" Jones, and Mitchy "The Kid" Freimark.
I don't know what I'd do without the love and support of you guys. Thank you!

The Voss Family
Back row: Bernie, Jack, Jerry, and Ben; Middle: Barb, Donna, Johnny, and Buzz;
Front: Brenda, Betty, Becky, and Bonnie.

Brenda